A Traveller's History of Poland

JOHN RADZILOWSKI

Series Editor   DENIS JUDD
Line Drawings   *PETER GEISSLER*

Interlink Books

An imprint of Interlink Publishing Group, Inc.
Northampton, Massachusetts

First published in 2007 by
INTERLINK BOOKS
An imprint of Interlink Publishing Group, Inc.
46 Crosby Street, Northampton, Massachusetts 01060
www.interlinkbooks.com

Library of Congress Cataloging-in-Publication Data
Radzilowski, John, 1965–
    A traveller's history of Poland / John Radzilowski. – 1st American ed.
      p.   cm. – (Traveller's histories)
    Includes bibliographical references.
    ISBN 1-56656-655-X
    ISBN 13: 978-1-56656-655-1
    1. Poland—History.   I. Title   II. Title: Traveler's history of Poland.
III. Series: Traveller's history.
    DK4140.R33   2006
    943.8–dc22   2006011521

Printed and bound in Canada by Webcom

To order or request our complete catalog,
please call us at **1-800-238-LINK**, visit our web site at
www.interlinkbooks.com or write to us at:
INTERLINK PUBLISHING
46 Crosby Street, Northampton, MA 01060-1804
e-mail: info@interlinkbooks.com

Contents

Preface

Polish people possess a rich, complex and thriving historical tradition. The same cannot be said of the history of Poland as a state. The wry observation that, 'Poland does not have a history, only neighbours', contains an essential and painful historical truth, especially when for much of the period from the late nineteenth century the western neighbour was a united, efficient and expanding Germany, and the eastern one an ambitious yet fearful Tsarist then Soviet Russia. The brutal partition of Poland from 1939–40 between Hitler and Stalin might serve as the most potent symbol of the long-standing 'Polish problem.'

Despite this, the Poles have managed to build and maintain, against the odds, an unbroken if often blood-stained cultural heritage. This process began at roughly the same time that Carolingians, Vikings and Saracens were asserting their power in differing ways in Europe, and a full century before the Norman Conquest of England. Positioned dead centre in geographical Europe, Poland was obliged simultaneously to face both west and east. Thus on the one hand it was an important part of the Christian West, and on the other needed to confront and accommodate the predominantly Orthodox and Islamic east. In the process, Poland absorbed a clutch of minority groups, of which easily the largest, before 1940, was Jewish. This latter demographic fact, as well as the notion that the Nazi's dirty work could best be done in conquered territories, led to the establishment of three of the most notorious extermination camps on Polish soil.

Poles were not, however, simply the passive victims of other nations' aggression. Often they stood foursquare against invaders and bullies.

Although the country ceased to exist for much of the nineteenth century, and under the rule of Nazi Germany, there were eras when Poland flourished and really counted for something in the balance of continental power – for example, at its height, its power stretched from the Baltic to the Black Sea.

Far too often, however, Poles were obliged either to submit to foreign domination, or to leave their homeland in order to enjoy political and religious freedom and to prosper overseas. The Polish Diaspora has established significant populations in the United States, Canada, Australia, the United Kingdom and several European states. With the enlargement of the European Union in 2004, hundreds of thousands of Poles have availed themselves of the right of domicile and work within the European community, in the process establishing the contemporary icon of the 'Polish plumber' – efficient, well trained and inexpensive.

Foreign observers might wonder whether these chronic traumas have fundamentally left the Poles insecure, notoriously hostile to outsiders in their midst, and marked by nothing more glamorous than dogged resistance and the capacity to survive.

But this would be to see only the shadows that fall across Polish history rather than the brilliant and cheering interludes. As John Radzilowski points out in this lucid, sane and eye-opening book, Poles are keenly aware of the contrast in their history, 'of the glorious achievements and tragic disaster, of great victories against impossible odds and decline brought on by internal bickering and corruption.'

What they, and the traveller to Poland ought to see, is a highly cultured country, with some of the most unspoiled countryside in Europe, with great rivers, primeval forest, and towering mountain ranges at its borders. There are also beautiful cities and towns, some of them superbly restored, where museums and galleries recall the past and cherish it.

For the rapidly increasing number of annual visitors to the new and apparently stabilised Poland, this fascinating book will indeed be essential reading.

Denis Judd
London

Acknowledgements

The complex history of Poland is not well known in the English-speaking world, making efforts to present it to the general public in an accurate, interesting, and readable format all the more daunting. I was therefore grateful to have had the examples of two previous masters of the craft to follow. The works of Norman Davies and the late Oskar Halecki have weathered well the changeable winds of academic fashion and set a benchmark that the present book strives to reach.

Grateful thanks are also due to the many colleagues, family, and friends whose comments, suggestions, and advice have improved this work in ways great and small. Thanks goes first of all to my wife Kasia who aided the process of writing with her constant encouragement and correction of my Polish grammar. My father, Professor Thaddeus Radzilowski (Piast Institute), has been a mentor and source of stimulating ideas about Polish history and culture since I was a small boy. My brother, Professor Paul Radzilowski (Madonna University), provided sources on the medieval period. Friend and colleague Professor Marek Jan Chodakiewicz (Institute for World Politics) likewise provided information on new revelations from the communist era. Over the years many friends and acquaintances have proven a source of ideas and critiques. Though we did not always agree, through conversations and email exchanges, they have helped me think through many important issues. Among them are John L. Armstrong, Professor Roman Solecki, the late Professor Stanislaus Blejwas, Marcin Zmudzki, members of the Friends of Poland listserv, the board and members of the Polish American Cultural Institute of Minnesota, and my colleagues and students at the University of St Thomas. (Naturally, any errors or omissions in this work are the responsibility of the author.)

The author also extends his thanks to Professor Norman Davies and Professor Leonard Kress (Owens University) and his online journal *Artful Dodger* for allowing him to use previously published English translations of the poems of Edward Slonski and Jan Kochanowski, respectively. My gratitude also goes to the Piast Institute (www.piastinstitute.org) which has helped to encourage and promote this work.

The author thanks Victoria Huxley and the staff at Arris Books for their skill and patience in the editorial and production process. Books are more than a structured collection of prose. Though unseen by the reader, the work of editors, graphic designers, cartographers, and typographers has contributed immeasurably to the work you now hold.

Lastly, and most important, however, I am profoundly grateful to my grandmother, the late Genevieve Radzilowski – to whom this work is dedicated – and to her father the late Jan Ochalek. Though they possessed no higher education, they imparted to our family and to me a love of books, learning, and a fascination with Polish literature and history.

I have been blessed to stand on the shoulders of giants.

John Radzilowski
Minneapolis, Minn., USA

Introduction

Poland is a paradox. It has played a crucial role in European history. Yet, its history and culture are almost unknown in the English-speaking world and what is popularly believed about Poland's past is often inaccurate. Despite this, Poland's independence has been at or near the heart of modern Europe's political crises. Ignorance, language barriers, and the Cold War division of Europe explain part of this lacuna, but part of the problem has been Western scholars who have been traditionally sympathetic to Poland's major rivals, Germany and Russia.

Poland is located at the geographic centre of Europe, though it is often wrongly referred to as being in 'Eastern Europe'. It has been part of the Latin, Christian West for more than a millennium. Poles have viewed themselves as the Bulwark of Christendom and have twice repelled major invasions that would have altered or destroyed European culture as we know it. Poles have been among the most profoundly Christian of nations. Yet Poland has had close ties to the east – especially the Orthodox and Islamic worlds. It has also provided a home for what was once the world's largest Jewish community – who termed their adopted homeland, 'Polin', a place of rest – as well as a myriad of smaller religious and ethnic groups. Whereas the old, aristocratic conservatives of the nineteenth and early twentieth centuries saw Poles as in the words of German Chancellor Otto von Bismarck the 'general staff of world revolution', the European and American left has viewed Poles as inveterate reactionaries for their staunch anti-communism and opposition to the Soviet Union. During the communist era, the country became known as a nation of heavy industry. Yet, Poland is also one of Europe's last agrarian societies where over a quarter of the population is involved in farming, often at a subsistence level. Though heavily settled for centuries, the country possesses Europe's last stand of primeval forest and some of its most important remaining wild places. While deeply attached to their homeland, Poles have migrated across the world, settling on every inhabited continent, sometimes in huge numbers.

Polish history is one of glorious achievements and tragic disasters, of great victories against impossible odds and of decline brought on by internal bickering and corruption. It is not a story of steady and sure progress, but of constant ups and downs. At Poland's height its kings and the ruling gentry class presided over a vast inland empire stretching from the Baltic Sea to the Black Sea. Yet, throughout the nineteenth century Poland was wiped from the map of Europe and existed only in the minds and culture of its people. For Poles, the past has been like a cyclical Shakespearean tragedy, good and evil, nobility and beauty, horror and ugliness.

Poland's history begins and ends with its geography, yet Poland's boundaries have changed so dramatically over the centuries that historians often speak of 'the Polish lands'. These encompass the territory of present-day Poland, from the Oder-Neisse border in the west and including lands historically ruled by Poland: modern Lithuania, Latvia, Belarus, most of Ukraine, and even Moldova.

This land is primarily flat, with rolling hills, a landscape formed by successive European ice ages. This broad plain forms a natural highway from central Asia to central Europe, running between the Baltic Sea and the Carpathian Mountains. In the north, the land is dominated by thick forests interspersed with marshes and lakes which since ancient times retarded travel, invasion, and economic growth. To the south, the Carpathian mountain chain and the high peaks of the Tatra Range define Poland's southern boundary. Lower than their cousins, the Alps, the Carpathian Mountains present spectacular natural landscapes and the numerous passes have allowed trade and migration across the centuries. In between, the land is a mix of forest and meadow with the latter giving way to the former as human habitation has increased.

This broad, open land is cut by many rivers. The most significant is the Vistula (Wisła), running from the Carpathians south of Kraków,

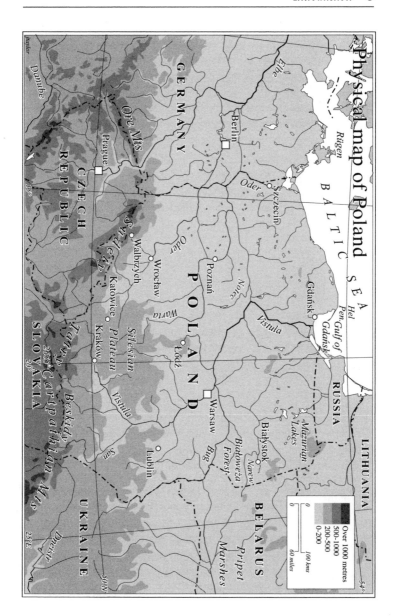

Physical map of Poland

through Warsaw and the Mazovian uplands and finally to the Baltic Sea at Gdańsk. Its major tributaries, the San and Dunajec in the south and the Narew and Bug to the east, drain the southern slopes of the Carpathian Mountains and the forest and marshes of the eastern border respectively. To the west is the Oder (Odra) with its major tributary the Warta.

In the north and northeast lie the picturesque Mazurian Lakes region, and great swathes of forest and marshland. Here is the Białoweża Forest, once the hunting preserve of royalty, now Europe's last stand of primeval forest and home to the European bison (żubr), the shy forest horse (tarpan), the wolf, moose, and lynx. In the southeast, stretching from Lublin eastward into Ukraine, is the beginning of the Europe steppe, the wide open land that would deeply mark the Polish psyche.

The regions beyond today's Polish border played a crucial role in Poland's history. Known as the Kresy ('borderland'), this multi-ethnic land was ruled by Poland for centuries. Though often a minority, Poles from this region include Adam Mickiewicz, the great bard of Polish Romanticism; Tadeusz Kościuszko, hero of Polish and American history; interwar leader Marshal Józef Piłsudski; and poet and Nobel laureate Czesław Miłosz.

History is to Poles what food is to the French. Debates over seemingly arcane points of history have often revealed deep fault lines in Polish society. In the nineteenth century, debates over why the partitions had occurred and at what point Poland's freedom had been truly lost helped to define whole political and intellectual movements. During the communist era, history became a tool of state propaganda as well as a means of resisting the power of the state. As Poland moved toward freedom, a Polish pope would point his people back toward the core of their historical experience. After 1989, among free Poland's first governments were a disproportionate number of historians serving as ministers and ambassadors. Today, how one stands on the issue of treating the crimes of the communist period bears an eerie resemblance to the historical debates and consequent political fault lines of the nineteenth century.

Yet, Poles are often amazed and frustrated that people from other countries know so little of Poland's past, especially considering the size of the Polish diaspora in the English-speaking world. As Poland has again emerged on the European and world stage, it is perhaps time for Europeans and North Americans to look again at a land that is at once both distant and very near.

CHAPTER ONE

Early Poland,
Origins to 1138

Pre-Slavic Origins

Much of the prehistory of Poland is based on informed guesses, augmented by archaeological and paleolinguistic studies. A variety of cultural groups made their homes in the lands between the Dnieper, Vistula, and Oder. Waves of Indo-European peoples migrated through toward the West, some putting down roots, but rarely completely subsuming or displacing earlier populations.

The first people of the Polish lands were prehistoric hunter-gatherers who followed game across the plains of northern Europe. The first settled populations, however, were groups of Neolithic farmers who migrated into the Vistula and Oder basins, probably from the region of the Middle Danube (modern Hungary and Austria) between 5,000 and 4,800 BC. These farmers were part of the so-called Linear Pottery culture. Its major centres (at least those presently discovered) were north of modern Toruń, in the Kujawy region, and south and west of Szczecin. These early people chose a belt of land with rich loess soil and settled alongside rivers or lakes, often choosing to settle on islands or other defensible locations.

By about 4,500 BC the Linear Pottery culture was succeeded by the Lengyel culture, whose best-known locations were at Brześć Kujawski and Osłonki. The Lengyel people grew grain and kept a variety of livestock, the most important being cattle with pigs, sheep, and goats kept as well. They also consumed a variety of wild animals – ducks, geese, turtles, fish, deer, and small mammals.

The Osłonki settlement, excavated by Polish and American

archaeologists, consisted of at least thirty longhouses surrounded by fortifications consisting of a wide ditch and wood and earth palisade. Graves at the site revealed rich treasure troves of copper jewellery, probably imported from sources in the Carpathian Mountains. Radiocarbon dating puts the site at about 4,300 to 4,000 BC.

The established Lengyel farming communities seem to have given way to the less settled Funnel Beaker culture (named after its distinctive pottery) by around 3,900 BC While the Lengyel people seemed to have been concentrated at relatively few sites in northern Poland, the Funnel Beaker people were more widely dispersed and seem to have represented a halfway point between hunter-gatherer and agrarian societies. They may have been semi-nomads, occupying sites for brief periods of time before moving onto greener pastures when the soil was depleted or game grew scarce.

These early cultures also developed the first basic mining – digging for flint deposits in the Holy Cross Mountains of central Poland, and panning for salt near Kraków. Such commodities could be traded for copper from Slovakia. Larger, more settled communities, such as Brześć Kujawski, even developed workshops that smelted copper ore and then cold hammered it into ornaments.

They also set a pattern of life in north central Europe that would endure for thousands of years, though with many local variations and new cultures moving into and out of the region. Farming settlements were relatively scattered without a well-developed hierarchy. While larger communities developed, they consequently divided into smaller satellite settlements due to pressure on available resources. Hill forts, protected by massive earth and timber fortifications provided protection against raids rather than permanent homes. Long-distance trade in rare commodities such as copper brought goods from hundreds of miles away, but local trade was more often in the form of gifts to secure peace and cement alliances.

Farming and stock herding provided the main sources of food. Grains such as barley and wheat were commonly grown (with rye, now a staple of Polish life, introduced later). Cattle, used for meat and milk, were the most common forms of livestock. Pigs were kept semi-feral and herded into the forest during the summer and fall to fatten up on roots and acorns. Most people lived in simple houses made of wood and dug partly into the ground as shelter against winter's cold, with a roof of timber covered with turf.

At the dawn of the Bronze Age, the Funnel Beaker people were gradually succeeded by the Lusatian culture in the north of present-day Poland by around 2500 BC and in the south by the Mierzanowice culture. It was the latter who built the massive hill fort at Trzcinica (near the modern Polish-Ukrainian border). Trzcinica's hill fort, undoubtedly the residence of a powerful chieftain, covered 0.6 ha and was protected by an earth and timber rampart 2.5 m thick. Its inhabitants had close trade and cultural ties with regions south of the Carpathians. Around 1600 BC migrants from the south gradually absorbed the local population and expanded the Trzcinica site, both in size and in economic and social complexity.

The inhabitants of these regions maintained regular trade with the Greeks, Romans and other Mediterranean cultures from the Bronze Age onward. The most prized commodity was amber, culled from the shores of the Baltic Sea. Honey, wax, furs, and slaves were also traded. Settlements such as Kalisz were well established by the first millennium AD (if not earlier) and were mentioned by Roman sources. Occasional caches of Roman coins found in southeastern Poland attest to a lively trade that had been in existence for centuries.

During the first millennium BC the region witnessed the migration of Germanic and Celtic peoples. The latter exercised some cultural influence on the local population but are chiefly remembered in the name often given southern Poland, Galicia, or 'land of the Gaels.' The Germanic influence was stronger and the Przeworsk culture, which spread over much of present-day Poland during the first millennium had a distinct Germanic flavour.

The Slavs

Until the first millennium BC the primary ancestors of the Poles had not appeared on the scene and their origins have been a matter of much academic debate. Poles are Slavs, part of the largest ethno-linguistic group in Europe. Slavs and Balts were probably the last Indo-European groups to leave their original homeland in central Asia. When they did so is a matter of some speculation, perhaps as early as 2000 BC or as late as 500 BC. Over the course of several centuries they moved westward in a gradual migration that would eventually bring them to eastern Europe. It is likely that they reached the territory of present-day Ukraine by the end of the first millennium BC. At that point, the Balts (the ancestors of today's Lithuanians and Latvians) separated themselves and continued moving north toward the Baltic Sea.

The early Slavs (or proto-Slavs) may have been described by Greek chroniclers as the Vendi or the Scythian farmers and lived north of the Black Sea but were separated from the Greek world by such nomadic groups as the Scythians. They had close contact with Persian-speaking peoples such as the Sarmatians and Scythians and at some point may have been allies or subjects of those nomads. Slavic languages, including Polish, contain a significant number of loan words from Persian related to religion, hunting and feasting. Slavs also had close contact with Germanic peoples such as the Goths. There was probably significant intermarriage between Slav and Goth, and there are numerous loan words in Slavonic that date from this very early contact.

At the beginning of the first millennium AD, the Slavs lived in a belt of territory between the steppes around the coast of the Black Sea and the vast forests of northern Europe. The mix of open land and forest was ideal for subsistence farming, herding, hunting and gathering. In the fifth century as more and more barbarians were able to breach the borders of the Roman Empire, the Slavs came under increasing pressure from new invaders who sought to move through their lands to the rich pickings of the Roman world. In addition, Germanic neighbours to the west began to move further west and south into the Roman Empire, opening up opportunities for Slavic migration. These pressures perhaps combined with a growing population resulted in the Great Migration.

Throughout the fifth and sixth centuries, a mass movement of Slavic tribes dispersed throughout central and eastern Europe. The ancestors of the East Slavs (Russians, Ukrainian, Rusyns and Belarusins) moved north and east, though many remained in the original homeland. The ancestors of the South Slavs (Bulgarians, Croatians, Macedonians, Serbs and Slovenes), driven in part by alliances with other nomads, travelled into the Balkans where they assaulted the Eastern Roman Empire, even raiding the Greek islands.

The West Slavs, the ancestors of the Poles, as well as the Czechs, Slovaks and Sorbs, moved into present-day Poland, Czech Republic, Slovakia, Austria and eastern Germany, occupying most of the territory east of the Elbe. Along the way, they absorbed and Slavicized remaining Germanic settlements.

The ancestors of the Poles and other Slavic group did not exist as nations, but lived in tribal societies. These tribal groups were led by chieftains whose power was based on military prowess and the ability to attract and keep a sufficient retinue of followers. Like earlier inhabitants, the Slavs lived in scattered farming communities but maintained a series of central hill forts that would serve as refuge in case of raid or invasion. Slavic settlers also built forts on islands in lakes and rivers or in marshes to provide additional protection. Although some existing hill forts were adapted for use by the Slavs, the existing archaeological record shows that the newcomers greatly expanded the number and range of such forts.

Slavonic society did not have a well-defined hierarchy. There were numerous chiefs and many tribes and subgroups who would unite only if threatened from the outside. Major population centres emerged only gradually, usually due to economic or religious reasons. Trading ports on the major rivers or the Baltic coast grew quickly. Wolin, near the present-day German-Polish border, grew into a major trading centre by the ninth century, with its own harbour, lighthouse and a wide range of merchants and craftsmen. Its several thousand inhabitants traded with Russia, Germany and Scandinavia. Further up the Baltic coast, at Arkona on the island of Rugen in present-day Germany, comes evidence of another major Slavic centre – this one a cult site to the god Svantovit which existed until it was sacked by Danish invaders in 1168.

Slavic pagan beliefs are known only in their broad outlines as a mix of nature worship, animism, ancestor worship and the existence of a few major deities shared by most Slavs. The centre of Slavonic spirituality was the family hearth. Personal and family spirits (*domowy*), if properly honoured and fed, protected the home and its inhabitants and may have been seen as embodiments of departed ancestors. Beyond the home were the generally benign but capricious spirits of the fields. Further afield, lurking in the forests and marshes, were the dangerous *leshy* who could lead travellers astray and even to their deaths. Worship was often connected with sacred trees or groves, though larger cult sites were not unknown. In the Holy Cross Mountains south of Warsaw, pagan pilgrims continued to visit the site of a strange rock barrow 1300 meters long well into the twelfth century much to the chagrin of local Christian monks.

The established pantheon of gods and goddesses memorized by students of classical Greece and Rome, did not have a Slavic counterpart. A range of major deities was worshipped by the Slavs but without the (admittedly artificial) structure known in classical studies. Major gods in one tribe were minor figures in another and unknown to yet others. Only toward the end of Slavic paganism as contact with Christianity grew did the worship of major deities take on a form that would be familiar to our eyes. That said, a number of major deities did emerge during the pre-Christian period. Piorun was the god of war and the thunderbolt, worshipped in sacred groves of oak trees. Mokosh, whose name means 'the moist one,' was the earth goddess, patroness of childbirth. Svarog was the god of the sun or of fire (depending on the location). Svantovit was the god of magic and prophecy. Svantovit, also known as Triglav (lit. 'three headed') like some Slavic deities, was portrayed as having multiple heads, reminiscent of Hindu gods and perhaps recalling an earlier Indo-European practice.

THE ORIGINS OF POLAND

The name Poland (or Polska in Polish) derives from a single Slavic tribe living in western Poland between the Vistula and Warta rivers. The Polanie took their name from the Slavic word for field, *pole*, and were thus 'dwellers in the fields.' Their original territory was indeed one of rich soil, well watered by numerous lakes and rivers. The seat of tribal power was the town of Gniezno. The name meant 'nest,' appropriate because the emblem of the tribal chief was the white Baltic Sea Eagle.

Through some combination of strong leadership, military success, diplomacy, good marriages or just plain luck, the chieftains of the Polanie were able to conquer or win over neighbouring tribes into a kind of confederation that encompassed much of west central Poland. Despite this, local lords retained significant power within their territory. Leaders of Polanie were referred to by medieval chroniclers as 'dukes', a term best understood in its original Roman meaning of war leader. The authority of the chieftain was largely dependent on his ability to mobilize, lead and reward a band of loyal warriors.

It is likely that leadership within the Polanie and other neighbouring tribes was not hereditary and was certainly not based on the principle of the eldest son inheriting his father's mantle. This was particularly true as early Slavonic rulers, as embodiments of the fertility of the land, had numerous wives and concubines and usually fathered many children. War leaders were probably chosen from within a circle of powerful men, though at least one legend hints that a few women may have held leadership positions. Even down to modern times, Polish inheritance traditions stressed equality among all siblings, which, while seemingly egalitarian, often resulted in fragmenting the family patrimony. Although the notion of hereditary rulership eventually took root in Poland, it was never particularly strong and later would result in a unique political experiment that would set the Poles on a very different course from many other European nations.

Sometime in the ninth century the Polanie tribe broke with this tradition and established a form of hereditary rulership. According to legend, the land was ruled by the cruel and inept King Popiel (King Ashes). Popiel and his wife murdered his uncles who he thought were plotting to take over the throne. The result was chaos and as the country fell apart, the couple shut themselves inside their tower where they were devoured by the mice who had grown strong feeding on the corpses of the king's murdered relatives. In his place, the people chose a peasant wheelwright named Piast to be their ruler.

The dynasty that bore the name of the legendary wheelwright would claim rulership of Poland more or less continuously for the next four hundred years. The blood of this dynasty would intermingle with nearly every European royal or princely house so that virtually every modern monarch can trace some ancestry back to the sturdy peasant of legend.

Accurate dates in early Polish history are difficult to come by, but it is likely that the house of Piast rose to power sometime in the early 800s AD. Legends aside, the name itself may mean 'guardian' or 'tutor', perhaps deriving from a title rather than a proper name. (It would not be the first European dynasty to begin as guardians or instructors of the prince's children. The first Carolingian king of France, Pepin, also began his career as tutor.)

The first Piast whose name is recorded is Ziemowit who was succeeded by his son Leszek, and then by his grandson Ziemomysł. Ziemomysł was the father of Mieszko, the first Polish ruler for whom solid historical evidence exists.

Poland first appears in historical chronicles in 962. It was already a local power under Duke Mieszko I (922–92) with a household guard (*drużyna*) of 3,000 well-equipped warriors. His main stronghold at Gniezno was defended by strong fortifications. Mieszko ruled over what was then the largest of the west Slavic states that extended over most of the territory between the Oder and Vistula. To the north and east, the Slavic Pomeranians, Kujavians and Mazovians remained independent under their own rulers, though occasionally subject to Mieszko's stronger Polanian state. To the south was the centre of the Vistulanians, Kraków, destined to play a major role in Polish history. The people of Kraków had strong ties to the Czech/Moravian state south of the Carpathian Mountains.

To Mieszko's west he faced a series of northwestern Slavic tribes inhabiting what is today eastern Germany. By the middle of the tenth century, however, these fiercely independent and staunchly pagan

Mieszko I, the first historic ruler of Poland

tribes were coming under increasing pressure from the expanding German empire under Otto I. After more than a century of bloody wars, these tribes were being destroyed or Germanized. (Their only remnant today, aside from place names and archeological sites are the 50,000 or so Sorbs of southeastern Germany.)

Though the Polanians themselves had faced these western neighbours on the battlefield, the western tribes had also provided a buffer against the more powerful German empire. So the appearance of Mieszko and the Polanian state in the chronicle literature coincided with the moment in time when the Polanians faced a significant challenge to their existence. One of Mieszko's first responses to this threat was to contract an alliance with the Czechs. In 965, Mieszko married the Czech princess Dabrowka to seal the deal.

THE SOUTHERN CONNECTION

To the south of the growing Piast state was the major city of Kraków, seat of the Vistulanian princes. Kraków's history stretched back to the legend of the clever farmer, Krak, who defeated the great dragon Smok and used his bones as the foundation for his stronghold. Founded in the fourth century, the city was strategically located near one of the best north-south routes across the Carpathian Mountains and on the Vistula River, making it a natural location for commerce. Because of its location, Kraków had close ties to the Czech lands and probably allied with or was subject to Czech rule during its early history.

With their closer proximity to the Roman world, the Czechs, Moravians, and Slovaks developed powerful but short-lived states as early as the seventh century. In 862, the Christian missionaries Saints Cyril and Methodius reached Moravia and brought Christianity. They also created the first Slavic written language (the basis of the Cyrillic script used in modern Russian and Ukrainian) and created a Slavonic liturgy that would have immense cultural and linguistic influence in the centuries that followed. Christianity gradually spread north, from Byzantium and Rome. Individual Christians as well as missionaries carried the faith north of the Carpathians. By the end of the eighth century, the prince of the Vistulanians had converted to Christianity and the faith made significant inroads in the Kraków region.

At the time of Mieszko's marriage, Christianity was filtering into Poland from three directions: from Byzantine missionaries, from the expanding German empire, and from Czech and Moravian territories. The German option was perhaps the least attractive, given cultural and linguistic differences and the political influence German churchmen might wield on behalf of the emperor. Both the Poles and Czechs worked hard to avoid falling under the sway of the German Holy Roman Empire, so adopting the faith from German missionaries was not in Mieszko's interest.

The influence of Byzantine Christianity on eastern and central Europe during the tenth century was undeniable. Byzantium was the world's most important city, with a population of over one million. Its wealth and learning were a magnet for many of the region's developing states. This represented a clear alternative to the Latin Christianity, for although the schism between Eastern and Western Christianity was not final until after Poland's conversion, tensions and rivalries had already emerged. Yet, at the very moment Christianity began to make serious inroads into the Piast lands, direct contact between Poland and Byzantium was made difficult if not impossible, by the invasion of the Magyars in the tenth century. Poland would therefore adopt Christianity from Rome via their Czech and Moravian neighbors. Czech loan words, rather than German, would form the basis for the Polish liturgical vocabulary.

966

Poland's conversion to Christianity in 966 was not a foregone conclusion. Some of Poland's Baltic neighbours remained pagan well into the fourteenth century. Nevertheless, Slavonic paganism with its endless heterogeneity and its ties to locality and family was increasingly ill-suited to the Polish ruling class. In particular, it yielded little pragmatic power for the new world of cross-border trade, new ideas, and international alliances. Christianity provided a common cultural and political vocabulary that allowed Mieszko and his followers to become part of a larger and more vital world. It also represented a bold assertion of Mieszko's personal authority. After all, neither his tribe nor his nascent princedom had ever officially adopted paganism. It was simply the faith that had always existed. Now Mieszko proposed to change this and in the process expand the power of his rule over his people.

The tenth century was a time in which religious faith was far more than a matter of private belief. It was the medium through which society functioned. It bound individual to family, family to community, community to prince. It was the source of art and learning, and provided solace, comfort and inspiration in times of trouble and darkness.

The problem was how to join the Christian world without losing independence to more powerful Christian princes. In an age when secular rulers often chose bishops, accepting Christianity from the Holy Roman Empire would place Poland's leading religious figures in the hands of Mieszko's most serious foe. While the Polanie had always had rivalries with other Slavic peoples, the Czechs and Moravians represented the lesser of two evils. Mieszko's Christian wife, Dąbrowka, also seems to have played a major role in his decision. According to a German chronicler of the time:

> When, after they were already married, Lent came around, Dąbrowka wanted to offer freely to the Lord abstention from meat and mortification of the flesh, but her husband tried to induce her by sweet promises to break her pledge. She yielded to him so as to be able to win his consent on more important matters. ... She worked patiently for her husband's conversion and God heard her prayers, causing the man who had denied Him to repent, abandon through his wife's patient persuasion the heathen venom and cleanse himself of original sin by holy baptism. The example of their beloved ruler was immediately followed by his errant subjects.

In 966 Mieszko accepted Christianity from Rome and placed his lands directly under the Holy See. This was a canny political manoeuvre and a clear shot across the bows of the German emperor. It established Mieszko as an independent prince and a direct subject of the pope rather than the emperor. In 968, the first independent Polish bishropic was established in Poznań, near Gniezno. Having an independent bishop was a crucial sign of independence, even if the man filling the role was not a native Pole. Neither Bohemia nor Moravia had their own bishoprics and when a diocese was established in Prague in 975, it was initially subordinate to the German see of Meissen.

Mieszko's adoption of Latin Christianity had enormous consequences for Poland's future. Poland would represent (along with Hungary and eventually Lithuania), the eastern border of Latin Christianity. The Poles would join the West and while they would remain closely tied to the Orthodox and Muslim East, they would look west for their cultural and religious inspiration. As in Western Europe, the Poles would eventually adopt clear ideas about individual liberty and limitations on the power of the ruler, be it king or president. Although faith would have an important impact on Polish politics, unlike in Russia where Church and State became one, in Poland faith and politics remained in separate though complementary spheres.

When Mieszko died in 992, his state consisted of most of modern west-central and central Poland including the provinces of Wielkopolska (Greater Poland), Kujawy, and the southern part of Mazovia. In addition to his capital at Gniezno, Poznan was emerging as a major economic and ecclesiastical centre, and his rule also extended over the cities of Kruszwica and Kalisz.

BOLESŁAW CHROBRY

Polish rulers after Mieszko were often given nicknames by which they are rendered more memorable. Mieszko's sceptre passed to his son, Bolesław I Chrobry or Bolesław the Brave (r. 992–1025). The state his father left to him was clearly a powerful and united one. It was made more so when Bolesław had all serious rivals for the throne exiled or blinded. In the final years of Mieszko's rule, the Piast ruler began to expand his territory. Beginning in the 980s, Pomerania was gradually subordinated to Polish rule, including the key cities of Szczecin at the mouth of the Oder and Gdańsk at the mouth of the Vistula. Mieszko's influence also began to extend south into Silesia, including the city of Wrocław.

Bolesław's mission would be to expand his patrimony and bring it closer to the Latin West. The new king had spent part of his young adult years at the court of the German emperor and understood contemporary politics, both secular and ecclesiastical. He was also an accomplished warrior and leader who mobilized and inspired the men under his command and staged impressive acts of political pageantry to impress visitor and local alike.

Bolesław cemented his rule over Silesia and Pomerania. His most important acquisition, however, was Małopolska (Lesser Poland). This well-settled and prosperous territory included the city of Kraków and its inclusion extended Piast rule from the Baltic Sea to the Carpathian Mountains. Małopolska had been previously under the sway of Bohemia and the expansion of Piast rule over Silesia and Małopolska helped sour Polish-Czech relations.

Another major irritant was the presence of Czech exiles at the Polish court. They had fled or been banished following internecine struggles in their homeland. One of these was Wojciech (Voytech), a prince of the Czech Slawnikowiec family. Wojciech (939–97) was a well-liked and intensely religious man who had been appointed Bishop of Prague then forced to flee due to political and clerical rivalries. He was a friend of the Holy Roman Emperor Otto III and close to Pope John XV. Though inclined toward a life of prayer, Wojciech's princely birth did not allow for the quietude of contemplation. In 995, most of his family was massacred by political rivals. He was released from his episcopal duties and volunteered to go to Poland. He was appointed Bishop of Gniezno but relinquished his office in favour of missionary work.

In 997, with the support Bolesław I, Wojciech attempted to convert the pagan Prussians living on Poland's northern border. He was murdered at the behest of local pagan priests, becoming Poland's first known Christian martyr. His death shocked both the imperial and papal courts, where he had been well known and an immediate effort to promote his canonisation began.

The canny Bolesław, though doubtless equally shocked by Wojciech's gruesome murder, exploited the tragedy for all it was worth. A Ruthenian chronicler of the time described him as so large in size as to tax any horse, but nimble in mind. He ransomed the martyred priest's body from the Prussians (supposedly for its weight in gold) and buried him in the church in Gniezno. While promoting the canonization of Wojciech, he embarked on a campaign to gain for Poland a separate independent archbishopric and three additional dioceses. At the time, Bohemia, with a far older Christian tradition, had only a single diocese subordinated to a German archbishop. Bolesław's effort paid off. St Wojciech (known in English as St Adalbert) was canonised in 999. In 1000, at the turning of the millennium, Pope Sylvester II permitted the establishment of dioceses in Kraków, Wrocław, and Kołobrzeg on the Baltic coast. Gniezno was made an archdiocese. This coup greatly enhanced the external prestige of the monarchy and increased internal cohesion.

That same year, Bolesław played host to Emperor Otto III (r.980–1002) and a large retinue of European nobles and churchmen who came on a pilgrimage to the shrine of the new saint. The emperor was greeted, not by barbarians dressed in furs as many of his retinue had expected, but by well-equipped knights and ladies and courtiers dressed in fine clothes. According to one chronicle, Otto III 'cried in wonder, "Upon my imperial crown, what I see here is beyond what I had heard about".' He is said to have stated of Bolesław that 'It is not fitting that a man of such stature be called prince or count, as one of many, but he merits the royal throne and crown.' Later, Otto III placed his own crown on Boleslaw's head, recognizing him as a sovereign ruler.

The Polish monarch then accompanied the emperor on his return journey to Germany and an embassy to Rome succeeded in securing a papal crown for Bolesław. However, imperial and papal politics intervened and the crown went to Hungary instead. Bolesław would remain without the final symbol of royalty until the very end of his reign.

BOLESŁAW'S CONQUESTS

In 1002, Bolesław's ally Otto III died and a struggle began over the imperial succession. Bolesław took advantage of the confusion and marched into Lusatia. He then added Bohemia and Moravia to his possessions, creating a single West Slavic state stretching from the Baltic to the Danube. Bohemia proved too much for the young Piast state to control and slipped from Bolesław's grasp by 1004. Moravia remained in his hands until 1020.

Bolesław's seizure of imperial territory was backed by some local German leaders and the Polish monarch took part in the deliberations to select the new emperor, Henry II (r.1002–1024). He even proposed to offer his daughter's hand to Henry's son to cement the alliance begun under Otto III. These plans broke down after Bolesław was assaulted by enemies within the imperial court. Bolesław escaped with his retinue and this began a protracted Polish-German conflict.

Henry II launched an invasion of Poland in 1005. Although the Poles were no match for the heavier German knights in the open field, they lured their foes into well-planned ambushes and harassed the invaders without mercy. Their massive earth and timber fortresses proved immune to German siege tactics. The campaign ended in a peace treaty that allowed Bolesław to keep Moravia but returned Lusatia to Henry. Two years later, Bolesław broke this treaty. Another large German army tried without success to force the Oder River. The conflict dragged on for four years. Another peace treaty returned Lusatia to Poland but as an imperial fief and Bolesław was recognized as a monarch by Henry II.

This peace treaty lasted until 1014 when a new conflict broke out. Two imperial armies crossed the Oder but the wily Bolesław kept them from linking up while his lighter forces bled the invaders white with ambushes and raids. In 1017, Henry himself took the field with an imperial host that included Czech forces and contingents of pagan Slavic allies (much to the chagrin of the newly Christian Poles and some of Henry's own bishops). The imperial forces tried to force the key fortress of Niemcza south of Wrocław. The small community's inhabitants reinforced by a contingent of Bolesław's knights staged an epic defence, throwing back every attack of Henry's superior forces. As the emperor's army exhausted itself at Niemcza, Bolesław cut off his opponent's supplies and lines of retreat. Finally, Henry had to beat an ignominious retreat to Bohemia with his battered army. A final peace treaty was concluded in 1018. The fifty-year-old Polish king regained Lusatia and a German princess as fourth wife. Henry even agreed to support his next campaign against Kiev.

By then Bolesław's attention had also turned eastward toward Kievan Rus. One of his daughters had wed a son of the Grand Prince of Kiev. When the couple were imprisoned by dynastic rivals, Bolesław mounted an expedition in 1013 to free them. His unlucky son-in-law

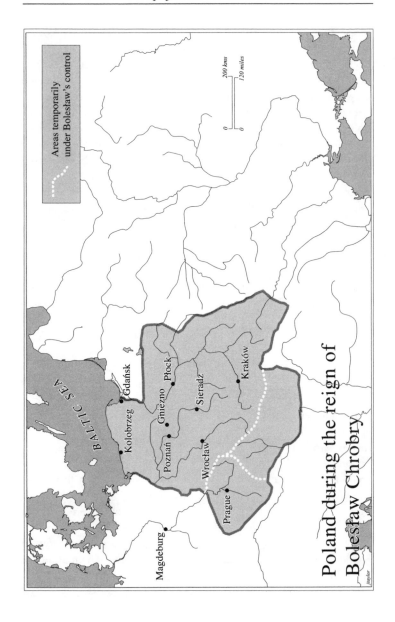

Poland during the reign of
Bolesław Chrobry

was expelled from Kiev a few years later and the Kievans raided eastern Poland in retaliation. In 1018, Bolesław, now freed from the German threat, mounted a major expedition against Kiev. His forces crushed the Kievans and Bolesław seized Kiev, then one of the largest and wealthiest cities in eastern Europe. He reinstalled his son-in-law and proceeded to rob the city. According to a chronicler, Bolesław 'was constantly sending money to Poland and took the rest of the booty when going back.' Unlike his previous fiasco in Bohemia, however, Bolesław had learned his lesson and never tried to directly control Kiev.

On Easter Sunday 1025, Bolesław was formally crowned king of Poland by the Polish bishops. The now aged monarch died shortly thereafter. During his remarkable reign he had expanded his kingdom dramatically, turning it into a regional power capable of repelling even the might of the Holy Roman Empire. As a military commander he proved capable of outfoxing larger, more powerful foes time and again. His conquests brought prosperity to Poland, but the strength of his rule was based on military victory. His campaigns often proved unsustainable and drained resources and manpower. In the hands of lesser men the large state he built through his personal leadership would not last.

Fragmentation and Restoration

Bolesław left his crown to his son Mieszko II (990–1034), known as Mieszko the Slothful, passing over an older son, Bezprim. Though a capable commander, Mieszko had neither the skill nor the luck of his father. In 1030 Poland's enemies took advantage of the old king's death to take back lands they had lost. Simultaneous attacks by imperial forces in the west and Kievan forces in the east, sent Mieszko into exile in Bohemia and Kievans managed to install Bezprim as ruler. Bolesław's older son proved both incompetent and unpopular and was assassinated after a short reign. Mieszko returned to the throne in 1032 but was never able effectively to put his late father's empire back together.

The disparate possessions of Bolesław I had been held together by personal loyalty to the old king who governed potentially fractious local potentates with a strong hand. When that glue disappeared, local provinces and their nobles grew increasingly independent. This fragmentation was quite common in medieval Europe but was especially pronounced in Poland which lacked a strong tradition of kingship. Weak rulers were forced to buy the loyalty of their knights and nobles by granting privileges, offices, and additional lands. These local leaders often grew strong enough to ignore their overlords.

The structure of the early Polish nobility is not clear. Local nobles emerged from tribal leadership. Although many noble families would later claim legendary ancestors of foreign pedigree – stretching back even to classical Rome – most grew from local Slavic stock. Noble or knightly families in Poland were bolstered by clan membership. Though the exact origin and nature of clans are the subject of heated scholarly debate, they were probably originally based on common ancestry or kinship but soon evolved into a complex of relationships that bound powerful and weaker members of the nobility together through mutual obligations of support and patronage. Members of clans fought together under a common banner and bore the same coats of arms (with minor variations).

Unlike the nobility of western Europe, the Polish nobility was quite large, encompassing 8 to 10 per cent of the population. Polish nobles almost never held titles (such as count or duke) and came to resemble in some respects the Japanese samurai class. Their status was tied to their right to bear and use arms. Collectively they were referred to as *szlachta*, an obscure term that seems to denote 'those who serve'.

During the eleventh century, this class was still in its infancy and local tribal loyalties, reinforced by dialect and custom, remained strong. Although nobles sought greater independence from the monarch, their own subjects could also rise in revolt in the face of repression and cruelty. Without a strong monarchy as a check on the power of the nobles, some became petty tyrants in their own right.

After Mieszko II's death in 1034, Poland was convulsed by a series of internal revolts, including some aimed at overthrowing the Church and restoring pagan rule. The revolts were often started by petty nobles and aimed at over-mighty regional lords who had spent the decade since the death of Bolesław I amassing power at the expense of their less powerful neighbours. The revolt was strongest in Silesia and western Poland, but weaker in Małopolska where

Christianity was much better established and in Mazovia. The chronicler Gallus Anonymous wrote:

> While Poland suffered defeat and wrongs from others, it was even more shamefully tormented by its own people. Slaves rose against their masters, the low born against the noble, taking high office themselves and turning their victims into servants, or taking lewdly their wives after having killed them and wrongfully seized their property. Even worse, they abandoned the Christian faith – of which we cannot speak without tears and sorrow – rebelling against bishops and God's priests; some of them, as though worthy of a death in dignity, they slew with swords, other – judged less worthy – they stoned to death.

Mieszko's successor, Prince Kazimierz, was forced to flee the country. Thousands of refugees fled the carnage in western Poland and went to Mazovia. In 1038, the Czechs took advantage of the chaos in Poland and invaded, sacking Poznań and Gniezno. They stole the relics of St Adalbert and brought them back to Prague, along with many skilled craftsman and their families who were forcibly relocated to Bohemia. Although Czech forces eventually withdrew from Wielkopolska, they remained to occupy most of Silesia.

Prince Kazimierz I, known as the Restorer (1016–58), returned the following year with the support of the German emperor Conrad II (r.1024–39), whose own interests were not served by the instability on his eastern frontier. With the traditional Piast strongholds of Poznań and Gniezno devastated by revolt and invasion, Kazimierz relocated his power base to the important southern city of Kraków. It would remain Poland's capital for the next five centuries. Kazimierz then proceeded to recover the provinces that had broken with the monarchy. It took ten years of war to win back Mazovia and Pomerania. In 1050, Kazimierz attacked Silesia and drove out the Czech garrisons. He managed to appease Emperor Henry III and hold onto the province, though at the price of paying a yearly tribute to Bohemia.

Like all early Polish rulers, Kazimierz the Restorer played a careful game of cat and mouse with the German empire. At times, they acted as vassals of their powerful neighbour while defying the emperor at others. The empire was close enough to be a serious threat, but Poland was too distant and too strong to be easily subjected to direct rule (as happened in Bohemia). Polish rulers could be masters in their own house but abroad had to act with caution, especially when confronting imperial vassals such as Bohemia. As the conflict between the papacy and the empire heated up in the late eleventh century, Polish rulers would attempt to separate themselves yet further from the German empire's shadow.

Kazimierz I died in 1058. Although never formally crowned as king, he managed to reconstitute a significant part of his grandfather's state through a combination of warfare and diplomacy. He left his eldest son and heir, Bolesław II, an undivided patrimony.

THE ECONOMY OF MEDIEVAL POLAND

The majority of Poland's population lived in small villages, often small clusters of dwellings with a dozen or fewer families. Larger villages and towns had a church and perhaps a few craftsmen and merchants. Only in larger cities and around castles could a significant community of merchants and craftsmen be sustained.

People came in a bewildering array of classes. Peasants could be free or unfree in varying degrees. Yet, freedom did not always imply prosperity. There were prosperous unfree peasants and poor free ones. Their obligations also varied according to who was their overlord or where they lived. For example, some peasants were obligated to pay the *stróza*, an obligation meant for the upkeep of castles. This could come in the form of taxes paid in coin or agricultural goods, or as labour. In some villages, particular families were required to pay the *stróza,* others not. In some cases, peasants were also required to serve as guards in time of war or unrest.

Most people made their living through subsistence agriculture. Farming was carried on in the three-field method where about one field in three was left fallow each year and used as pasture in order to restore the soil's nutrients. Millet was the most common grain since it grew under even difficult weather conditions and could be easily processed into gruel, a dietary staple far more common in the eleventh century than bread. Wheat, oats, barley and rapeseed were also commonly grown. Rye was introduced in the early Middle Ages. Crops like wheat and rye were often grown to be sold or used to pay feudal obligations.

Fruits and vegetables were commonly grown. Major vegetables included onions, lentils, field peas, cabbage, fava beans, kale, white carrots, beets, parsnips, alexanders, skirrets, turnips, radishes, cucumbers, and melons, as well as mushrooms (which were found wild in the forests). Orchards of apples, pears, cherries, plums, and peaches were reported even before the adoption of Christianity. Grapes were introduced into southern Poland with the advent of Christianity and native wine production existed until a cooling of the climate in the sixteenth century made it impossible to continue. While beer became a staple of Polish life for both nobles and commoners, it was usually made without hops, but was flavoured with herbs and resembled some forms of archaic ale. The earliest known drink among the Poles was mead, a by-product of the region's ancient tradition of beekeeping.

People of all classes kept livestock. Cattle were kept for meat and milk and as beasts of burden. Pigs were raised semi-wild and fattened in forests during the autumn, while sheep and all forms of poultry were common. Fish was introduced with Christianity as a staple food for meatless fast days and the trade in salt, smoked, or pickled fish was a lucrative one.

In early Poland, there existed specific villages dedicated to certain crafts or tasks, such as fishing, hunting, baking, horsekeeping, or barrelmaking. These were usually established by a lord or nobleman early in the Piast period to encourage such crafts. Over time, they gradually lost their economic function, but retained a historical memory of their former crafts.

Major estates began to emerge by the eleventh century and though few in number at first, played an important role in the development of trade and agriculture. Of equal, if not greater importance, was the introduction of the monastic system in Poland. The first monastery, the Benedictine Abbey at Tyniec near Kraków, was established as early as the 1050s. Monasteries provided a conduit for new methods of farming and husbandry, as well as being repositories of learning, art, music, and prayer. Through monasteries, new technology, such as the heavy plough, spread rapidly throughout Europe, gradually improving crop yields through the fourteenth century.

Poland's first monastery, the Benedictine Abbey at Tyniec, near Kraków was
established in the 1050s

In the decades following Poland's conversion, trade and industry
grew quickly. Iron working had existed in central Poland for centuries
but expanded with the growth of medieval Poland. Iron mines in the
Holy Cross Mountains expanded their production and by the eleventh
century Polish smiths were turning out a wide range of weapons, tools,
and everyday objects. Pottery and tilemaking also developed rapidly,
rivalling the sophisticated production centres of contemporary
Germany.

Poland's major trade in the early Middle Ages followed the old
north-south amber route. Polish honey, wax, amber, furs, and salted
herring moved south while Hungarian copper and wine and finished
goods from Italy, Bohemia, and Austria moved north. The Polish
upper classes developed a liking for Hungarian wine that has been
passed down to Polish wine lovers over many centuries. East-west trade
was restricted by long distances but trade routes between Kiev and
Germany were active from the tenth century. Trade routes between
Germany and Kiev passed through southern Poland, enriching cities
such as Kraków and Przemyśl. Sea trade on the Baltic was slowed by
piracy as the remaining pagan Slavs turned to the way of Vikings,

ravaging the now-Christian shores of Scandinavia as the Scandinavians had done in western Europe in earlier times. Over time, however, these problems declined.

Coinage had been introduced as early as the reign of Mieszko I. Jewish craftsmen arrived from Western Europe or perhaps the Mediterranean to develop the prince's mint. (This was the origin of what would later become one of the world's largest Jewish communities.) Some early Polish coins featured inscriptions in Hebrew as well as pictures of the monarchs and other symbols of state authority, including the Piast eagle. The first meaningful Piast coins were minted in the reign of Bolesław II. They used native silver from the Legnica region of Silesia and were known as 'thick' *denars*. There were 240 *denars* to a *grzywna* which amounted to between 182.5 and 197.68 grams of silver. During the periods of Poland's fragmentation these coins were gradually devalued and eventually scrapped by later monarchs.

The Two Bolesławs

Kazimierz the Restorer's eldest son, Bolesław the Bold, assumed the throne in 1058. Bolesław II (1039–81) was gifted with tremendous personal energy – to the point of recklessness – as well as boundless pride. During the first years of his reign, despite another failed expedition to Bohemia, Bolesław managed to secure Poland's borders and install his uncle on the throne of Kiev.

Bolesław's reign occurred during the most intense period of conflict between the Papacy of Gregory VII and the Empire of Henry IV. Bolesław allied Poland with Pope Gregory in the hopes of reducing the power of his mighty next-door neighbour. He developed alliances with Hungary, launched raids into Bohemia and supported German princes rebelling against the emperor. His support was rewarded with the establishment of a new diocese in Płock. In 1076, he was crowned king with the blessing of the Church. The king fostered the expansion of the monastic system. The economy flourished.

Yet all was not well. Bolesław's obsession with his wars in Bohemia, Hungary and against the emperor led him to neglect affairs elsewhere. He lost the province of Pomerania and made no real attempt to regain it. The return of royal power in the person of a strong monarch was also a threat to many powerful nobles. The king's foreign enemies encouraged resentments at home and with royal forces dispersed, Bolesław's internal enemies mobilized against him in 1079. One of these was Stanisław, Bishop of Kraków. When the king realized the danger, he seized the bishop and had Stanisław hacked apart with swords. This move, however, only strengthened the opposition. The murdered bishop became a martyr of a cruel and oppressive ruler and was later canonised.

Bolesław fled to Hungary as his support at home collapsed. He took refuge at the court of his ally, but soon died under mysterious circumstances, perhaps murdered by agents of his Polish rivals.

In place of the deposed Bolesław, his brother Władysław Herman (1040–1102) became the reigning prince, though his chief lieutenant Sieciech was, according to some sources, the real ruler. The king's political weaknesses and the deposition of his brother meant that power devolved increasing to powerful nobles, such as Sieciech. These 'magnates' frequently pursued their own ambitions, which in some cases included the complete deposing of the Piast dynasty. Władysław reversed his brother's policies and moved Poland back toward the imperial orbit. The internal affairs of the country, however, remained in turmoil and a series of internal struggles tore the ruling classes into factions. Local revolts forced the king to buy the support of nobles who could help him to put down insurgents. Władysław's eldest sons Zbigniew and Bolesław the Wrymouth attempted to displace his father's powerful Palatine Sieciech, whose ambitions had grown apace. After they removed their father's favourite, they effectively divided the country between them.

When Władysław Herman died in 1102, his two sons were fully prepared to fight each other for the spoils. Zbigniew held Mazovia, Płock and Kraków while the younger Bolesław controlled Wrocław and Sandomierz. Both princes sought outside allies. Bolesław proved the more effective or lucky military commander. By 1107 he had exiled his brother to Bohemia and was recognized as the senior prince of Poland. That same year, Bolesław III (1086–1138), who was given the name Wrymouth perhaps due to some deformity, attacked Pomerania, a semi-independent province which had supported his brother's cause. Although he gained some successes, attacks by the Czechs and Germans kept him from exploiting his victories.

In 1109, Emperor Henry V (r.1106–25) invaded Poland with a large imperial army, determined to crush Bolesław and put Zbigniew on the throne as a direct imperial vassal. The Germans and their Czech allies failed to take the heavily fortified cities of Bytom and Wrocław. When the imperial forces reached Głogów, they seized hostages, including the garrison commander's son, and lashed them to their siege machines in hopes of forcing the defenders to stay their archery, but the citizens shot their own kin rather than surrender. Henry's failure at Głogów left his army vulnerable to Bolesław's guerilla tactics. The heavy imperial forces were harassed without mercy, drawn into ambushes and cut off from their supplies. At Psie Pole – the 'field of the dogs' – Bolesław administered a humiliating defeat on the imperial invaders, effectively ending the empire's ambitions to incorporate Poland. Zbigniew was sent back to Poland by the terms of the peace treaty. Bolesław had his brother blinded, brutally ending the conflict over succession.

For the next twenty-plus years, Bolesław engaged in a series of protracted campaigns to regain Pomerania and to keep his Bohemian rivals at bay. He managed to place Gdańsk firmly within his control and seized Wolin and Szczecin, among the last strongholds of Slavonic paganism.

On Bolesław's death in 1138 he left five sons. Mindful of his own experiences and those of his predecessors, the prince sought to end the bloody conflicts over succession that had divided the country into rival camps and threatened the future of the dynasty. While the concept of primogeniture (inheritance by the eldest son) was being gradually adopted by Polish nobles, Bolesław reached back into Slavic tradition and divided the kingdom among his five sons. The eldest son would hold the title of senior prince and serve as the acknowledged leader of the others. Nor would individual princes be allowed to necessarily pass on their holdings to their children. By giving each prince his own semi-independent territory, Bolesław apparently hoped to quell the ambitions of disinherited princes and ensure that the Piast dynasty rather than local nobles would hold the reigns of power.

Though Bolesław had devised a creative solution, in hindsight it proved a disaster, adding to the fragmentation of the country and leaving Poland divided and without a crowned king for almost two hundred years.

CHAPTER TWO

From Fragmentation to Rebirth, 1138–1333

Bolesław III's Legacy

Bolesław the Wrymouth's creative attempt to end the struggles over succession within the Piast dynasty merely added to the problem of fragmentation. His new provinces criss-crossed longstanding regional divides and may have been an effort to break down regional separatism. If so it largely failed. It did end efforts to overthrow the Piast dynasty but simply split the house into multiple lines of succession. Although a senior prince who held the largest and central province was supposed to lead the junior princes, powerful nobles were able to play the various princes off against each other.

The old king's eldest son by his first wife, Władysław (1105-59), became senior prince and four sons by his second wife became junior princes. Within a few years Władysław and his brothers were in conflict. By 1145, Władysław had been defeated and fled to the Holy Roman Empire, where he was to remain, earning him the nickname Władysław the Exile. His half-brother Bolesław the Curly (r. 1146–73) – named after his flowing locks – became senior prince but was no more effective in uniting the country.

Poland was not unique in its lack of internal cohesion. Fortunately, many of its neighbours shared the same problem. The age of powerful and aggressive German emperors was coming to an end. In place of the imperial threat, however, the Polish princes faced their local German counterparts who were eager to expand their personal holdings at the expense of those on their borders. The German princes of Saxony and Brandenburg soon destroyed the last of the pagan Slavic strongholds and turned their sights on their Polish Christian neighbours.

Meanwhile fragmentation proceeded apace. Władysław the Exile died in 1159 and his sons, Bolesław the Tall, Mieszko the Stumbler and Konrad the Lame, divided their father's province of Silesia among themselves. Their conflicts with their uncle Bolesław the Curly pushed them toward closer alliances with German patrons. Bolesław the Tall, a renowned knight, was a favourite of Emperor Frederick Barbarossa (r. 1152–90). While remaining in the hands of the ever-widening Piast family, Silesia began to gradually draw apart from Poland proper.

In 1173, Bolesław the Curly died and the role of senior prince was assumed by his brother Mieszko the Old. He proved to be an efficient administrator. His reform of the treasury was carried out with the help of Jewish contractors, who minted coins bearing the king's name in Hebrew. This marked the first significant Jewish settlement in Poland. He also worked to keep the province of Pomerania in the Polish fold against increasing Danish and German interests.

It was partly Mieszko's effectiveness at rebuilding central authority that led to a revolt against his rule in 1177 by a coalition of southern Polish nobles. They drove Mieszko from the country and made his younger brother Kazimierz the Just senior prince. The new prince, with strong ties to the Sandomierz region, turned his attention eastward and he sought to acquire lands in Galicia. Parts of Pomerania slipped further from the Poles' grasp as local princes increasingly sought protection and patronage within the empire. Kazimierz's entanglements with Kiev and Hungary led to a coup in 1191 that briefly replaced his brother Mieszko on the throne. Kazimierz returned to power with the backing of Kievan troops. The last three years of his reign were the most successful. He was able to restore some measure of internal order and defeated the pagan tribes that had been raiding from the north. The prince died suddenly in 1194 after a banquet amid rumours of poisoning.

Although the house of Piast had remained in power for two centuries, the price was increasing division within the dynasty itself. Numerous local branches proliferated and grew increasingly independent and focused on local concerns. The fragmentation of medieval

Poland was reflected in the fragmentation of its ruling family. The lack of a clear tradition of succession further complicated the picture. Princes could choose their own successor from among their sons – a perfect invitation for interfamily rivalry and skulduggery. Yet, the leading noble families also felt they had a right to help choose the prince and to thus restrain the power of the senior prince to intervene in their affairs. At issue were such matters as who would administer justice and collect taxes. The result was that nobles sought to play off potential heirs to the throne against one another. Each of the greater noble families sought power for themselves by backing a particular candidate but as a class the nobility desired a weaker central authority.

Similar trends were apparent throughout Europe. Kings and princes were in constant conflict with their mightiest subjects and only a few were able to rule unchallenged. The experience of King John of England who was pressured into granting his nobility a range of rights in the Magna Carta in 1215 would have been painfully familiar to his contemporaries in the Piast dynasty.

Poland in the Thirteenth Century

After the death of Kazimierz the Just, his brother and rival Mieszko the Old again became senior prince and lived to usher in the new century, dying in 1202. Traditionally historians categorized thirteenth-century Poland as a mess. The country was divided internally without strong political leadership and suffered repeated invasions from external foes. Yet, it was also a time of cultural achievement, the expansion of the Church, immigration and new settlement, and growth in the economy. Poland became increasingly tied into European networks of trade and intellectual exchange.

Poland's cultural achievement was already visible at the end of the twelfth century. The great bronze doors of the Gniezno cathedral were made sometime during the 1170s, probably in the reign of Mieszko the Old. The doors show scenes from the life of St Adalbert and are among the most significant examples of bronze relief work in medieval northern Europe. Although its artist is unknown, it is likely he was a French or Flemish master or a native Pole trained in western Europe.

The entrance to the cathedral in Gniezno with its great bronze doors

Romanesque art and architecture arrived in Poland with the coming of Christianity and was the dominant style for most major religious buildings. The original cathedrals of Poznań, Wrocław, and Gniezno were created in this style. Although few have survived the ravages of time, history, and changing stylistic tastes, one that has survived is the Church of St Andrew in Kraków. Built in the 1000s and renovated in 1200, it is a late Romanesque gem that served successively as a royal chapel, a parish church, and a monastic church. Beginning in the 1250s, monks of the Cistercian order brought the Gothic style to Poland. The full flowering of Gothic art and architecture in Poland would not take place until the fourteenth century, but the foundations were already being laid in the 1200s.

Changes in the economy and land tenure underlay the new cultural and artistic trends. The patchwork of feudal obligations owed by most peasants were gradually simplified (though never fully done away with) in such a way as to emphasize more economically lucrative crops such as wheat and rye. New privileges were granted to encourage further productivity that would result in the production of crops that would yield more money.

As Poland was still relatively sparsely inhabited, nobles and princes encouraged settlement of new agricultural lands by peasant migrants through granting exemptions from various taxes and obligation. The obvious profitability of turning empty land into productive farms led to the recruitment of settlers from Germany and Flanders. Although German settlement in Poland was not unknown earlier, significant immigration dates from about the 1220s. The heaviest German settlement occurred in Silesia and Wielkopolska, though over the course of the succeeding centuries German migrant communities would be found in many areas of Poland. Although the more isolated German settlements were gradually Polonized, in Silesia and parts of Wielkopolska the newcomers gave some areas a distinctly Germanic character in language and customs.

German immigration was also significant in many towns and cities. German merchants and craftsmen were encouraged to settle as a means of economic development. Although the exact proportions and impact of the new arrivals are often disputed, over the next few centuries, cities such as Kraków, Wrocław, Poznań and Gdańsk clearly had a mixed German-Polish character with both languages spoken on the streets.

By the early 1200s Polish towns and cities had begun to expand in size as well as in economic and political power. Following models first developed in central Germany, cities were granted so-called German-law charters. Though they came in many local variants, they generally allowed cities a much higher degree of self-government under elected councils and mayors. Although still beholden to the ruling prince and the bishops, it allowed city leaders to gain some independence from local nobles and greater control over their own finances and trade. The first such charters were granted in the early thirteenth century in Silesia, but in the second half of the century expanded throughout central Poland.

Although even smaller towns benefited from the new economic conditions, the most prominent cities grew into hubs of international commerce and culture. Cities such as Wrocław, Poznań and Lublin promoted annual trade fairs on the feast days of prominent saints, drawing merchants and wares from throughout the region and as far away as Venice, Flanders, and the Middle East. Both Wrocław and Gdańsk joined the Hanseatic League, northern Europe's most prominent trading bloc, as full members.

During this era the Church in Poland began to shed some of the features of a missionary outpost on the edge of Christendom and took on the characteristics of its more sophisticated European counterparts. Among the most crucial aspects of this change was the Church's independence from secular power, a fact cemented by the divided nature of Polish politics. Princes in need of support had much to gain and little to lose by ceding rights to the clergy in religious matters. In 1207, the priest and historian, the Blessed Vincenty Kadłubek, was elected bishop of Kraków by members of the cathedral chapter without any intervention on the part of secular authorities. The principle by which kings and princes did not have total authority over the Church and religious observance was thus gradually established, becoming a seed-bed for limiting the rule of the ruler and more representative forms of government. The Church gained further rights in 1210 and 1215, including an independent judiciary to govern Church matters, guaranteeing the clergy greater independence. Leszek the White and other princes also placed Poland under the protection of the Holy See and made sure to send their tithes regularly to Rome. In doing so, they sought to create a hedge against foreign intervention.

Reform of the clergy took on new significance. The practice of valid clerical marriages was gradually done away with by the middle of thirteenth century. New monasteries were endowed and new orders arrived bearing the fruits of new learning, art and science. The Cistercian order was particularly important in influencing Polish religious and secular architecture. In this atmosphere, cultural development continued apace. The first Latin histories appeared: the chronicle of Gallus Anonymous and the *Chronica Polonorum* by Bishop Kadłubek. There was also a tradition of vernacular poetry, especially cycles of songs and epic stories. Little of this has survived and is known to us only second hand. Better known are hymns and sermons. The first preserved written work in Polish, *Bogurodzica*, or Hymn to the Virgin Mary, was already known by this period.

THE FOLLIES OF PRINCELY RULE

Following the death of Mieszko the Old, the role of senior prince fell to Leszek the White, Prince of Sandomierz, a son of Kazimierz the Just. He managed to live in peace with his brother Konrad of Mazovia who supported him in rivalries with Władysław the Spitter, the nephew of Mieszko the Old. In 1227, these rivalries ended in murder as supporters of the Spitter assassinated Leszek. His brother, Konrad, attempted to assume his brother's role without much success. Instead, Władysław Spindleshanks, eldest son of Mieszko the Old, took over.

Konrad would have been largely forgotten in Polish history – he was only senior prince for two years, 1241–43 – save for one fateful mistake. His home territories of Mazovia were suffering from raids by the pagan Prussians, a Baltic tribe living in the forests, swamps, and lakes of the Mazurian Lakes region of modern Poland. Polish settlers had been increasing penetrating and colonizing parts of this territory, bringing Christian missionaries with them. The local lord who had been organizing their defence fell afoul of Konrad, who had him executed. The colonists' defence system then fell apart, creating a crisis for Konrad who needed to defend these new lands but did not want a popular lord as a rival.

In 1225 he initiated negotiations with the Teutonic Order – known to Poles as Krzyżacy, literally 'the Cross Knights' from the order's symbol of a black cross on a white field. The Teutonic Knights had been founded in 1190 in Palestine to help care for wounded and ill German crusaders and pilgrims, but it soon became a military order with a thirst for earthly power. In 1211, the Order shifted its base of operations to Europe. The Hungarians invited the knights to Transylvania to help defend against incursions of pagan tribes from the steppes, but the Order sought its own state and began to meddle in the country's internal affairs. In 1225, the king of Hungary expelled the knights and they began to search for a new home.

Konrad granted the knights land around Chelmno as his vassals with the understanding that they would help defend the border and assist in the ongoing missionary activities in Prussia. The Teutonic Knights took possession of their new territory in 1228. Unbeknownst to

The symbol of the Teutonic Knights known to the Poles as the Krzyżacy –
literally the Cross Knights

Konrad, however, the Order had secured from the Holy Roman
Emperor a charter that granted them permission to hold Chelmno and
all conquered lands as their own. Although the emperor had no
standing to grant land that was not his to give, in thirteenth-century
Europe such legal niceties were often not honoured unless they could
be backed up with force.

Among the knights' first acts was to seize a man who had supposedly reverted to paganism, cut open his belly, nail his intestines to
a tree, and chase him around the tree until he died. Although later
German historians would attempt to downplay the knights' bar-
barism, their ruthlessness and political ambition can hardly be denied.
They largely ignored Konrad and did as they pleased in their new
lands.

The knights quickly moved to crush the pagan Prussians, waging a
virtual war of extermination against them. Few of the hapless Prussians
were even allowed to convert to Christianity, most were simply
slaughtered or enslaved. In their place, the Teutonic Knights brought
in German settlers. Within fifty years, the Prussians, who had resisted all

invaders for centuries, were almost gone. Even their name was taken as Prussian became almost synonymous with German.

From the beginning, the knights were overtly hostile to the notion of a strong, unified Polish state and did their best to keep the Polish princes off balance with a combination of warfare and diplomacy. Few Polish leaders were a match for the Teutonic Order, either on the battlefield or at the negotiating table. The Order drew on the best knights from throughout Europe and practised the latest in military technology. Throughout Europe, as monarchies grew gradually stronger and private warfare and raiding were outlawed, many European knights found fighting with the Teutonic Order the ideal outlet for their warlike tendencies. Slaughtering peasants for sport was not only legal, it came with the alleged blessing of being a crusader fighting the enemies of Christendom. Although their mandate had been to battle pagans as crusaders, when necessary the Order spread the idea that the Poles were really not Christian at all or had somehow lapsed into paganism to justify their policies.

In 1237, the Order absorbed a second German crusading order, the Brotherhood of the Sword, which had already conquered most of modern Latvia and Estonia. In addition to threatening Poland, the combined Order also turned its attention to Lithuania, the only remaining pagan state in Europe, and the Russian city states. This expansion was checked only temporarily in 1242 by the forces of Novgorod under Alexander Nevsky at the famous Battle on the Ice at Lake Peipus. Whereas in the past the Poles had faced occasional German expansion combined with long periods of peace, the Teutonic Order with its unified, military state represented a permanent threat.

The Mongols

While Polish princes fought among themselves for power a sudden new threat emerged from the east. Under Genghis Khan, the Mongols had rapidly expanded their empire, conquering China and Persia. In 1237–40 his successors smashed the Russian principalities one by one. In 1240, the great centre of Rus, Kiev, was sacked and burned to the ground. The speed and ferocity of the Mongol advance terrified and paralyzed their opponents. Their novel tactics of mobile warfare and their ability to collect vital political and military intelligence were far in advance of anything then practised in Europe. In 1241, under Khan Ogedei, the Mongols set their sights on central Europe, aiming for the fertile plains of Hungary. Believing that the Poles and Germans might come to Hungary's aid, the Mongols launched a diversionary attack into Poland in 1241.

The Mongols struck in February, before many of the princes could gather their forces together due to the winter conditions. The invaders took Sandomierz and massacred most of the population. A month later, they smashed the forces of Małopolska and sacked Kraków. It was during this siege that a legendary event took place that would forever make its mark upon the city. As the Mongols poured into the city, a trumpeter tried to sound the hour from a church tower. When he reached the seventh note a Mongol arrow struck him in the throat. Whether it truly happened is irrelevant. To this day, on the hour, the seven notes of the *Hejnał* are sounded from the church tower only to be cut off abruptly.

The Mongols swept on. The citizens of Opole fled to the forests and abandoned their city to be burned. The people of Wrocław burned their own city and retreated to an island in the river where the Mongols could not reach them. The senior prince of Poland, Henry the Pious of Silesia, gathered Polish forces along with contingents of Templars and Teutonic Knights. The two armies met at Legnica on 9 April, 1241. The Poles attacked the Mongols who promptly drew them into a trap, encircling them. A furious struggle ensued but the outcome was never in doubt. Prince Henry was cut down on the field, his head placed on a pike.

The Mongols then withdrew. They had achieved their objective of disrupting Poland and the sudden death of Khan Ogedei resulted in a power struggle among his successors who hurried their armies out of central Europe to participate. To the people of Europe it seemed almost miraculous. Among Poles a myth was born that Polish resistance had cost the Mongols so dearly that they were forced to call off their savage campaign of conquest. Although it was a nice fable, in truth the country had been spared. To the east, Poland's neighbours in Ruthenia and Kiev – who had long been part of the system of regional alliances and whose rulers had intermarried freely with Polish princely families – virtually disappeared from the scene. The devastation suffered by Kiev in particular, shifted the centre of gravity among the east Slavic principalities north to cities such as the mighty commercial city of Novgorod and a lesser-known one named Moscow. The consequences of this would be fateful indeed.

Provincial Poland

In the wake of that Mongol invasion Poland less and less resembled a unified state than a collection of principalities. Few strong leaders emerged and different regions experienced varying levels of economic and cultural development. Fortunately, Poland's neighbours were never strong enough to absorb the whole country, though they actively coveted pieces of Poland for themselves. From the east and the north came Lithuanian and Tartar raids. The Czechs and the Margraves of Brandenburg coveted Silesia while the Teutonic Knights threatened Pomerania and Kujawy. Yet, the biggest threats faced by Polish princes during this era were from their fellow princes.

Mazovia and Pomerania both faced threats from the Teutonic Order and the Mazovians also had to defend themselves against Lithuanian raids. Gdańsk was the major port for Pomerania. Traffic along the Vistula was a lucrative source of income for its princes and thus a bone of contention with the rapacious Teutonic Knights. Mazovia by contrast remained relatively poor without major towns or cities. Local warrior nobility made up the backbone of the province's social elite and were its major shield against external foes. They also proved highly fractious and difficult to rule, fighting amongst themselves as often as against invaders.

Wielkopolska and Kujawy had remained untouched by the Mongol invasion and there the economy developed quickly. New towns were chartered and forest and swampland were cleared for agriculture.

Silesia split into three smaller duchies, each ruled by a sub-branch of the Piasts – Wrocław, Legnica and Głogów. Each became increasingly tied to Czech and Germanic neighbours through bonds of economics, culture and political alliance. The three duchies often competed against each other and their rulers sometimes resembled petty brigands more than scions of a once-royal family. Wrocław remained the region's leading city and experienced dramatic growth throughout the thirteenth century as new inhabitants – Poles, Germans, Jews, and Walloons – came to work or to establish trades or businesses.

Małopolska had suffered the most from that Mongol assault. Sandomierz had to be rebuilt and Kraków, too, had to make up serious losses. Kraków rebounded faster than many other cities due to its political influence, location on major trade routes, lucrative salt deposits, and an influx of new immigrants. By the end of the thirteenth century, the city had more than doubled in area, all of which was enclosed in new fortifications.

Jewish Immigration

Among the new immigrants to Poland, Jews would have perhaps the most lasting impact. Jews had settled in Poland in small numbers a century earlier, but the first major influx came by the middle of the thirteenth century. Poland's developing economy was a major attraction. Jews filled positions as craftsmen, merchants, and moneylenders, becoming an important force in the economy.

Polish princes strove to attract these newcomers through the usual means of granting economic privileges that were offered to other groups, such as Germans. But they also provided guarantees of religious tolerance and the rudimentary beginning of Jewish community self-government. The first official act securing Jewish rights was the so-called Statutes of Kalisz granted in 1264 by Bolesław the Pious (d. 1279), Prince of Kraków. This set of laws allowed Jews the right to travel freely throughout the prince's domain (a right not enjoyed by many Christian peasants), freedom from serfdom or enslavement, and the right to practise their faith freely and openly (including worship in synagogues, ritual slaughter, and Jewish burial rites). These rights were guaranteed by the prince who took the Jews under his personal protection, and thus violators were subject to harsh punishments, including the death penalty. City authorities could still restrict Jewish residence and Jewish merchants were not necessarily on an equal footing with Christian competitors.

Although the statutes were not applied across all of Poland until almost a century later, the act was remarkable in its medieval context and it provided the basis for the rapid growth of Polish Jewry.

The Bohemian Intervention

In 1243, following the disaster at Legnica, Bolesław the Chaste (1226–79), Prince of Sandomierz, assumed the mantle of senior prince. He proved a relatively weak if long-lived prince. Under his rule, Poland was able to recover economically, but efforts toward re-establishing national unity amounted to little.

The only significant entity that was able to transcend Poland's growing regional differences was the ecclesiastical structure of the Church. This helped to thrust the clergy into the unusual role of champions of national unity at a time when this seemed a distant dream. Many clergy also came to resent the influx of German customs and habits, especially since German princes had a history of hostility toward Rome. Invasions by the Mongols and pagan Lithuanians also helped to awaken a sense of national loyalty among the clergy.

Following the death of Bolesław the Chaste in 1279, the country was dominated by three powerful princes who would each in turn assume the role of Poland's leading man. The first was Leszek Czarny (the Black) of Łęczycza and Kraków. He was an able warrior, but internal divisions within his own provinces limited his power. The second was Henryk Probus (the Righteous) of Silesia who had assumed power in his home province in 1270 and brought most of Silesia back under his suzerainty through skilful diplomacy and tough arm-twisting of his neighbouring princes in Legnica and Głogów. The third was Przemyśl II, prince of Wielkopolska, who had managed to draw his lands into close alliance with the princes of Gdańsk and Szczecin.

By chance, none of the three princes had a legitimate male heir, though Przemyśl II had a daughter who wed the king of Bohemia. Facing the same serious problem, the three princes negotiated a deal – when one died, the others would inherit. This was a significant step toward reunifying the country. When Leszek Czarny died in 1288, Henryk Probus assumed control of his land. He was challenged in this inheritance by Leszek's little-known half-brother Władysław Łokietek (1260–1333) (Władysław Elbow-High). The former was supported by the Czechs while the latter gained support from the Ruthenians, the east Slavic ancestors of today's Ukrainians and Carpatho-Rusyns. Henryk Probus managed to overcome some early setbacks and nearly captured the unlucky Elbow-High when his forces infiltrated and seized Kraków. The short prince allegedly escaped disguised as a monk.

Prince Henryk immediately tried to restore the monarchy and petitioned the Pope for a crown. However, he died in 1290 before he could make any further progress toward this goal. Przemyśl II (1257–96) assumed control in Kraków as the unsuccessful Elbow-High was still smarting from his previous defeat. Przemyśl again petitioned the Pope for a crown. Yet, Przemyśl's claim was about to be challenged by a yet more powerful foe.

Vaclav II (1271–1305), king of Bohemia, had long had designs on the Polish crown. He had also advanced a somewhat dubious claim on Silesia based on an earlier agreement with Henryk Probus. Unlike other claimants, however, he also had a large, secure power base in Bohemia and significant military and financial resources. In 1291, the Czechs invaded Poland and drove Przemyśl from Kraków, although the Polish prince took the Polish royal regalia with him to Poznań. Władysław Elbow-High challenged the Czech king's move, but the short prince's military skills were not up to keeping his own troops under control. Their riotous behaviour alienated the populace at large and superior Czech forces compelled him to surrender and he was exiled to Hungary. The Czechs established control over Małopolska and most of Silesia.

In 1295, Pope Boniface VIII, who opposed Vaclav's power grab for his own reasons, granted a royal crown to Przemyśl II. He was crowned in Poznań. For the first time in more than two hundred years Poland had a king. Przemyśl and Władysław Elbow-High patched up their differences to make common cause against the Czechs. Yet, less than a year later, Przemyśl II lay dead at the hands of attackers sent by the Margrave of Brandenburg. Władysław Elbow-High was called to the throne but confusion reigned and efforts were made to depose him. Seizing the moment, Vaclav II invaded central Poland, marching all the way to Gdańsk, bringing almost the entire country under his control. In 1300 he had himself crowned king of Poland.

ELBOW-HIGH

Władysław Łokietek or Elbow-High was not a brilliant military leader. He lost at least as many battles as he won. Chroniclers did not remember him as a gifted orator or a great patron of the arts. He was not especially lucky in politics and faced repeated reverses throughout his life. But what he lacked in these areas he made up for in determination and an ability to learn from his mistakes. Time and again his efforts to gain the Polish crown and reunify the country suffered crushing defeats at the hands of powerful foes like Vaclav II. Yet, time and again the short prince refused to accept the inevitable and survived to try once more. Although overlooked by more appealing figures in Polish history, for this alone he yet stands as one of Poland's greatest leaders.

Vaclav was an absentee king. Although he was a capable ruler his appointed agents in Poland proved corrupt and rapacious. Where Małopolska had supported the Czech king thanks to generous tax exemptions, it now had cause to regret this. The German-speaking archbishop of Kraków, John Muskata, one of the king's major supporters, was adept at looting his own parish churches, allegedly claiming that a soldier's axe was the best 'key of St Peter' for opening church doors. Vaclav's administrators favoured German-speaking burghers over their Polish counterparts, driving an ethnic wedge between the two groups in an effort to 'divide and rule'.

Following Vaclav II's coronation, Władysław was forced into exile as his fortunes waned. He went to Rome where he obtained the support of Pope Boniface VIII who was eager to curb the growing power of the Bohemian dynasty as it was a key pillar of the Holy Roman Empire. He then went to Hungary where he had friendly relations with many of the nobles. At this time, Hungary was engaged in its own struggle over royal succession. Vaclav II had laid a claim to the throne of St Stephen in an effort to create a dynastic superstate that would include Bohemia, Poland and Hungary. But this time, the ambitious Czech king had over-reached himself. He was opposed by Robert of Anjou who had his own powerful European connections. As an enemy of Vaclav II, Władysław's appeal for assistance caught the attention of Robert of Anjou. Seeing a chance to divert Vaclav II's attention, the Hungarians provided Władysław with the backing he needed. In 1304 he re-entered Poland leading an army of Hungarian troops.

The short prince was able to establish a base and began to expand his support. Those tired of the rule of Vaclav II's men flocked to his standard, including many peasants and members of the petty nobility. Within a year, Władysław had regained Sandomierz, Sieradz and most of Małopolska. Czech power was further weakened when Silesia broke away under the rule of Prince Henry of Głogów. In 1305, Vaclav II died and was succeeded by his son Vaclav III. Władysław besieged Kraków in the spring of 1306 and the city soon fell to his forces. As the younger Vaclav prepared to mount an expedition to once more drive the short prince from his father's Polish domain he was assassinated. This not only ended Vaclav's native Czech dynasty, it spelled the effective end to Bohemian opposition to Władysław's rule. By the end of 1306, he held all of southern Poland, save Silesia, including the royal city of Kraków and its lucrative salt mines.

Władysław then sought to regain Wielkopolska and Pomerania, but continued to struggle to hold on to southern Poland. In 1311, he faced a major revolt among the German burghers in Kraków with the support of the new Bohemian king John of Luxemburg. It took Władysł aw almost a year to put down the revolt. When he finally recaptured Kraków, he took revenge on the leaders of the rebellion – those unable to pronounce Polish words with the unique soft 'L' sound were beheaded. German was replaced by Latin as an official language of the city.

Meanwhile, the Teutonic Knights had not been idle in the north. When the Margrave of Brandenburg launched an attack on the city of Gdańsk in 1308, the Teutonic Knights came to the city's aid and promptly drove off the invaders. But the knights had not come as saviours. On 14 November, 1308 they seized the city by force, massacring Władysław's supporters and driving out most of the Slavic inhabitants. They followed this by seizing other strongholds in Pomerania. Within a few years, the entire province was under the

Knights' control. Many of the Polish and Slavic inhabitants were killed, driven out or dispossessed and German settlers imported to take their places. With this move, Poland lost its access to the sea.

Things went much better for the short prince in Wielkopolska. When Henry of Głogów died in 1308, he made his move and began to drive out Henry's sons. In 1314 he took Poznań and with it, the province was his. Although Wielkopolska had been the seat of the first Piast kings, under Władysław's rule, the centre of power in Poland shifted to the south to Kraków. Nevertheless, the old Piast stronghold was an important and rich province and holding the old capital of Gniezno had crucial symbolism for any prince seeking the royal crown.

In Europe's ongoing political struggles, Poland had strong support from the Papacy. Having made itself a direct vassal of the Holy See during the long period of princely rule, Poland was also one of the few lands in Europe that collected and paid Peter's Pence, an extraordinary tax that helped support the Papacy. The stronger Poland became, the more valuable it was to the Popes, be they in Rome or Avignon. In 1319, Pope John XXII granted Władysław his crown. On 20 January, 1320 Władysław Elbow-High and his wife Jadwiga were crowned king and queen of Poland in the cathedral of Gniezno. The long period of fragmentation had ended.

Following his coronation, Władysław opened a long campaign to regain territory lost to the Czechs, Brandenburgers, and Teutonic Knights. The campaigns against Brandenburg and Czechs proved inconclusive. The campaign against the Teutonic Knights was a disaster. Polish forces were simply no match for the heavily armoured, superbly mounted, well-organized Teutonic Knights. Although the Poles won a symbolic victory at Płowce in 1331, most of the periodic conflicts between Poland and the Order were chronicles of the Knights marching at will across Poland, sacking, burning, and massacring wherever they went. Dozens of towns and villages were destroyed and the territories of Dobryzń and Kujawy occupied. In 1332, the two sides, facing other pressing issues, agreed to a brief truce.

During the winter of 1333, Władysław, now age seventy-two, fell prey to illness and died on 2 March. He had survived defeat after defeat, outlasting or outmanoeuvring his numerous and far more powerful foes to reunite his kingdom. He was the first Polish monarch in almost three centuries to pass on an undivided patrimony to an uncontested, legitimate heir. On 25 April, 1333 Władysław's twenty-one-year-old son, Casimir (Kazimierz) was crowned king in Wawel Cathedral.

CHAPTER THREE

From Wood to Stone,
1333–1466

Kazimierz Wielki – Casimir the Great (1310–70)

Perhaps not much was expected of the young Casimir when he took the throne in 1333. He had received a basic education, especially in law, and had gained some administrative experience under his father as a regional officer (*starosta*). The new king had seen battle, both successful and unsuccessful. He had an eye for beautiful women and had got himself in trouble during a diplomatic visit to Hungary when he seduced the daughter of a powerful nobleman. There was nothing unusual or unique in his *curriculum vitae*. The troubles he faced – powerful external foes and a country divided and partly ravaged by war – certainly did not bode well for his rule.

Yet, in the history of every land and people, there emerge leaders whose ability and vision change their countries forever. Casimir would reign for thirty-seven years and where many of his predecessors were granted derisive or unflattering nicknames, the new king would be remembered simply as Kazimierz Wielki, or Casimir the Great. His rule would completely transform Poland.

At the time of his father's death, Poland faced conflict with its powerful neighbours – Bohemia, Brandenburg, and the Teutonic Order – each of which could have destroyed Poland on its own. Bohemia and the Order had even developed an anti-Polish alliance, although a temporary truce restrained the dogs of war. Without giving up his father's goals of reunifying the country and recovering her lost territories, Casimir chose diplomacy over war. The last years of Władysław's reign had conclusively demonstrated that Poland could

51

not win back Pomerania and Silesia with force of arms. The Teutonic Order was far too powerful and the kings of Bohemia had the vast resources of a prosperous and well-organized land to call against Poland. After a series of protracted negotiations lasting years, Casimir eventually agreed to give up Pomerania to the knights in return for the territories of Kujawy and Dobryzń which they had occupied. It was a humiliating treaty, made worse by the knights' supremely arrogant treatment of the Polish king, and many of Casimir's subjects would never wholly resign themselves to this peace.

On the other side, Casimir paid off King John of Bohemia to renounce his claims to the Polish throne. He also had to give up control of much of Silesia to the Bohemians, though he managed to keep the Duchy of Świdnica independent and under the control of his ally and cousin, Duke Bolko, which was an effective check on King John's ambitions.

Casimir's goals were two-fold: first to break up any potential alliance between Bohemia and the Teutonic Knights and second to give his

Casimir the Great

country breathing space to recover from years of war and build up its resources. Although the loss of Silesia and Pomerania was bitter, Poland was too weak to retain effective control over these provinces in the face of powerful enemies. There was every hope that Poland could recover them sometime in the future.

TERRITORIAL CLAIMS

As Casimir was forced to give up territories in the west and north, new opportunity beckoned to the east. The ruler of Halicz-Ruthenia, a principality on Poland's eastern border, died without an heir. As a relative of the ruling house, Casimir quickly advanced his own claim to this territory. In 1340 and 1341, the king mounted expeditions to secure his control, bringing cities such as Lwów, Przemyśl, Chełm and Vladimir under Polish control. This territory had been technically under the overlordship of the Khan of the Golden Horde whose Tatar horsemen represented a major threat to Poland. However, the Tatars were faced with internal strife of their own and proved unable to mount sustained expeditions to keep Halicz under their thumb.

A more serious challenge came from Lithuania whose pagan rulers had been successfully pushing back the remnants of Mongol control and claimed parts of Halicz, especially Vladimir and the fortress town of Bełz. Local boyars (gentry) were divided, some preferring the Lithuanians, other backing Casimir, and still others favouring neither. A protracted struggle followed and the Poles mounted regular expeditions into this new territory to repel Lithuanian incursions. By the 1350s, most of the territory was under Polish control, though Bełz, Vladimir and Chełm took longer to secure. Eventually, an agreement was struck that Lithuanian princes would rule these cities as vassals of Casimir.

The new territory represented a major expansion of the kingdom. Halicz-Ruthenia provided new resources and population. It was also the first Polish territory with a significant population of Orthodox Christians. Practical considerations overrode any notion of following the Teutonic Knights in their practice of conversion by the sword. Casimir needed the co-operation of local leaders both lay and clerical. Although the Catholic population would increase over time, the ancient faith of the inhabitants would be respected.

The acquisition of Halicz also changed Poland's traditional westward orientation. The growing weakness of the Golden Horde left a new power vacuum in this region which, although sparsely populated, had important resources and provided access to trade routes stretching to the Black Sea, Central Asia, and Persia. Although Poland remained firmly anchored to the West, it was the first step in a long process that caused Poland to develop in ways quite different from its western neighbours.

Casimir did not neglect his western and northern frontiers either. He began the process of reabsorbing Mazovia into the kingdom, turning its local princes into royal vassals. He also acquired a number of small but important territories in Pomerania that effectively separated the Teutonic Knights from a common border with Brandenburg and the Empire.

INTERNAL REFORMS

As important as these military and political steps were, however, it was Casimir's internal reforms that put Poland on the path to greatness. He completely reformed royal administration, basing royal power in the provinces on *starosta*s, an office introduced to Poland during the brief rule of the Bohemian kings at the start of the fourteenth century. Old offices were consolidated, making the king's rule more effective and its enforcement based on appointed men loyal to the throne rather than local gentry. He also modernized the military structure of the kingdom, creating a single *levée en masse,* with obligations for providing troops specified from the richest nobles down the modest village headmen. Where the country had been vulnerable to attack, during Casimir's reign Poland built sixty-six castles of the most modern type, rebuilt the defences of twenty-three cities, and supplemented this with lines of field defences and watch towers, closing off every major invasion route into the country.

In 1347, Casimir undertook his most ambitious project – completely rewriting the Polish law code. Until that time, there had been no uniform code of law, but a jumble of custom and local laws. Cities were often organized under German-style law codes and surrounding rural areas handled under noble or ecclesiastical courts. During the period of

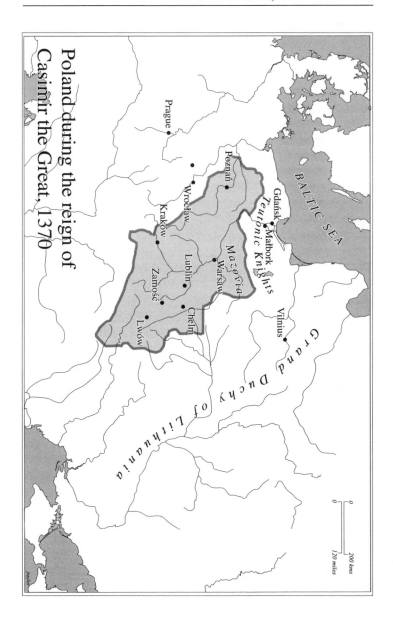

Poland during the reign of
Casimir the Great, 1370

fragmentation, local princes enacted provisions that applied to one region but were absent in another. Abuses were rampant and common folk without legal training stood little chance of getting justice. According to the chronicler Jan Długosz:

> The king convenes an assembly ... attended by all the bishops of the kingdom, its voivodes, castellans, officials, and eminent personages. The king presides and has with him experts in canon and civil law. The assembly then sets about organizing Polish law, writing it all down and publishing it. ... All are written in clear, simple language so that their meaning cannot be cleverly twisted or distorted. Various confused enactments of his predecessors are carefully corrected and clauses that have been overlooked are added, while those that are unnecessary are removed. ... All courts of justice, however small or large, and their judges ... are to conduct their cases solely in accordance with the written, published laws and to give their verdicts accordingly; also, that everyone, even the poor and those of humble origin, are to be free to appeal to the written law.

A BENEFICIAL RULER

Casimir's rule was particularly beneficial to peasants and tradesmen as he restrained the abuses of the gentry. One chronicle noted 'Under his reign no powerful lord or squire dared harm the poor, for justice was even for all.' He was also a friend to the country's small but growing Jewish population. During his reign, Jewish immigration grew steadily as Jewish communities were placed under royal protection and royal justice. During the same period, as the Black Death raged across much of Europe, Jews were persecuted in western and central Europe. Many fled to the safety of Casimir's Poland, where for reasons that are unclear, significant parts of the country were spared the worst ravages of the plague. The earlier Statutes of Kalisz were expanded. Penalties for attacking or robbing Jews were increased and firmly enforced. A common legend has it that Casimir's actions were motivated by his passion for a Jewish mistress named Esther, but this is merely a convenient myth. Casimir's interest was not only justice but economic growth. Jewish migrants brought skills the country needed and provided a bit of free market competition for local craft guilds (which many of them, of course, resented).

Casimir's policies and the expansion of Polish rule into Ruthenia and Mazovia resulted in economic growth and increased trade that had a ripple effect across the entire country. Royal tax revenues increased and the additional money was ploughed into new building and new projects which in turn created additional jobs. The king as well as bishops and nobles founded sixty-five new towns and about five hundred new villages. Canals were built, marshes drained, forests cleared for new farmland, new mills and mines created. Nobles and merchants had more money in their pockets, resulting in greater spending on arts and culture. New churches and monasteries were endowed. The new law codes and the expanding royal administration created a huge demand for trained scribes, scholars, and lawyers. In 1364, with the approval of the Pope, Casimir founded a university in Kraków to produce a cadre of skilled, literate men who would administer the new Poland he was creating. The school, later to become the famous Jagiellonian University, was only the second university in east-central Europe, following Charles University in Prague by only a few years.

Poland's growing power and wealth allowed Casimir to practise diplomacy on a grand scale. In 1363, Casimir played an important role in brokering a peace treaty between the Holy Roman Emperor and the king of Hungary that was to be sealed by the marriage of one of Casimir's granddaughters to the emperor. The wedding would become the largest summit of medieval European royalty. Kraków played host to the kings of Hungary, Poland, Denmark, and Cyprus, and the Emperor Charles as well as numerous princes, dukes, bishops, and knights. Guests were provided with sumptuous lodging, mountains of food, and gifts:

> At the end of all this banqueting, which lasts more than twelve days, the kings and princes, having established friendly relations and sworn to make a pact of eternal peace, exchange gifts, give cordial thanks and praise to King Casimir for the honour done them and the gifts they and their people have received, and so depart for home, again provided on the way with all their needs by the king's *starostas*.

Casimir's one signal failure, however, was to produce a legitimate male heir. The king had children by many mistresses, but only daughters by a succession of wives. Only Casimir's first wife, the Lithuanian princess Aldona, seems to match the king's lively and passionate temperament. After her death, his marriages were loveless dynastic affairs. To secure his succession, he turned to his nephew and ally, Louis of Hungary (r. 1342–82). Louis was designated Casimir's successor as his heir. To secure the agreement of the Polish gentry, Louis promised to grant them a wide-ranging series of privileges.

In 1370, the king was sixty years old, but still vigorous and active. In September he went hunting and while pursuing a deer was thrown from his horse and broke his leg. A fever set in. The king seemed to recover but returned to his royal duties too soon and suffered a relapse and his condition went steadily downhill. On 5 November, 1370, Casimir the Great died and was buried in Wawel Cathedral in Kraków.

It was popularly said that Casimir found a Poland made of wood and left behind a Poland made of stone. Długosz wrote:

> King Casimir was so eager to make his country illustrious and rich that he went to great expense building churches of brick or masonry, as well as castles, towns, manors, etc. so as to make Poland, which he found dirty and with buildings only of clay or wood, a place of brick and masonry and famous. This he did. He was particularly concerned that prelates, canons, and rectors of parish churches should build their private residences near their churches, and that peasants and villagers should not suffer injury from the nobles and knights. So, too, the peasants and settlers ... whenever they were oppressed by their masters, obtained some protection from him. The knights and nobles called him 'the King of the peasants.'

With Casimir's death, the line of Piast rulers, begun with Mieszko I four centuries earlier, ended. Yet, the last Piast was the greatest. In thirty-seven years, a land that had been little more than a collection of squabbling principalities had become a powerful, unified kingdom. Casimir established his country as a player on the chessboard of European politics. He rebuilt its governmental, economic, legal, educational, and military structures. It is little exaggeration to say that without Casimir the Great, Poland would never have become a significant European state.

The Angevin Interlude

As an absentee monarch, Poland's new ruler, Louis of Anjou, king of Hungary, needed the support of the nobility. To secure this, he was fully prepared to grant wide-ranging concessions that weakened royal power. The immediate impact was to undo some of the progress made under Casimir. Poland became less able to defend itself and attacks from Lithuania and Brandenburg resulted in the loss of some border areas. The longer-term effect was to confirm a tendency that had long been a feature of Polish political life – strict limits on the power of the monarch and an abhorrence of absolutist rulers.

In an age of limited communications, Louis' practical ability to exercise control over Poland was small and his main focus remained on Hungary. The two realms coexisted in relative harmony thanks to a similar strategic orientation and (in spite of linguistic and ethnic dissimilarity) a certain cultural sympathy. Although clashes between Poland and Hungary were not unknown during different periods in history, Poland and Hungary have been each other's most consistent allies. A saying that rhymes just as well in Polish as in Magyar runs 'Pole and Magyar/like two brothers stand/whether with sabre or tankard in hand.'

Under local Polish administrators, the government machinery set up by Casimir functioned smoothly. The economy grew and colonization of new lands in Halicz continued. A major Lithuanian invasion in 1376 caused significant destruction but a Polish-Hungarian counterattack seized Bełz and Chełm, making them a permanent part of the realm.

Louis' major problem was the same one faced by Casimir – lack of a legitimate male heir. Unlike Casimir, however, Louis' solution was to insist on the succession of his daughters. This practice was followed more readily in Western Europe (whence the House of Anjou originated) but was largely unknown in Poland. In 1374, representatives of the Polish gentry agreed to the succession one of Louis' daughters. His daughter Elizabeth would have the Hungarian crown and his younger daughter Jadwiga the Polish crown. Prior to Louis' death in 1382, however, he made his daughter Maria regent since his other daughters were still children. This seemingly undid the previous accord with the

Polish nobility. Maria was the wife of the Margrave of Brandenburg, which further complicated matters and raised serious opposition in some quarters. A virtual civil war broke out with several factions vying for control over the succession process. In 1384, a compromise was reached and a council of nobles would act as the regency. In 1384, Louis' daughter Jadwiga (1374–99) was crowned queen of Poland. She was not yet eleven years old.

Lithuania

To Poland's north and east lay the Grand Duchy of Lithuania, Europe's last remaining pagan land. In the far distant past, Poles and Lithuanians had shared a common Balto-Slavic heritage. In the early years of Poland's history, there was little direct contact between Poles and Lithuanians. Baltic tribes such as the Prussians and Jadzwingians were a more immediate problem for the Poles and at times the semi-independent duchy of Mazovia acted as a further barrier. The coming of the Teutonic Knights had changed this picture. The knights destroyed the native Prussians and reduced the Jadzwingians to a shadow of their former power. In addition to their ongoing assaults on Poland, the knights' major objective was the destruction and subjugation of Lithuania.

Yet, the Lithuanians proved a difficult foe. Although unable to face the heavily armoured Teutonic Knights in the open field, fighting from the fastness of their native forests and swamps and from the massive ramparts of their earthen forts, Lithuanian warriors brought the Teutonic juggernaut to a virtual halt. Although the knights could easily ravage peasant villages, they faced fierce ambushes and raids that took a yearly toll of their forces and made besieging Lithuanian strongholds difficult.

Under two great warrior princes, Gedymin (1316–41) and Olgierd (1345–77), the Lithuanians took advantage of the growing weakness of the Mongols and their successors, and expanded to the southeast. From their base in Vilnius (Wilno), these two princes captured huge territories, including the cities of Vitebsk, Smolensk and Kiev, pushing the Golden Horde back to the shores of the Black Sea. In 1362, under

Prince Olgierd, the Lithuanians smashed Mongol forces at the decisive battle of Blue Waters. This new territory was sparsely inhabited and most of its residents were Slavic Orthodox Christians. This rapid expansion also put the Lithuanians on a collision course with the powerful princes of Moscow (Muscovy) who had served as local Mongol vassals and later threw off Mongol rule.

Although facing a common foe in the Teutonic Knights, Poland and Lithuania were also rivals. Lithuania was a loosely organized state and local princes undertook frequent raids into Poland with or without the approval of their overlord in Vilnius. Wealthier Poland was an attractive source of booty, cattle and slaves. Casimir the Great's expansion into Halicz was a further irritant, blocking Lithuanian ambitions.

At the same time, there had been occasional peaceful overtures. Casimir's marriage to his Lithuanian wife Aldona resulted in the release of a huge number of Poles held as slaves in Lithuania. Adventurous Polish merchants willing to risk life and limb found Lithuanian princes ready customers for European luxury goods as well as weapons and armour. Polish missionaries also journeyed north to spread the word of God, hoping to achieve by persuasion what the Teutonic Knights had failed to do with the sword. Poland increasingly became Lithuania's window on Europe. Over the years, the Lithuanians had periodically flirted with Christianity. Individual princes would convert, sometimes sincerely, sometimes for short-term gain before reverting to their ancient beliefs. Yet, the baptism of the entire country remained an elusive goal.

Following the death of Olgierd in 1377, he was succeeded by his sons, chief among them Jogaila (Jagiełło). He sought to push Lithuania's borders further east while keeping the Teutonic Knights at bay. Yet, at the same time it was clear that without coherent organization and administration the sprawling warrior state would exist only as long as its rulers were successful on the battlefield.

Jadwiga and the Birth of the Jagiellonian Dynasty

To the powerful coterie of nobles who ruled Poland in the name of the young Jadwiga, it was clear that they needed a king and husband for their charge. There were many potential suitors, including a prince of the rising House of Habsburg from Austria. Yet, involving Poland in the dynastic squabbles of Europe was not an attractive option. All potential suitors brought a ready-made list of allies and enemies. Moreover, the privileges and freedoms gained during Louis' reign might be lost if a new king emerged from the dominant political traditions of western Europe where monarchies were gaining greater strength.

It was these factors that turned Polish eyes toward Lithuania. At the same time, the Lithuanians were looking toward Poland. Realizing that they could not fend off the Teutonic Knights, the Muscovites and the Poles at once, they chose Poland as the lesser evil. In a series of protracted negotiations in 1385–86, the Polish barons agreed to elect Jogaila king of Poland on his marriage to Jadwiga. In return the two countries would be joined in a dynastic union. Jogaila would be baptized as Władysław Jagiełło (r.1377–1434) and along with him his entire nation would become Christian. Polish captives would be released from Lithuania, cross-border raids would cease, and the two countries would form a common front against the Teutonic Knights.

What the young Jadwiga thought about this is not recorded. Her future husband was nearly three times her age. Yet, she was a young woman of deep faith and the conversion of Lithuania had been a goal of the Church in east-central Europe for at least a century. The marriage would also greatly strengthen her country in its mortal battle against the Teutonic Order. It was for these reasons that she gave up chances for romantic love and agreed to the marriage. Her decision would open a new chapter in European history.

In 1386, Władysław Jagiełło converted to Christianity, he married Jadwiga, and was crowned king of Poland. His people soon followed and became Christian. In a single stroke, two large nations had been joined into one. While that union would take many years to cement, it would occur far more smoothly than many dynastic unions. Poland was a compact, well-organized state. Lithuania was a sprawling country with a low population but rich in resources. The new combined state stretched nearly from the shores of the Baltic Sea to the Black Sea in the south, making it easily the largest state in Europe at the time.

In the years that followed, numerous Polish institutions were adopted in Lithuania, perhaps the most important being the organization of the Church. Polish clergy streamed north to teach the faith and catechisms and other religious writings were translated into Lithuanian at the king's behest. Churches and monasteries were built. Polish and Jewish merchants and craftsmen brought new skills and increased trade. Polish political culture was also gradually imported into Lithuania. In time, Lithuanian gentry would become almost completely Polonized though this process took at least a generation. Although this merger has been seen by modern Lithuanian nationalists as a dark chapter in their country's history, few people at the time thought of themselves as 'Poles' or 'Lithuanians' in the modern sense of the term.

Jagiełło's first order of business was to consolidate his rule. This was accomplished relatively easily within Poland since the Polish gentry had already agreed to his coronation. Within Lithuania, however, he faced a more difficult task. His brothers and cousins, especially his cousin, the able but crafty Witold, came from a tradition where local princes ruled virtually independent from the Duke. Jagiełło's more centralized style, reinforced with the power of the Polish kingdom behind him, did not meet with universal approval. Internal dissent within Lithuania was also fostered by the Teutonic Knights who were deeply concerned with the potential of the joint Polish-Lithuanian alliance. Eventually, the king, with the active support of Queen Jadwiga, was able to bring his homeland under a greater measure of control. The eventual compromise was to make Witold his surrogate in Vilnius.

THE DEATH OF THE QUEEN

Meanwhile, in 1399 Queen Jadwiga died from complications of childbirth (her newborn daughter lived only a few days). Despite her youth, the queen had taken an active part in advising the king. Known for her piety and charity, she gave special emphasis to missionary work among the Lithuanians. Her charity for the poor of Kraków was legendary and when she fell ill, the royal castle was besieged by crowds of peasants praying and offering home remedies for her recovery. On her deathbed, she pawned her jewellery to re-establish the university in

Kraków founded by Casimir the Great, which had become weakened in the years following his death.

The queen's death sparked a new political crisis since Jagiełło's legitimacy had flowed from his wife. Jadwiga had foreseen this on her deathbed and recommended that her husband remarry another descendent of Casimir the Great, which he later did. A new treaty of union was drafted and approved by the assembled gentry of both Poland and Lithuania and Jagiełło himself was re-elected by the Poles as their king, a vote of approval for the new dynasty.

The problems of consolidating royal authority in Lithuania and then Poland delayed a reckoning with the Teutonic Knights. Meanwhile, the knights had not sat idle. In addition to stirring up rebellions in Lithuania, they seized the Lithuanian province of Samogitia, cutting Lithuania off from the Baltic Sea. Claiming that Lithuania had not truly converted to Christianity and that Poles were aiding the pagans, they sought new recruits throughout Western Europe, luring them with promises of lavish living and easy victories against pagan armies.

Throughout the first decade of the 1400s relations deteriorated. Teutonic attacks into Lithuania and raids on Poland continued without pause. Meanwhile, Polish military assistance flowed north into Lithuania to help stiffen defences there. In 1409, a Lithuanian revolt in the captive province of Samogitia brought tensions to the boiling point. Negotiations between the sides broke down and the Teutonic Knights launched a full-scale attack on the Polish border province of Dobryzń, driving out Polish forces.

Grunwald

Throughout the winter of 1409–10, both sides prepared for a major showdown. The knights recruited a large number of west European nobles, hungry for glory and booty as well as units of cannon and elite Genoese crossbowmen. In the coming campaign, the Teutonic Order would field the best-equipped, best-trained, most technologically advanced army in Europe at that time. Backed by the Order's vast wealth and protected by the most formidable castles in Europe, to any observers it must have seemed their forces would easily sweep all before them.

Jagiełło, however, had not been idle. He began to systematically mobilize the forces of the Polish kingdom. It was then that the reforms of Casimir the Great bore fruit as Polish knights and commoners responded en masse. The king also stockpiled supplies and equipment. In Lithuania, Duke Witold organized the forces of the Grand Duchy. The allied armies, while slightly larger than the knights, were not as well equipped. Only the wealthiest Polish knights could match the Teutonic brethren in horses, arms, and armour. The Lithuanians and their auxiliaries, while tough fighters, tended to be lightly armoured and rode small but sturdy horses descended from the herds of Genghis Khan.

The Allies also faced a major strategic problem: their two armies were separated by great distances and the Vistula River which lacked permanent bridges in northern Poland. Getting the entire Polish army across the river in the face of the deadly Teutonic army would be dangerous and time-consuming. Unless the two armies could join forces they had little hope of victory and on their own could be easily defeated. But years of fighting against the descendants of the Mongols had imparted many military secrets to the king, secrets unknown in most of Europe. Throughout the winter, Polish engineers laboured in secret to create Europe's first pontoon bridge based on Mongol models. As the campaign began, the bridge was floated downriver to a point near Warsaw and the entire army of the kingdom crossed the Vistula in days instead of weeks. Soon they linked up with the forces of the Grand Duchy under Witold.

On 15 July, 1410 the two armies met at Grunwald, in present-day Mazury: nearly 30,000 Teutonic Knights and about 38,000 Allied forces. The knights were arrayed in a tight semi-circle, infantry, cannon, and crossbows backed by ranks of mounted men, the brothers of the Order clearly visible in their white cloaks bearing the black Maltese cross. In the ranks was the Grand Master of the Order himself, Ulrich von Jüngingen. Facing them on the right were the Lithuanian forces of the Grand Duchy under Duke Witold assisted by Tartar auxiliaries. In the centre stood the Smolensk regiment of Belarusin boyars fighting under banners bearing images of Orthodox saints. On the left stood the forces of the Polish kingdom, knights, townsmen, and armed peasants.

The royal guard remained in reserve while the king himself was positioned, like a Mongol general, on a hill overlooking the scene.

As morning broke, both forces remained in place, facing off across the field. From the Polish ranks, the ancient *Bogurodzica* could be heard sung by nobles and commoners alike. Legend has it, the Grand Master, seeking to taunt the Allies, sent a herald to King Jagiełło, bearing two swords with a message that he could have them to strengthen his resolve. The king was said to have replied that they would soon be put to good use, but the image of Jagiełło bearing two swords, symbolizing his two realms, would be reproduced in statues of the king over the centuries.

In the late morning, action was joined as Lithuanian forces on the right tested the Teutonic defences. For the knights seeing the foe that had eluded them for so long exposed in the open field was too great a temptation, and they counter-attacked. Given that the Lithuanians were well versed in the Mongol tactic of feigned retreat, it is possible that what happened next was planned well in advance. The Teutonic Knights with their heavy warhorses could not be stopped and the lightly armoured Lithuanians fell back but away from the Allied centre. It seemed as if the knights had triumphantly scattered half the Allied army and they began to pursue the retreating Lithuanians. Between the Lithuanian and Polish forces stood the three banners of the small Smolensk regiment. Though lightly armed like the Lithuanians, the Belarusins stood their ground against the Teutonic onslaught, suffering horrific losses. One banner fell under the hooves of the knights' horses, but the Belarusins, according to the chronicler, 'fight as befits knights and men and emerge victorious.' Thanks to their stand, the main thrust of the Teutonic charge was directed away from the Polish forces.

On the left, the Poles attacked. Peasants and impoverished members of the gentry advanced on foot under fire from cannon and a hail of arrows to cut through the makeshift field defences protecting the Teutonic lines. Through these gaps the mounted Polish knights, the main strike force of the kingdom, hit the Teutonic forces. The ranks of Teutonic foot soldiers were driven back by the momentum of the Polish attack into the lines of mounted knights behind them, leaving the Teutonic Knights little room to manoeuvre. As they were pressed back, Teutonic commanders were forced to commit their reserves to stop the Polish advance in ferocious close-quarter fighting.

Meanwhile on the right, the heavy warhorses of the Teutonic Knights began to tire and get bogged down in swampy terrain. Although the Lithuanians had been driven far from their original positions, their smaller horses had great stamina and Witold's men had not suffered major losses. As their pursuers began to fall back to rejoin the main body of the Teutonic army, the Lithuanians rallied and counterattacked. Soon, Teutonic forces were being hemmed in on both sides as the Allied forces gradually encircled the knights. King Jagiełło committed his reserves and the Teutonic army began to break. Lightly armed infantrymen and foreign knights began to lay down their arms or run away. But the fighting brethren of the Teutonic Order neither gave nor received quarter. Many battled to the bitter end as their army fell apart around them.

By the end of the day, the largest and most important battle of the European Middle Ages was over. The Grand Master and nearly all of his knights lay dead on the field. In a single day, the army of the most powerful military state in Europe had been crushed. For Poland, it would mark the dawn of her golden age.

The immediate aftermath of the battle did not result in the complete destruction of the Teutonic Knights, who still had powerful protectors in the Empire and in the Papal Court. Forced to sue for peace, the knights gave up Samogitia and Dobryzń. The failure to follow up on the brilliant victory was also the result of Jagiełło's thinking. As a Lithuanian by birth, he realized that complete destruction of the Order would benefit the Polish half of his realm far more than the Lithuanian portion. As Polish influence in Lithuania was already great, it is likely that he felt a need to maintain a 'balance of power' within the realm. A final reckoning with the Order would be put off for a second generation. Nevertheless, the power of the Teutonic Order had been broken. Its ability to recruit from European nobility was gone and in future campaigns it would depend largely on mercenaries. Never again could it launch a sustained offensive campaign and the days when Teutonic armies could march through Poland were over.

Late Medieval Culture and Thought

The re-establishment and flowering of a unified Polish state in the fourteenth and fifteenth centuries provided greater support for cultural and intellectual life. The founding of a university in Kraków was only the most obvious example of a maturing cultural and intellectual life. Prior to the 1300s, most books in Poland were Latin translations from Italy, Germany or France. During the late Middle Ages while new learning and ideas continued flowing into Poland from these countries, native Polish writers became increasingly active in both Latin and Polish.

The first text in the vernacular was *Bogurodzica* (Mother of God, or Hymn to the Virgin Mary), which originated in the thirteenth century and was unquestionably a native composition rather than an adaptation from Latin. This simple prayer in the form of a hymn functioned as the unofficial national anthem and was sung by soldiers before going into battle. Another early religious text was the *Holy Cross Sermons*, written down in the late thirteenth or early fourteenth centuries. The variety of religious and didactic poems and sermons written in the vernacular grew steadily throughout the fourteenth century. By the fifteenth century they were quite common. The best known was *Dialogue between Master Polycarp and Death* which included a heavy dose of social satire that zeroed in on the failings of corrupt clergy, doctors, lawyers and others. Secular poems which had circulated in oral traditions for centuries began to be written down as well in the fifteenth century.

Historical chronicles were the most common books of the day. The first work of critical history was written by Jan Długosz in the mid-fifteenth century, the twelve-volume *Annals,* in which the author attempts to use a broad range of sources, including legal documents and chronicles of neighbouring countries. Yet perhaps the most significant work of this era came from the Rector of the Kraków academy, jurist Paulus Vladimirus (*c.* 1370–1435). Called on to represent Poland to the Papacy at the Council of Constance in the dispute with the Teutonic Knights, Vladimirus penned a series of treatises. Based on Polish experiences in Lithuania and Ruthenia, he interpreted Church teaching to condemn the entire practice of 'conversion by the sword' as practised by crusaders. Conversion could only be legitimate, he argued, if conducted in accord with Christ's model: 'It is inadmissible to force pagans to convert by force of arms or any form of violence ... evil cannot be used for good ends.' Moreover, he advanced the then innovative concept that all nations, regardless of faith or language, had inalienable natural rights. His argument was to prove the cornerstone for the concept of universal human rights that emerged out of the Christian tradition.

Throughout the fourteenth and fifteenth centuries, Poland experienced a tremendous flowering of Gothic art and architecture. The great cathedral of Gdańsk, built by the city's wealthy German-speaking burghers, was the largest church-building project north of the Alps in the fifteenth century. Local builders created a style called 'Vistula Gothic' which used native red brick in place of the most common stone and masonry buildings found in western Europe. Poznań cathedral and Wawel cathedral in Kraków were notable architectural achievements. The Poznań cathedral, built entirely from brick, featured an especially sophisticated use of space to create the kind of soaring architecture for

Poznań cathedral built in the local 'Vistula Gothic' style

which the Gothic style is noted. Kraków's Collegium Maius, is the only extant example of a Gothic-style university building.

In art, native artists absorbed influences from Germany, Flanders, and Italy and beyond and began to create a unique regional style. Talented local artists found work from local merchants, nobles, and the royal court. Others travelled abroad, finding commissions throughout northern Europe. Workshops in western Poland, such as those of the 'Wrocław Painter,' show the clear impact of Dutch, Flemish, and German contemporaries. The Wit Stwosz altarpiece in Kraków's St Mary's Church and the Beautiful Madonna of Kruźlowa were brilliant examples of Gothic religious carving.

In eastern Poland, with its growing contacts with the Orthodox world, a second style of Gothic art emerged. The best example is the stunning frescoes in the royal chapel in Lublin Castle. Endowed by Władysław Jagiełło himself, they show clear Italian influences reminiscent of Giotto combined with styles drawn from Orthodox Ruthenian icons. The frescoes show scenes from the life of Christ and the Old Testament as well as portraits of saints and prophets. The larger scenes have a more Italianate flavour, while many of the individual portraits of saints have a more icon-like quality. Several of the saints were purely from the Eastern Christian world, their veneration virtually unknown in the Latin west. The eastern influence is also evident in text fragments on the frescoes, which are all in Old Church Slavonic. At the same time, the frescoes were created for a Latin-rite church and include a picture of the king, as the patron, being presented to the Blessed Mother by St Władysław, a convention found only in western art. The chapel shows the true blending of diverse cultural influences that would become a hallmark of Poland in the centuries that followed.

THE JAGIEŁŁONIANS

In the short run the battle of Grunwald seemed more of a catastrophe for the Teutonic Knights than a success for Poland-Lithuania. The two nations had to struggle with a complex internal situation and properly codify the systems of government for the sprawling new country that was being born. In 1413, leading nobles of the two nations signed the Union of Horodło, the most significant step toward accomplishing that goal. The Lithuanian nobility were granted new privileges, giving them a status much closer to their Polish counterparts than ever before. Lithuanian gentry were further Polonized by being adopted into Polish gentry clans, creating a kind of brotherhood between the leading classes of both countries. Moreover, a parliamentary system was developed for Lithuania modelled on Polish lines and local administrative offices were created that matched their Polish counterparts in form and function. The office of the Grand Duke was retained and Lithuania remained theoretically independent, though subordinate to the Polish crown. The Lithuanians retained local autonomy and gained important new political rights while at the same time moving much closer both politically and socially to their Polish neighbours. This was accompanied by a cultural Polonization of the Lithuanian elite that included gradual adoption of Polish as their primary tongue.

Like his immediate predecessors, Louis of Anjou and Casimir the Great, Władysław Jagiełło entered his later years without a legitimate male heir. Three of his wives had died either childless or after bearing only daughters. In 1424, however, he married a Lithuanian princess who bore him two sons, Władysław (1424–44) and Casimir (1427–92). Because the new heirs had no blood tie to the Piast dynasty, the assembled Polish nobility would not immediately accept them as Jagiełło's heirs without additional concessions and guarantees of liberty. Though strongly resistant to further erosion of his power, the king could not budge them. In 1430 he granted additional rights in return for the parliament – or *sejm* – of nobles agreeing to the succession of one of his sons provided they confirmed all of the gentry's privileges.

In May 1434, Władysław Jagiełło fell ill and died. He was over eighty-years-old and had ruled Poland for forty-eight years, the longest reign of any monarch in Polish history. His rule had been characterized by patient and steady efforts to develop a new system of internal governance that could incorporate both his realms into a single entity. He had built steadily on the foundation laid by Casimir the Great and had at last brought to bay Poland's greatest external foes, particularly the Teutonic Knights. At the same time, this was not accomplished by the king alone. The legal anomaly of having a monarch without a direct blood claim to the throne opened the door to the power of the assembled gentry. To rule effectively, Jagiełło had needed their support and co-operation, which they freely gave but, in return, the gentry placed firm limits on the power of the king, marking the beginning of a political experiment unique in contemporary Europe history. This experiment would significantly shape Poland's future.

In July 1434, the ten-year-old Władysław III was crowned king. His accession to the throne was supported by a powerful group of nobles led by the archbishop of Kraków, Zbigniew Oleśnicki. The archbishop, in cooperation with the queen mother, Sophia, and a coalition of gentry, would hold the levers of power during the years of the young king's minority. The first task was to defend Lithuania from a new threat from the Livonian branch of the Teutonic Knights who launched an invasion in support of a separate pretender for the crown of the Grand Duchy. The German knights, with the support of the Holy Roman Emperor, were joined by a large Russian contingent who all shared the goal of breaking the Polish-Lithuanian union. Their forces were defeated by a combined Polish-Lithuanian army, ending a major threat to the union.

With threats from the north and east in check, Archbishop Oleśnicki turned his attention to the south. In Bohemia, the Hussite rebellion had seriously weakened imperial power and had spread to Silesia. This movement of religious dissent also had some support in Poland proper. Hussite armies made raids into south Poland, even attacking the shrine of the famous Black Madonna of Częstochowa. While some Polish gentry wanted to use the unrest to reattach Silesia to the Polish crown, Oleśnicki's main goal was a dynastic union between Poland-Lithuania and Hungary. The Hungarian throne lacked a male heir and the Hungarians faced a serious threat from the Ottoman Empire which was rapidly crushing Christian resistance in southeastern Europe. In 1440, the Hungarian nobles elected the sixteen-year-old Władysław their new king. This led to the outbreak of a brief civil war. While Władysław's supporters emerged victorious, Hungary was seriously weakened by the strife.

Meanwhile, Zygmunt, the Grand Duke of Lithuania (who had ruled since the death of Witold) died. According to a previous agreement, King Władysław was to have been elected the new Grand Duke. With the king engaged in Hungary, however, his younger brother Casimir was sent to Lithuania in his stead. The Lithuanians promptly elected Casimir grand duke, creating a confusing situation. In 1444, Władysław, though his presence was badly needed back home, set out on a crusade against the Turks at the head of a Hungarian army. At Varna, in present-day Bulgaria, the army met defeat at the hands of a much larger Ottoman army. The young king was killed along with most of his Hungarian supporters.

For more than two years, Poland remained without a crowned monarch. Casimir was the obvious choice, but the young prince sought to retain his position in Lithuania in addition to holding the Polish throne, while Archbishop Oleśnicki sought to retain his power either by advancing alternative candidates or making Casimir give up his new Lithuanian power base. In 1447, however, both countries bowed to the inevitable and Casimir was elected king of Poland. While both countries remained theoretically independent, and there were significant conflicts to be resolved, the political structures were increasingly harmonized and they were now ruled by a single monarch who was both king of Poland and grand duke of Lithuania. Casimir completed the process of making the Lithuanian and Ruthenian gentry of the Grand Duchy the legal equals of their Polish counterparts, with rights that included immunity from confiscation of property, fines, or imprisonment without due process of law.

Under its new king, Poland faced an old problem – the Teutonic Order. With its financial power in decline following its military losses, the knights had turned to taxing their own German subjects to pay for their military and political expenses. To accomplish this required more than a little coercion. The burghers of cities like Gdańsk and Toruń saw the increasing freedoms enjoyed by the Polish elite to their south, which contrasted sharply with their growing tax burdens and their lack of political rights. In 1454, a widespread revolt broke out in West Prussia with the goal of seceding from the Teutonic state and joining Poland. The rebels appealed to Casimir for protection and it was granted.

This act initiated the Thirteen Years' War with the Teutonic Order. By this time, the order's armies were mostly mercenaries, but this also meant they were professionals. Polish armies, by contrast, were often made up of nobles without experience in fighting together. As a result, the early years of the conflict went poorly for the Poles. An initial invasion of Prussia met with a humiliating defeat at Chojnice in 1454 and the knights received another boost when Denmark entered the war in an effort to destroy Gdańsk as a potential commercial rival. This forced a re-organization of the military structure and an effort to professionalize the kingdom's war-making ability.

The city of Gdańsk proved a valuable asset. As the most important port on the Baltic, it also gave Poland its first navy. In 1456, the city's fleet defeated a combined Danish-Teutonic fleet off the island of Bornholm. Soon the financial and military power of Casimir's combined realm was being brought to bear on the Teutonic Knights. In 1460, the mighty fortress of Malbork surrendered to the Poles after Casimir agreed to pay its mercenary garrison the back wages that the order had failed to provide. In 1462, the Poles defeated the knights at the battle of Świecino. In 1463, a flotilla of twenty-five Polish ships defeated a much larger Teutonic fleet of forty-four ships at Elbląg. After this, the Poles were able to take fortress after fortress. In 1466, the knights were forced to sue for peace. The peace treaty that followed ended the power of the Teutonic Knights for good. Poland regained the province of West Prussia (eastern Pomerania), lost over a hundred and fifty years before. It also gained the province of Warmia. The mighty port of Gdańsk and the commercial centres of Toruń and Elbląg were now in Polish hands. The Vistula flowed unvexed to the sea entirely within the kingdom and Poland's access to the sea was restored. The knights were forced to pay tribute to Poland and their holdings reduced by half.

The defeat of the mighty Teutonic Knights set the stage for the rise of Polish power which would dominate east-central Europe for the next two centuries.

CHAPTER FOUR

The Golden Age,
1466–1576

Noble Rule

By the conclusion of the Thirteen Years' War Poland was an established and powerful state. Its greatest enemy for the last century and a half – the Teutonic Order – had been smashed and rendered mostly toothless. New foes would emerge soon enough and there were plenty of internal conflicts to occupy the ruling elite, but for the time being Poland stood as the great power of east-central Europe. During the Renaissance it would be known as the Commonwealth of Poland and Lithuania.

The country had developed a unique political system with a hereditary monarch whose power was limited by a parliament made up of the assembled nobility and leading churchmen. Although the relationship between king and parliament was often fraught with strife – nothing unusual in a parliamentary system – it served Poland well. This made Poland the only state in Europe that could claim a political structure that came closest to what modern eyes would view as democracy. Although the elements of this system did not come into place immediately and evolved slowly over time, the underlying concepts were in place by the end of the fifteenth century. It was a system that encouraged restraint of power, moderation, tolerance, and a disinclination to indulge in dynastic ambitions.

For most of its existence, the Polish system did not have the advantage of a written constitution that carefully set out the rules of political exchange. Instead these were worked out piecemeal, often as a result of kings who need support for particular projects or who wished to ascend smoothly to the throne and needed to mollify potential opposition in parliament. Yet, there were a few key laws that helped to codify the rights of the nobility. The first of these was *Neminem Captivabimus*, analogous to Habeas Corpus. Enacted in the early fifteenth century it prevented the seizure of a nobleman's person or property without a proper ruling of a court. The second was *Nihil Novi* which came a century later in 1505. As its name suggested 'nothing new' could be imposed on the gentry without the consent of the parliament, or as the contemporary slogan went 'nothing about us without us.' By the late sixteenth century, the system had produced even more radically democratic acts. *De non praestanda obedientia* declared that the nobility had the right to disavow allegiance to the king in cases where he exceeded his powers or violated the law. To protect rights that might be trampled by excessive power of the executive, noble citizens had the right to protect themselves by force if needed by forming a 'confederation.' This was a temporary expedient meant to correct injustices that could not be otherwise addressed through normal legislative means.

Finally, there was *liberum veto* in which acts of legislation could be rejected by the vote of a single member of the parliament. *Liberum veto* was the most infamous of these acts, blamed for much of the disorder that engulfed the Commonwealth in its final phase. Its original purpose was to restrain the potential tyranny of the majority over the individual. Despite the bad press it has received from historians over the years, it was rarely used until the final century and a half of the Commonwealth's existence. It existed rather as a last resort, a guarantee of rights. It was not until the entire system began to break down that it was significantly abused to the detriment of all.

Under this system, the king was the supreme judge and commander-in-chief of the army. He could mobilize the assembly of nobles (*pospolite ruszenie*) for war, but only with the consent of parliament. The king also convened parliaments and set the agenda for its deliberations. Although he was the chief executive and appointed major civil officers, the king could not marry, divorce, or travel abroad without consent of parliament. Nor could he confer with foreign representatives without the presence of members of the nobility. Foreign relations were to be closely overseen by the senate, the upper house of parliament.

The most common officer of government was the *starosta* who served as local sheriff and judge. The next level of office holder was the castellan, who was the leader of the nobles in a particular district and held senatorial rank in the parliament. The most important local official was the *voivode*. *Voivodes* were provincial governors. They enforced laws and standards in their jurisdiction, led provincial military forces and had oversight over Jewish affairs.

At the national level were the king's royal ministers. The most important of these was the chancellor, who was the king's main representative and intermediary with the parliament and his subjects. The grand marshal guarded the king's person and administered royal justice. The treasurer handled the government's finances, minted money, and collected revenues and paid bills as approved by the parliament. These offices were assisted by under-chancellors, under-treasurers, and under-marshals. Military operations were lead by *Hetmans*, one for Poland, a second for Lithuania. They were assisted by Field *Hetmans* who also oversaw the security of the country's borders.

Parliamentary representation began at the provincial level in local assemblies, or *sejmiki*. These bodies (consisting of nobles and bishops from each province) voted on local matters and sent representatives to the national parliament. The national parliament met as the occasion demanded and was summoned by the king. Parliaments (or *sejms*) could occur once several years or every other year. At the end of the Thirteen Years' War, *sejms* usually lasted a few days but in later times sessions could last for months. The upper house of parliament, the senate, consisted of all ministers, bishops, castellans and *voivodes*. The *sejm* itself included all members of the senate and the representatives of the local *sejmiki*.

Revenue was raised mainly from the land tax, but other taxes were important as well: especially taxes on mining, dwellings, commercial activity, and manufacturing as well as tolls on transport. The Jewish community had a separate tax based on population. Clergy were exempt from taxes until the Saxon era in the early eighteenth century although the Church occasionally made donations to the state treasury in times of need. The rent and other income from properties belonging to the Crown provided revenue for the king's own purse.

THE NOBLE ESTATE

The noble estate, which made up about 8 to 10 per cent of the population (compared with 2 or 3 per cent in much of the rest of Europe), possessed the right to vote and ran the affairs of state. Although voting rights were restricted to male members of the gentry, noblewomen possessed greater power and rights to property than most of their sisters in Western Europe.

The petty nobility were the largest share of the noble estate. Most petty nobles were small landholders. From this class came the lower-level officials in the country's military and administrative structure. Although not quite a yeomanry, the petty nobles were in a sense the backbone of the Polish-Lithuanian state. The second group of nobles was the magnates who held much larger tracts of land and the highest offices. In theory, the two groups were political equals as each member of the estate possessed but a single vote and titles such as duke, prince, count or earl were not used and considered a foreign importation. In practice of course, the magnates had greater power and influence. Yet, they could not disregard the will of their lesser peers whose personal pride and sense of honour and duty toward country would not allow the magnates to rule unchecked.

The nobility collectively referred to itself as *naród* or 'the nation'. Everyone else was the 'the people'. Members of the nation were citizens, which implied having the right to vote, bear arms and engage in public affairs. Citizenship, however, implied being a member of the gentry and belonging to an accepted heraldic clan. The Polish gentry of this era looked directly or indirectly to the ancient republic of Rome as a kind of political ancestor of their own system. Although possessing noble status gave rights, it also entailed serious responsibilities and a duty to serve the nation, to uphold the faith and to protect the weak. Like the medieval knights they in some sense were, members of Polish gentry did not always uphold these ideals, but the ideals themselves were very strong and gave the gentry – despite fierce political divisions – a kind of social and cultural cohesion.

Polish gentry were largely rural, though the wealthiest families maintained residences in major cities as well as country estates. Wealth depended on land and on the peasants who worked it. Most nobles possessed a limited amount of property – a house, some farmland, and perhaps a village. Many poor nobles were economically indistinguishable from wealthy peasants. In regions such as Mazovia, it was not uncommon to have entire villages made up of gentry. The wealthiest nobles, such as the Radziwiłłs, the Potockis, or the Sapiehas, possessed vast territories that sometimes dwarfed the smaller kingdoms of Western Europe. A man on horseback could ride for days without leaving the land of some magnates.

Above all else, Poland's gentry prized personal honour and courage. It was no shame to be poor, but dishonour was unbearable. The gentry could be touchy and prone to violence over small matters of honour, yet at the same time extremely generous to each other as well as to guests and strangers. Hospitality was legendary. For nobles stuck on remote country estates, it was not unknown to fête guests for days, begging them to stay longer, or even temporarily sabotaging their carriages. Nobles, rich or poor, would bankrupt themselves rather than turn away an honoured guest, following the old Polish maxim 'A guest in the house is God in the house.'

As the Polish-Lithuanian state expanded its control over Ukraine and regions around the Black Sea, the nobility came into increasing contact with the Islamic world – especially central Asia, Persia, and Turkey. Over the course of the sixteenth century, the Polish gentry developed a taste for the eastern style of clothing and decoration. While some eastern influences had always been present, during Poland's Golden Age these became especially pronounced. The trade in textiles was so great that Persian carpet makers and silk weavers – many of them ethnic Armenians – devoted their workshops to commissions from the Polish elite. Some simply relocated to Poland to be closer to their primary market and it was through Poland that Persian carpets entered European homes.

Eastern styles helped to emphasize the differences the Polish gentry felt they had compared to their counterparts in other countries. In Russia, nobles became the servants of the tsarist state. In Western

Europe, nobles lost power to the new centralized monarchies and to the growth of the great commercial cities. In Poland, by contrast, the decentralized power of the gentry grew while the power of the state remained severely limited. Polish gentry contrasted this 'liberty' with the 'servitude' of other lands. This difference was further explained by a mythical genealogy in which the Polish gentry were said to be descended from the ancient Sarmatians – warrior nomads who allegedly practised a form of tribal democracy. The term 'Sarmatian' became almost synonymous in some uses with 'Polish.'

Casimir the Jagiellonian (1427–92)

The first great event of Casimir's reign had been the subduing of the Teutonic Order. Yet, his greatest struggles would be waged internally to cement the union with Lithuania. The two segments of his realm did not fit together smoothly. The Union had endured for almost a century but Lithuania had a significantly different set of problems from Poland. Within the kingdom itself, Casimir exercised significant authority. The middle gentry had grown in strength in the mid-fifteenth century and proved to be a natural constituency for the king in balancing the power of magnates. In Lithuania, the great lords still dominated the local councils and were less tractable.

While Poland enjoyed a sizable, compact population, a prospering economy and relatively secure borders, Lithuania did not. The Grand Duchy's rapid expansion to the east and south had left it with long, undefended borders and vast stretches of land with few inhabitants. Potential enemies, especially Moscow and the Ottoman Empire and its vassals in Crimea, abounded.

Previously, the Jagiellonian Grand Dukes had brought Novgorod, the great commercial city of north Russia, under their nominal control. This was an obvious irritant to the rulers of Moscow who considered Novgorod a rival and valued its access to the Baltic trade. In 1478, the city fell to Tsar Ivan III who destroyed both its wealth and its political power. Smaller independent principalities with ties to Lithuania, such as Tver, also suffered the same fate. Lithuania was simultaneously threatened from the south by the Ottomans and the khan of Crimea. In

1484, the Ottoman Sultan, Bajazet II, took control of the Moldavian coastal cities, cutting Lithuania's direct access to the Black Sea.

The Lithuanians simply did not have the resources to fend off these threats and increasingly relied on Polish support. Casmir, however, was not about to commit Poland to a multi-front war with powerful foes like the Ottomans to protect Lithuania while neglecting the security of Poland itself. While the Poles mounted successful expeditions against the Crimean khan, Casimir realized that protecting Novgorod against Ivan III would overstretch his resources. Nor was he about to take on the Ottomans who had systematically crushed Christian resistance in the Balkans.

More significantly, Lithuania's internal situation remained unstable. A plot to assassinate the king and his sons by a group of Lithuanian magnates was nipped in the bud in 1481. Many of the plotters were either sympathetic to Moscow or in the pay of the tsar. Sympathies for an Orthodox ruler played a part in the plot, but more important were internal divisions, greed, and rivalries among the Lithuanian elite.

Much of the later years of Casimir's reign were taken up with pacifying Lithuania and once again attempting to secure the thrones of Hungary and Bohemia for princes of the Jagiellonian house. His reign increased the power of the state, but also tended to put dynastic concerns above the security of the realm. The large, sprawling Polish-Lithuanian Commonwealth was a potent force, but it faced powerful foes in Muscovy, the Tartar Khanite of Crimea (backed by the Ottomans), and the Habsburg dynasty which saw itself as the natural ruler of central Europe. In his final actions, however, he left the complete union of Poland and Lithuania hanging by recommending one son, Jan Olbracht, to be king of Poland, and a second son, Alexander, to be Grand Duke of Lithuania. Casimir the Jagiellonian died in Lithuania in 1492.

THE PERILS OF SUCCESSION

Casimir's son Jan Olbracht (1459–1501) was elected king of Poland following his father's death and while his brother Alexander (1461–1506) ruled Lithuania, Jan Olbracht was considered the senior partner of the diarchy. The new king was an experienced military commander and enjoyed strong support in the parliament. His goal was to break the alliance between Crimea and Moscow. His first aim, however, was to strike at Moldova whose ruler had joined the anti-Polish front. The king's expedition in 1497 was unsuccessful, and the political fallout greatly emboldened Poland's enemies. Tartars and Ottoman forces ravaged Ukraine and southeast Poland, taking many slaves to the markets of central Asia and the Middle East. The Hungarians joined the anti-Polish alliance. The Muscovites under Ivan III renewed their assault as well. Even the Teutonic Knights made an effort to regain some of their lost territory. The king remained calm, however, and faced down the knights with a show of force and made peace with the Ottomans and Hungarians while developing an anti-Habsburg alliance with France. However, the king was struck down in 1501 by disease, possibly syphilis.

His brother Alexander succeeded him on the throne, though like a number of Polish kings throughout history who came to power suddenly or in moments of crisis, he had to make significant political concessions to gain the throne. This weakened royal power and undid some of the gains made by Alexander's brother and father. Alexander was an unimpressive figure, but knew how to appoint good advisors and subordinates. During his rule in Lithuania, he appointed a Jewish convert Jan-Abraham Ezofowicz as treasurer. Ezofowicz's financial skill and loyalty kept the duchy financially solvent during even the worst crises. His court marshal, Michał Glinski, delivered a crushing defeat to the Crimean Horde at Klecko in 1506.

Yet, the most significant achievement of Alexander's reign was the Parliament of Radom in 1505, which enacted the statues of *Nihil Novi* and approved a new law code, the first since Casimir the Great. The parliament set clear boundaries on the king's authority and created the precedent that new laws, decrees or major policy changes had to be approved by parliament. This parliament also created a relative balance among the different factions of the gentry – especially the magnates and the middle gentry. Finally, it made the gentry equally subject to the laws of its own parliament.

In foreign policy, events began to shift again in Poland's favour.

Muscovite efforts to take Smolensk were rebuffed and in 1505 Tsar Ivan III died and the anti-Polish coalition began to come apart. The Moldavians made peace and the Crimean Tartars were defeated. In 1505, the king was struck down by paralysis and never regained his strength, dying the following year shortly after hearing news of the victory at Klecko.

Zygmunt the Old and the Origins of the Polish Renaissance

Prince Zygmunt, the son of King Casimir, was forty-two-years-old when he came to the throne in 1506, hence his nickname Zygmunt Stary or Zygmunt the Old (1467–1548). Prior to his accession, he had managed royal possessions in Silesia for his brother, and had done so conscientiously. Nevertheless, the king's many years as a minor prince had made him a rather passive man, disinclined to make tough decisions. However, this would soon become necessary. By 1512, the new Russian tsar, Vasil III (1479–1533), began to renew his father's campaign to seize Lithuania's eastern provinces. Vasil again allied himself with the Tartars, but this time enjoyed the active support of the Habsburgs as well as Saxony, Brandenburg, and Denmark. Zygmunt managed to alienate Glinski, the victor of Klecko, who offered his services to Moscow. In 1514, the tsar's armies captured the fortress of Smolensk, dealing a major blow to Lithuania's defences. A relief force arrived too late to stop the fall of the city. Under Konstanty Ostrogski, 20,000 Poles and Lithuanians then faced a Muscovite army four times its size. At Orsza, Ostrogski's men conducted a daring crossing of the Dnieper in front of the enemy forces and achieved a brilliant victory, totally destroying the tsar's army and halting any further Russian invasion. The following year, Poland signed a treaty with the Habsburg emperor, which again stymied the anti-Polish coalition, though Smolensk remained in Russian hands and hostilities with the tsar continued.

In 1517, Zygmunt married Bona Sforza, daughter of the duke Milan, cousin of the king of France and niece of the emperor's wife. Though young, the well-connected Italian princess had grown up in a world of high political intrigue. As queen she helped provide some direction to Zygmunt's increasing hapless nature and as the years went on would become a real power behind the throne. She also successfully produced a male heir, Zygmunt August, born in 1520.

Faced with ongoing wars against the Tartars and Muscovites and their allies, the Poles decided to take down one enemy that was both close and unprepared – the Teutonic Order. Despite having lost much of its former power, the Order had continued to intrigue against Poland, working in concert with Denmark and Moscow. The weakened Order had little chance against the Poles. Its powers had been further depleted by the growth of the Reformation in German-speaking lands. Prussia, under the harsh rule of the crusading knights, had proven very receptive to Lutheranism, further undercutting the Order's power. Nevertheless, the indecisive Zygmunt did not press his advantage to the full. Contemporaries, including the Order's Danish allies, believed Prussia was finished. Yet, Zygmunt allowed the Order off the hook. In 1525, a final peace was signed. The Order's territory was transformed into a secular Lutheran duchy under the former grand master, Albrecht Hohenzollern. The new duke became a vassal of the king. However, Prussia remained nominally independent and old medieval ties of vassalage were becoming increasingly anachronistic. Moreover, the new duke was related to the Hohenzollerns of Brandenburg who were long-time enemies of Poland. Although the Teutonic Order was gone from Poland's doorstep, the seed of a new threat had been planted by the king's leniency.

In the east, Poland signed a new treaty with Muscovy, but faced a continuing threat from the Tartar horde in Crimea. Years of violent Tartar raids forced a reorganization of the defences of Ukraine. Parliament approved funds for a standing army to defend the border, but in typically decentralized Polish fashion, placed these forces in the hands of local inhabitants. In Ukraine, officials recruited a mixture of local brigands, minor nobles, freed peasants, and others. This new force would come to be called 'Cossacks.' Tough, resourceful and with excellent knowledge of the local terrain they would prove an effective barrier to Tartar incursions.

CULTURAL FLOWERING

As king, gentry, and parliament worked to patch up the Commonwealth's defences, Poland was undergoing a major cultural flowering.
The wealth brought by increased trade and growing contacts with east
and west could be seen in the royal court and in the households of the
gentry and wealthy city dwellers. During the late 1400s, late Gothic art
and architecture had flourished in Poland. With the king's marriage to
Bona Sforza, the Italian connection, which had always been strong,
grew stronger. In 1519, architect Bartolomeo Berrecci designed the
Sigismund Chapel at Wawel Castle for the king and queen, creating
one of the architectural gems of the northern Renaissance. Every inch
of its stone walls and dome was covered with sculpture: floral arab-
esques, grotesque creatures, and mythological scenes. The chapel was
further enhanced with a massive silver altarpiece with scenes from the
life of the Virgin created by the silversmiths of Nuremburg.

The new queen brought many artists, poets, cooks, and musicians
from her native land to the royal court. But they followed a path that
was increasing well-travelled. As Italy became a battleground for the
great powers of Spain, France, and the Empire, many talented Italians
left their homeland in search of opportunity elsewhere. In addition, a
large number of Poles who had received schooling in Italy also brought
back new learning and ideas. Another influence came from Holland via
Gdańsk, where the sophisticated Netherlandish style of painting had
numerous patrons and a local school of painters who incorporated
Polish, German, and Dutch influences.

To be sure, many gentry households remained very provincial, but
others, especially among the wealthy magnates, became Renaissance
princes. With money and land to spare, they could dream great dreams
and bring them to reality. Among the most ambitious was Jan
Zamoyski (1542-1605), royal *hetman* and a member of one of Poland's
greatest families. Zamoyski's ambition was to create an 'ideal city' – the
pinnacle of Renaissance urban planning. In 1589, he founded the city
of Zamość on the old trading routes between Poland and the Black Sea.
His Italian architect combined northern Italian and central European
architectural styles and local materials in an effort to create a town that

was both visually harmonious and functional. One part of the town was devoted to noble residences, especially the founder's own family. The remaining sections of town were organized around three large town squares. Zamoyski populated his town with ethnic Poles, but also included sections for Poland's major ethnic and religious minorities including Orthodox Ruthenians, Jews, and Armenians. To complete his city, the prince founded an academy of higher learning, the second in Poland.

Although few nobles could achieve the scale and magnificence of Zamoyski's vision, nearly were all were touched by the spirit of the times. It became increasingly important to educate one's children in the basics of the catechism, as well as rhetoric, poetry, and the classics. Treatises teaching appropriate manners began to appear in Polish and Latin closely following Baldesar Castiglione's *The Book of the Courtier* (which also circulated in Poland). Printing reached Poland two decades after Gutenberg published his first book and expanded rapidly. Books were printed in Latin, Polish, German, and Cyrillic. Kraków printers produced the first Cyrillic type and the first printed books in Cyrillic. By the end of the sixteenth century, Polish publishers had produced an astonishing two million volumes.

REFORMATION AND RELIGIOUS REVOLT

The religious revolt sparked by Martin Luther also had a significant effect on the Commonwealth. The writings of Luther and other dissidents reached Poland very quickly via the country's urban centres where German was widely read and spoken. From there it quickly diffused into the Polish population. Criticisms of the worldly abuses of churchmen and of practices such as indulgences found fertile ground in the Commonwealth, aided by the spirit of religious tolerance that was one of Poland's hallmarks. (There had been precedents for this, as the earlier Czech heretic Jan Hus had gained adherents in Poland and Hussitism was well known in western Poland.) Although exact numbers are not known, as much as a third of Poland may have converted to Protestantism, Lutheranism and more importantly, Calvinism. These numbers were increased by the admissions of groups of radical Protestant dissenters, who fled to Poland after being persecuted elsewhere in Europe by Catholics and other Protestants.

The Reformation was especially strong in cities and among the middle gentry. Unlike in Western Europe, however, conversions and subsequent reconversions occurred without bloodshed. In the late sixteenth century, Poland experienced one of the most successful counter-reformation movements in Europe. Led by skilled orators such as the Jesuit Father Piotr Skarga, large numbers of Protestants returned to the Catholic Church. Yet, the influence of the Reformation on Polish life was immense. Poland became a true meeting place of religious ideas. Debates over theology and matters of faith came to occupy a central place in Polish thought and public discourse, more so perhaps than in any other European contemporary country. From Poland, new ideas percolated eastward to the Orthodox world. Polish Jesuits in Kiev produced a new, more accurate translation of the Bible into Old Church Slavonic that would help spark reforms in the Russian Orthodox Church. The Reformation also dramatically increased the use of the vernacular in Polish writing. Although use of Polish had grown gradually over the previous two centuries, in the 1500s it became the language of the nation's most important literature.

The Age of Copernicus and Kochanowski

The flowering of Polish Renaissance culture found its highest expression in the written word. This intense burst of creativity brought forth poets, humanists and scholars. At first, local books were written mainly in Latin, but Polish became increasingly common as the language of literature during the course of the sixteenth century. As author Mikołaj Rey put it: 'Among other nations let it always be known/That the Poles are not geese/and have a tongue of their own.'

The best known Pole of this age was Mikołaj Kopernik – or Nicholas Copernicus (1473–1543). Born in Toruń in 1473, the young Copernicus studied at the Jagiellonian University in Kraków and later at the universities of Bologna and Ferrara. During studies for medicine and canon law, he became fascinated with astronomy. After 1512, as canon of Frombork cathedral, he devoted himself to astronomy. In 1514 Copernicus published a small, handwritten volume for a few

Nicholas Copernicus, the great astronomer

friends called the *Little Commentaries* in which he set forth a series of axioms that placed the sun, not the earth, as the centre of the universe and further explained that the apparent retrograde motion of the planets was a result of observers experiencing the movement of the earth from which they observed.

Shortly thereafter, Copernicus began work on his magnum opus, *De revolutionibus orbium coelestium,* published shortly before his death in 1543. The German mathematician Georg Rheticus had a chance to closely observe Copernicus' scientific method:

> My teacher always had before his eyes the observations of all ages together with his own, assembled in order as in catalogues; then when some conclusion must be drawn or contribution made to the science and its principles, he proceeds from the earliest observations to his own, seeking the mutual relationship which harmonizes them all; the results thus obtained by correct inference under the guidance of Urania he then compares with the hypothesis of Ptolemy and the ancients; and having made a most careful examination of these hypotheses, he finds that astronomical proof requires their rejection; he assumes new hypotheses, not indeed without divine inspiration and the favour of the gods; by applying mathematics, he geo-

metrically establishes the conclusions which can be drawn from them by correct inference; he then harmonizes the ancient observations and his own with the hypotheses which he has adopted; and after performing all these operations he finally writes down the laws of astronomy.

Though not immediately accepted by other astronomers, Copernicus' observations and his thesis that the earth revolved around the sun and not the sun around the earth formed the basis of the work of Johannes Kepler and Galileo Galilei. He was the first great astronomer of the modern era and as such laid the basis for future study of the heavens.

The second great figure of the Polish Renaissance was Jan Kochanowski (1530–84). Born into a noble family in central Poland in 1530, Kochanowski was educated at the university in Kraków and then Italy. During his early years, he proved a master of Latin and composed a number of Latin elegies. On his return to Poland, he accepted a position as a secretary at the royal court of Zygmunt August. When not performing his duties he began to write poems in Polish, inspired perhaps by Italian writers such as Petrarch. After his stint at the court, he married and retired to a country estate to raise his children and devote himself to his art. His best known works were *Psalms of David*, the *Horatian Songs*, and his Ovidian-styled *Satires*. In 1579, however, his young daughter Urszula died at the age of two-and-a-half. The grief-stricken Kochanowski tried to make sense of this tragic loss and putting pen to paper wrote nineteen heart-wrenchingly beautiful poems that came to be known as *Treny* (Laments). Unlike his previous efforts, the Laments followed no prescribed pattern known in Renaissance or classical verse – representing a completely new direction in Polish literature. In Lament V, Kochanowski wrote:

> Like a tiny olive tree
> in some vast orchard
> Following the path
> of its mother upward
> Not yet with branch or leaf
> barely a sprouted shoot
> That some zealous gardener
> might clip to uproot
> Prickly thorns

> or a dense patch of nettle –
> Soon it will drop
> losing the struggle
> Limp by the foot
> of its beloved mother.
> And so my *Ula*
> my own sweet daughter
> How did you get so tangled up
> in Persephone's anger and her grief
> That you fell to our feet
> like some pruned leaf?

(Trans by Leonard Kress,
http://www.wooster.edu/artfuldodge/poetsastranslators/kress.htm#5)

Prior to his death in 1584, he wrote the equally important *Dismissal of the Greek Envoys*, a tragedy that shared much in spirit with the Laments and which introduced unrhymed blank verse to Polish. Kochanowski was first great vernacular poet in any of the Slavic languages and laid the basis for Polish poetry of the early modern era with its strong sense of the tragedy and centrality of religious and classical imagery.

Polish Cities (Kraków, Gdańsk, Warsaw)

Poland's cities were centres of Renaissance learning and art. Some were economic powerhouses. But they lacked the political clout of their western counterparts. Polish cities rarely banded together to protect their own interests at the national level. City leaders were eager to enhance the power of their own communities, but rarely worked to further the status of the merchant class within the Commonwealth. The result was that, as a whole, Polish cities had a brief heyday in the fifteenth and sixteenth centuries but stagnated and rarely grew as large and wealthy as their Western counterparts. There were, of course, important exceptions.

The city of Gdańsk was the wealthiest city in the Commonwealth and held the title of the 'Royal City of Gdańsk' and enjoyed special rights unknown to other Polish cities. By the mid-seventeenth century, Gdańsk had grown to over 70,000 inhabitants, most of whom spoke both Polish and German. The city's wealth was due to the Polish grain trade with Holland and other major West European destinations. By the early 1600s, Gdańsk was the most important port on the Baltic. Ships from around the world came calling, but Holland, England, Germany and Scandinavia were the city's biggest trading partners. The city was also an important cultural hub, exposed to influences from around the world. Gdańsk had special ties to England. Some of the earliest performances of Shakespeare on the Continent were in Gdańsk. The city was also well known to adventurer John Smith, who probably recruited a group of artisans from the city to bolster his Jamestown colony in Virginia.

Kraków held pride of place among Polish cities as the capital and seat of royal power until 1596. During Poland's Golden Age, the city grew steadily, fuelled by trade routes from east to west and north to south as well as by the large number of people who came every year to the royal court. The city's magnificent Cloth Hall (Sukiennice) and its Main Market (Rynek Główny), as well as the chapels of the Wawel and the buildings of the Jagiellonian University, are among the best evidence of the city's zenith. With Poland's first and largest university, Kraków was also the nation's intellectual centre.

Among Polish cities, Warsaw, the present capital, was a late bloomer. It was the provincial seat of Mazovia in the Middle Ages and a minor

The great Cloth Hall in Kraków built during the city's zenith

trade centre. With the Lithuanian merger, however, Warsaw's central position between Wilno and Kraków gave the city increasing prominence. It proved an ideal location to hold elections and parliaments when large numbers of nobles would come from both sectors of the Commonwealth. In 1596, the first of the Wasa kings, Zygmunt III, made Warsaw the official capital. Thereafter, the city grew quickly in size. Nobles built palaces and townhouses to stay near the royal court. Merchants, bankers, courtiers and servants came too, swelling the city's population. Unlike Kraków, with its university traditions and cultural roots, and Gdańsk, with its orientation to international commerce, Warsaw was by nature an overtly political city. The nature of these three great cities would endure for many centuries.

Zygmunt, Father and Son

The reign of Zygmunt the Old was characterized by both great successes and missed opportunities. As Zygmunt aged, initiative for creating policy fell more and more to the queen. Brilliant and ruthless, Queen Bona (1494–1557) sought to make Poland the premier power in central Europe and to regain lost provinces such as Silesia. To this end, she was strongly opposed to Habsburg influence and was in some ways the leader of the anti-Habsburg party in Poland. This group sought alliances with France and sometimes Turkey to counter Austrian power. Throughout the sixteenth and seventeenth centuries, Poland would vacillate between seeking alliance with the Habsburgs and opposing them, depending on the shifting winds of political fortune and which faction held the upper hand within Poland.

Culturally and economically, Poland achieved greatness under Zygmunt's rule. The queen systematically rebuilt the fortune of the royal family and introduced many successfully economic and agricultural innovations. New settlements were founded, especially in the east borderlands in what is now Ukraine, and colonists were brought in from the heart of Poland and elsewhere to put more land under the plough and develop small-scale industry and crafts. It was during this era that Poles invented their own form of distilled spirit, called 'wódka' or vodka, and distilling became an important local industry. Not only

Germans, Dutch, and Jews settled in Poland during this period, but also Scots, Irish, Armenians, Czechs, and Tartars.

From a constitutional and legal standpoint, however, efforts at reform were largely unsuccessful. The role of king remained unclear in some areas and contradictory and outdated laws and acts that had crept in over the course of time remained unaddressed. During Zygmunt's reign, the great nobles, the magnates, grew more powerful, despite the bitter opposition of the queen. The queen's seemingly autocratic tendencies also met with a cool reception from the middle gentry, who otherwise would have been natural allies and saw a strong monarch as a check on the power of the magnates.

The problems were most obvious in efforts to defend the Commonwealth's far-flung borders. Parliament routinely failed to allocate enough money for defence until serious crises arose. The core of the country was kept safe thanks to the skill and dedication of Poland's relatively slender armies and their commanders. Great victories, however, were rarely followed up as parliament would fail to provide the resources necessary to win wars. In general, parliamentarians were preoccupied by local interests and often viewed defensive arrangements for distant provinces as a questionable adventure.

In 1548, on the death of Zygmunt the Old, his son Zygmunt August (1520–1572) took the throne. This succession resulted in immediate political upheaval, in part because a few months before, the new king had married Barbara Gasztołd-Radziwiłł, a daughter of the powerful Lithuanian Radziwiłł family. The match was based on love, but a close tie between the king and such a powerful family was viewed with suspicion by the gentry. Nevertheless, the king's opponents overplayed their hand and a reaction in the king's favour helped restore some of his prestige. In all events, the marriage did not last long and by 1551, Barbara was dead, poisoned according to some contemporaries who pointed the finger at Zygmunt's powerful mother, Queen Bona. The king married an Austrian Habsburg archduchess in 1553, but never really recovered from the loss of his beloved Barbara and would never sire a legitimate male heir.

The new king was a skilled diplomat and when Russia attempted to seize Livonia and the key port city of Riga, Zygmunt outmanoeuvred the tsar, Ivan the Terrible, and signed a treaty with the archbishop of Riga and the grand master of the Livonia Order which brought all of present-day Latvia and part of Estonia under Polish rule and prevented Muscovy from gaining a port on the Baltic. This Ivan would not stand for, and he attacked Poland with the help of the Swedes. The conflict dragged on with little advantage to either side until 1568 when the Swedes, concerned over a growing Russian threat to Finland, switched sides and signed a peace treaty with the Poles. This forced Ivan to sign a truce with Poland. The annexation of Livonia refocused Polish attention away from the eastern borderlands toward the Baltic. Polish diplomats began to press the issues of trade and maritime rights in the courts of northern Europe

The conflict over Livonia also forced the king into improved relations with the parliament and made him much more adept at the art of Polish-style representative government than before. This was especially important as Poland and Lithuania moved into the final stage of unification and the gentry sought to reform Poland's form of government. In 1569, the previously separate Polish and Lithuanian parliaments met jointly in the city of Lublin.

Up to this point, the Jagiellonian dynasty had provided a good portion of the 'glue' that held the two parts of the Commonwealth together, but the prospect of Zygmunt dying without an heir threatened to undermine previous arrangements. Although the magnates of Lithuania opposed a full legal union, the overwhelming majority of Lithuanian gentry favoured it. Moreover, the king gained the support of the gentry of Ruthenia (Ukraine) which was transferred from Lithuania and placed under the kingdom of Poland. On 1 July 1569, the Union of Lublin was signed and the separate status of Lithuania largely disappeared. The king would be elected by the gentry of both realms and parliaments would be unified and would meet at Warsaw. Lithuania retained a separate law code and public offices.

The remaining issue was succession to the throne. As it was clear that Zygmunt would not produce a male heir, various factions lined up candidates for the job. The Habsburgs were especially eager to secure the Polish throne, but the loss of freedoms by the nobility of Bohemia under Habsburg rule turned much of the Polish gentry against any

Habsburg candidate, fearing a repeat of what had happened in Czech lands. The issue remained unresolved when the king died.

Zygmunt August died in 1572, the last of the Jagiellonian dynasty. His remarkable reign was the end of an era of dynastic monarchy in Poland. His efforts, however, greatly strengthened the Polish state, which in many ways was at the height of its power in 1572. He had helped to create a single state entity and secured this with constitutional reform, thus ending the problem of a state with two separate governments. His acquisition of Livonia had stymied Muscovite expansion (at least for the time being) and made Poland into a moderately strong Baltic power.

During his reign, Polish Renaissance culture flourished and the forces of the Reformation and Counter-Reformation engaged in vigorous but largely non-violent debate in an effort to win souls for God. As Germany and Western Europe became increasingly torn by religious strife, Poland remained an island of tolerance – officially Catholic but with huge Protestant, Jewish, Orthodox and Muslim communities living side by side. When asked about this question, Zygmunt had once proclaimed 'I am not the king of your conscience', a statement that sounds remarkably 'modern'.

Succession to the Polish throne which had been hereditary, but only with the agreement of parliament, now became completely dependent on the will of the assembled gentry. Henceforth, to be elected, kings would have to swear to uphold the rights and freedoms of the gentry and accept limited power, a stark departure from the increasingly absolute power of other European and Asian monarchs.

In 1573, parliament elected Henry Valois (1551–89) the brother of the king of France as king. He arrived in Poland the following year, but as a young man and unaccustomed to Poland's unique political culture, his authority could never really be established and the king spent his days with wine, women, and song. When his brother died, Henry took the chance and fled in ignominy back to France, crossing the border in the dark of night. In 1575, parliament declared the throne vacant. The interregnum challenged the new parliamentary system, for a kingdom without a king was prey for all potential foes.

CHAPTER FIVE

The Silver Age and the End of the Commonwealth, 1576–1795

Stefan Batory (1533–86)

After the fiasco of Henry Valois' brief reign, the pro-Habsburg party in Poland made a major play for a Habsburg monarch. Support for electing Emperor Maximilian II came mainly from a group of powerful magnates, as well as a few other supporters, such as the city of Gdańsk. When a group of senators tried to stage an election of the emperor without consulting the mass of the gentry, the parliament revolted against even the slight hint of Habsburg affiliation. Instead they chose the most anti-Habsburg candidate they could find, Stefan Batory, Prince of Transylvania.

The new king was an able politician and a skilled general. He managed to win over the majority of the gentry and the pro-Habsburg faction collapsed. The city of Gdańsk refused to accept the election and rose up in revolt. Batory wasted no time in besieging the city and revoking its commercial rights. The spat ended in a negotiated settlement, but the king had proved to be a man of action.

During the conflict with Gdańsk, Ivan the Terrible had invaded Livonia in a new Russian effort to defeat the Commonwealth and gain control of the Baltic coast. Despite parliament's slowness in approving money for the armed forces, Batory assembled an army in 1578 and went on the counter-offensive. He seized the fortress of Polotsk that year. In 1580, the king took to the field again, striking deep into Muscovite territory and seizing Velikye Luki. Polish cavalry ranged far behind Ivan's lines, wreaking havoc wherever they went. In 1581, with parliamentary support weakening as the cost of the war grew, Batory resolved to take the 'impregnable' Russian fortress of Pskov, garrisoned by 30,000 of Ivan's best troops. The Polish army laid siege to Pskov throughout the fall and winter of 1581/82. Led by Jan Zamoyski, the army endured brutal cold and near starvation. Cavalrymen froze to death in the saddle along with their horses. However, by then Ivan had had enough and agreed to a peace treaty, returning all territory to Poland. Muscovite armies had lost more 300,000 men and Polish detachments ranged at will throughout the countryside. This defeat, combined with Ivan's brutality toward his own people, would result in a major crisis for Russia in the decades to come.

Although a warrior at heart, Batory was also a reformer. His experiences in the campaigns with Gdańsk and Muscovy led him to reform the military system, creating the nucleus of a standing army, the *piechota wybraniecka* or 'select infantry', made up of free peasants and based on modern military principles. He also reorganized the cavalry, laying the basis for the fast and deadly winged hussars that proved to be the mainstay of future Polish victories. He also strengthened the

Reformer and warrior, Stefan Batory

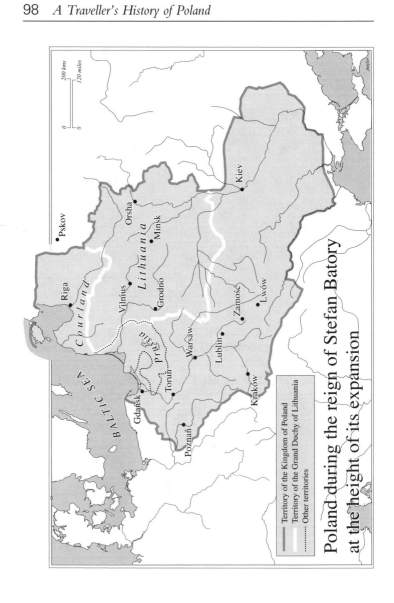

Poland during the reign of Stefan Batory at the height of its expansion

southeastern border by confirming the privileges granted to loyal Cossacks and enrolling a group of them as part of the regular forces of the Commonwealth.

As an administrator, he created new permanent supreme tribunals for Poland and Lithuania that played a significant role in speeding up civil suits, since litigants no longer had to wait for the next parliament. The elected tribunals also created a more uniform system of justice throughout the realm. In addition, Batory created a new administrative system for Livonia which was to be ruled as a separate part of the Commonwealth under royal control.

Batory introduced the Counter-Reformation into Poland in a significant way. He especially favoured the Jesuits who set up several new colleges and schools throughout the country. At the same time, he reconfirmed his predecessors' policies of religious tolerance and protection for the rights of religious dissenters.

In 1586, Batory died, leaving behind a vigorous legacy.

SOCIAL AND ECONOMIC CONDITIONS

The opening of the Vistula and the port of Gdańsk caused a tremendous expansion of the Polish manorial economy as demand for Polish grain grew with Europe's expanding population. Other key exports included timber and timber products, leather goods, and livestock. One response was the opening up of new lands, especially in Ukraine. Royal, noble and church estates grew in size. Another response was to seek to tie the peasants more closely to the land and thus increase the amount of labour devoted to grain production. This occurred gradually at first and did not have a major impact on the peasants. The wealth from the grain trade flowed in some degree to all sectors of society.

At the end of the sixteenth century, this system was beginning to fray around the edges. The costly war with Muscovy contributed to the problem, but a more significant factor was the crisis of Polish currency. Like its Hungarian and Bohemian counterparts, the Polish florin was silver and Spain's discovery of massive silver deposits in the New World and the subsequent flood of silver into Europe's economy caused a serious devaluation of the florin. As Polish grain became worth less, the

Polish gentry sought to further increase agricultural production to make up for lost income. This meant further enserfment of the peasants. At the behest of the gentry and especially the magnates, peasants' legal rights and ability to leave their farms were restricted. During the Middle Ages Polish peasants had enjoyed greater freedom than their Western European counterparts. Over time, however, as West European peasants became freer, Polish peasants became less free and a political system meant to protect the rights of the gentry worked against the rights of the great mass of the population. In addition, some peasant traditions worked toward further impoverishment – such as the practice of equal inheritance for all surviving children. This meant that farms were divided among a farmer's heirs, gradually creating ever smaller farms and leading to a class of landless rural labourers. By the end of the sixteenth century, peasants worked for their masters an average of two to three days a week, in addition to any extra duties that might be required.

A further weakness of the Polish manorial system was its increasing tendency toward massive estates, especially in Ukraine and Lithuania. Large owners became increasing removed from the operation of their landholdings. This was coupled with a strong cultural aversion to direct involvement in commerce. One result was that magnates increasingly relied on middlemen to run their estates, especially the revenue-gathering portions. These agents, who were most often Jewish, received concessions to collect taxes or operate mills, taverns or other village businesses. As these middlemen were required to deliver a certain income to the owner of the estate, there was strong pressure to exploit the peasants. Although many middlemen were honest, many were not. Regardless of their honesty, however, there emerged a natural tendency among the peasants to blame their troubles on the lord's agents with whom they interacted on an almost daily basis.

Industrial and craft production developed slowly. The guild system was not as well established in Poland as elsewhere, especially in smaller towns. This allowed a certain degree of freedom for journeymen but meant that the political influence of craftsmen was more limited. The largest industrial production was salt mining at Wieliczka and other mines. Glass, paper, and metal production were also significant. Some industrial enterprises were owned or partly owned by the gentry while others were in the hands of co-operative associations led by the master craftsmen who oversaw production. In general, industrial production remained underdeveloped, in part due to the small size and political weakness of cities within the Commonwealth.

The Wasa King

The election of 1587 once again pitted the pro-Habsburg faction against their opponents. The Zborowski family led the former. They had fared poorly under the reign of Batory and wanted to recoup their fortunes. The anti-Habsburg faction was headed by Jan Zamoyski (1542–1605), Batory's chancellor and grand *hetman*, and one of the most powerful and remarkable men of his age. Zamoyski and his supporters managed to thwart the Zborowskis and their supporters and elected Zygmunt Wasa (1566–1632), the twenty-one-year-old son of the king of Sweden, who was related to the Jagiellonians through his mother's side. The Zborowskis then formed their own parliament and elected Archduke Maximilian of Austria. Encouraged by his supporters, the archduke invaded Poland to forestall the succession of Zygmunt. In January 1588, Zamoyski decisively defeated Maximilian, captured the archduke, and sent his unwilling guest for a long stay in Zamoyski's new city of Zamość in east-central Poland.

If one goal of Zamoyski and his followers in electing the new king had been to check Habsburg influence, another had been to create an alliance with Sweden. This would help Poland against Muscovy while creating a dominant power in the Baltic. For his part, Zygmunt Wasa came to the throne as a devoted Catholic from a mostly Protestant country. Internal politics in Sweden had grown increasingly tense and the Catholic Wasas hoped that the Polish throne would provide a power base from which to restore their fortunes. The new king, however, was shocked by the weakness of the position he had accepted and spent a great deal of effort trying to undermine the power of parliament. Nor were the gentry willing to support their new king's Swedish ambitions. Odder still, though elected by Zamoyski and his supporters, Zygmunt III proved to have a strong affinity for the

Habsburgs, much to the chagrin of the anti-Habsburg majority in the parliament. This soon caused a break between the king and the chancellor, and the king began to side with those who had originally opposed his election.

Within a few years of his election, Zygmunt made a strange attempt to ally with the Habsburgs. Over the objections of Zamoyski and much of the parliament he married Austrian Archduchess Anna in 1592 and had her crowned queen. He then seems to have made an attempt to resign the throne in favour of another Austrian archduke. Behind this was a desire to return to Sweden, where his father King John III was already in poor health. The king's moves, however, alienated many of his own supporters and gave the chancellor the upper hand. Zygmunt was forced to back down in public, losing a great deal of his prestige. He publicly promised never to leave the country without the permission of parliament. He and Zamoyski were reconciled and the chancellor would serve the king well for many years.

At end of 1592, Zygmunt's father died, leaving him the throne of Sweden. The king received permission to return home and did so and was crowned king of Sweden in 1594.

The Union of Brest

Poland proved to have one of the most successful Counter-Reformation movements in Europe. Led by well-educated, articulate Jesuits like Fr Piotr Skarga (1536–1612), the Catholic Church not only won back many Protestants, but also had a growing impact on Poland's large Orthodox population. Eastern Slavs living in Poland were torn between different centres of Orthodox authority – Moscow, Kiev and Constantinople. Constantinople had been under Turkish rule since 1453 and its political influence was weak. Moscow claimed to be the new Rome of the Orthodox world, but few Ruthenian Orthodox leaders trusted Moscow. This position was only strengthened by the political unrest that swept Russia after the death of Ivan the Terrible as his long reign of terror had left the country weaker rather than stronger. Polish rule, the rapid development of Christian discourse in Europe, the strength of the Counter-Reformation and the introduction of innovations such as the printing of the Bible in Old Church Slavonic drew many Orthodox leaders back to Rome.

Initial overtures were made to Rome via the king in 1590 by a group of Poland's Orthodox bishops. These bishops drew up a document stating conditions under which they could reunite with Rome. In particular, these included retaining many of the rites and traditions of the Eastern Church and the need to have bishops and metropolitans drawn from the Ruthenian or Greek peoples. (Ruthenians, not to be confused with Russians, were east Slavic ancestors of today's Ukrainians and Carpatho-Rusyns.)

The bishops then visited Rome and were received in high pomp by Pope Clement VII. For his part, the king of Poland agreed that Ruthenian clergy would have the same rights as Catholic clergy and that the bishops would be given the rank of senators.

As might be expected, this move aroused considerable resentment from other Orthodox leaders, both religious and secular. The two sides had little middle ground and unrest threatened. Many religious leaders saw this effort as frustrating their own attempts at reform and revival within Orthodoxy. Secular Orthodox gentry were especially opposed to re-unification since they administered religious affairs in their own lands and would have lost this right under the Catholic Church.

In 1596 – the same year that Zygmunt III moved the capital to Warsaw – a large body of Orthodox leaders held a synod in Brest. The meeting drove the two sides into permanent schism. The Metropolitan of Kiev and the Bishop of Brest proclaimed their desire for unification with Rome and marched in procession to the local Catholic cathedral where they were met with open arms. Those who resolved to remain in the Orthodox fold excommunicated those who sought union and were in turn excommunicated by their opponents.

The Eastern Rite Catholic Church retained its eastern traditions in union with Rome. Its influence was the most pronounced among Ruthenians in the western-most parts of the Orthodox world where it became a vital and enduring presence. Orthodox religious leaders and the tsars of Russia saw it as a major threat to their power and an insult to their authority that time would never wipe away.

THE SWEDISH PROBLEM

Zygmunt III Wasa was never known as a personable man. By disposition he was morose, suspicious and even secretive. Neither the Poles nor the Swedes found him particularly likeable. His election to the Polish throne had been meant to draw Poland and Sweden into closer alliance. Zygmunt's succession to the Swedish throne in 1594, rather than the culmination of this plan, turned out to be its downfall. Zygmunt promptly alienated his Swedish subjects, especially on the subject of religion where it was clear that he was deeply opposed to the Lutheran faith that was then the majority religion of the country. After the coronation, the king returned to Poland – the only act most of his new Swedish subjects approved – and left the reins of power in hands of his ambitious and able uncle Charles.

Charles wasted no time in removing Zygmunt's supporters from office and introducing harsh measures against Catholics. Before long Charles was king in all but name. Zygmunt got little sympathy from the Polish parliament and the government remained in the hands of the able Zamoyski whose efforts were bent toward preventing the Habsburgs from drawing Poland into a major war with the Ottoman Empire. However, the king did manage to raise an army of mercenaries and invaded Sweden in 1598. He was promptly defeated by his uncle and fled back to Poland. Charles took complete control of Sweden and Finland. Estonia, however, remained loyal to Zygmunt and this prompted Charles to send troops to seize this territory in 1600, where they clashed with Zygmunt's forces. As a result, Swedish forces crossed the border and attacked Livonia, sparking a war with Poland.

At first the Swedes captured Polish forts throughout Livonia and menaced Riga in late 1600. Polish forces remained small, but in 1601 under able leaders such as Krzysztof Radzwiłł and Jan Karol Chodkiewicz, the Poles inflicted a series of defeats on the larger Swedish armies. The key to these victories was the Poles' innovative use of cavalry, especially the winged hussar.

Winged hussars were among the last great shock cavalry of Europe. Recruited from the gentry and mounted on horses that were both powerful and swift, the hussar charge was almost unstoppable. Swedish cavalry, used to exchanging volleys of pistol fire, were overwhelmed by the rapid charges of the hussars. The speed of their attack was such that contemporary firearms were rarely able to get off more than a single volley. Hussar lances outreached the pikes of defending infantry, allowing them to break pike squares. The most memorable aspect of the hussar's regalia, however, was the great wings attached to the back of the hussar's armour. Made of wood with vulture or eagle feathers, the purpose of the wings is hotly debated. Some argue that the sound made by wings during a mass charge frightened enemy horses, while others claim they evolved as a defence against Tartar lariats or lassoes. Regardless of their origin, the winged hussars would face Poland's enemies on many battlefields. Often outnumbered, they would save the Commonwealth time and again.

One of the unstoppable winged hussars

By the end of 1603, the Poles had cleared most of Livonia and Estonia of Swedish garrisons. However, lack of regular pay and supplies severely hampered Polish efforts to consolidate these gains. In September 1604, *Hetman* Chodkiewicz defeated a Swedish effort to seize Biały Kamien in Livonia. The following year, the parliament again failed to provide sufficient resources to defend Livonia as unrest over Zygmunt's continuing efforts to take the Swedish throne increased. Charles, having proclaimed himself king of Sweden, invaded Livonia in 1605 at the head of 12,000 troops – an army much larger than previous Swedish efforts. His goal was to take the port of Riga, the cornerstone of Polish control in the region. Opposing him, Chodkiewicz could field a mere 3,500 men.

On 26 September, the two armies met at Kircholm near Riga on the banks of River Dvina. The Swedes, having learned of the danger presented by Polish hussars, dug in their infantry and intended to use their cavalry to counterattack once the Polish cavalry had been halted by the infantry in its field defences. The first part of the battle was an exchange of infantry fire with the Poles unsuccessfully trying to draw the Swedes out into the open. Then Chodkiewicz ordered his infantry to withdraw, creating the impression that he was abandoning the field. King Charles, hoping to win a decisive victory, ordered his army forward. Polish infantry and artillery stopped the Swedish advance and Chodkiewicz's cavalry attacked. Polish light cavalry turned the Swedish left flank which then crumbled under the force of a hussar charge. On the right, the Swedes fought fiercely to hold off the initial Polish charge, but a second attack routed the remainder of Charles' army. The Poles pursued the fleeing infantry remorselessly, killing over 6,000 of Charles' men. The Swedish king and his remaining forces fled back to their ships. Once again, however, Chodkiewicz was unable to follow up on his victory as his unpaid and disgruntled forces refused further orders.

The stunning success of the relatively weak Polish army in Livonia fuelled King Zygmunt's ambitions. The chancellor, Jan Zamoyski, who had been able to maintain a balance between the various factions in the parliament and the king, had died the previous year, leaving Zygmunt to pursue his desires. He had begun to undertake diplomatic moves without consulting parliament and, after the death of his first wife, married a second Austrian princess. In 1606 he called a parliament and demanded significant constitutional changes, including regular allowance for a standing army and decisions based on majority vote. The king made it clear that he planned to lead an expedition to Sweden and take back the Swedish crown.

This proved too much for the gentry. A large group of nobles rebelled against the king but were defeated in 1607 by a royal army. Nevertheless, the king was unable to push his schemes forward and by 1609 had to agree to a compromise with the gentry that granted amnesty to the rebels and maintained the constitutional order exactly as before.

Zygmunt's poor political skill in handling the gentry was a godsend to his uncle King Charles of Sweden. After the disaster at Kircholm, Charles mounted several new expeditions into Livonia. Avoiding battles with the Polish cavalry, the Swedes used their infantry and superior artillery to capture a series of Polish strongholds. In 1609, as the political crisis in Poland eased, the Swedes made a new effort to capture Riga but were thwarted yet again by *Hetman* Chodkiewicz. Although the war would continue, this defeat effectively ended the first Swedish attempt to capture Livonia.

FALSE DMITRIS

Zygmunt's troubles at home were but a trifle compared to his counterparts on the Russian throne. Ivan the Terrible's ruinous wars and repression had left his successors in a precarious position. In 1598, Ivan's son and successor, Theodore, died and the nobleman Boris Gudunov took the throne. Theodore's younger brother, Dmitri, was murdered and suspicion fell on Gudunov who faced widespread unrest.

In 1603, a man claiming to be Prince Dmitri appeared in Poland at the court of the Palatine of Sandomierz, Jerzy Mniszech. He was probably a young monk named Grigogiy Otrepiev. 'Dmitri' married the Palatine's unusually ambitious daughter, Marina. Together, they recruited an army of Polish mercenaries and Cossack freebooters and invaded Russia in 1604. This army defeated Gudunov's forces and Gudunov died suddenly in early 1605. The remaining Muscovite armies accepted 'Dmitri' as tsar and he and Marina were proclaimed tsar and tsarina. Without any approval of the parliament or king, a Polish-backed candidate now sat on the throne of Muscovy. There is little record of 'Dmitri's' thoughts on his succession, but the real power seems to have resided in the Tsarina Marina who wasted little time in encouraging the Jesuits to begin the task of converting Russia to Catholicism.

The reign of 'Dmitri' and Marina did not last long. Days after the official coronation, the new tsar was murdered by a powerful Russian prince, Vasiliy Shuisky, who wasted no time in proclaiming himself tsar and started a pogrom of all Poles in Moscow that left five hundred dead. Tsar Vasiliy, however, proved even less popular than his two pre-decessors and had little authority beyond his own armies.

Meanwhile, Marina managed to escape back to Poland. She joined up with a supporter of her late husband, Mikhail Molchanov. Mol-chanov proclaimed that he was 'Dmitri', and had secretly escaped Shuisky's murderous rampage. Marina tearfully recognized her 'hus-band' – even though the new 'Dmitri' did not look anything like the old one. The 'reunited' couple recruited an army of some 18,000 Polish and Cossack adventurers, many of whom had participated in the rebellion against King Zygmunt in 1607. The second 'Dmitri' invaded Russia in 1610 and made a serious bid to take Moscow, gaining support from Shuisky's many enemies within Russia.

The participation of so many of his former opponents in the forces of the second 'Dmitri' finally managed to wrench Zygmunt's attention away from regaining the Swedish crown. Even before 'Dmitri's' invasion in 1610, the king made overtures to Shuisky and signed a truce with the tsar in an effort to undercut his opponents. Shuisky, however, was in desperate straits as 'Dmitri's' supporters gained ground. In 1609, he signed an alliance with Sweden, which promptly sent a force of 5,000 men to Moscow to open a new front against the Poles. Thus, the strange affair of the False Dmitris came home to roost in Poland.

With the entry of Sweden into the fray, Zygmunt acted quickly, but, as always, without much forethought. He proclaimed himself heir to the Russian throne and set about organizing an army to settle affairs with Russia. On the face of it, this plan could well have been the realization of Stefan Batory's ambition to end the Muscovite threat to Poland's eastern borders once and for all. It could also have resulted in a substantial reunification of eastern and western Christianity. But Zygmunt's main ambition seems to have been to draw on the resources of Russia in his bid to become king of Sweden. When the king consulted his *hetman*, the experienced Stanisław Żółkiewski, he was advised to move on Moscow at once, minimize civilian casualties and destruction of property, and depose Shuisky with all haste. The king ignored the advice and instead set out to besiege the heavily defended fortress of Smolensk.

Shuisky countered this move and sent an army of nearly 40,000 Russians and Swedes to relieve the city. At Kluszyn they met a force of 5,000 Poles under the redoubtable *Hetman Żółkiewski*. Once again, the Swedes threw up field defences to stop the hussars. Though outnumbered eight to one, Żółkiewski sent his infantry forward to hack through the Swedish lines. With the infantry clearing the way, the winged hussars charged the combined army. Once again, the hussars swept all before them. The Russians and Swedes panicked and fled, suffering huge losses. After Kluszyn, Shuisky's support among the Russian nobles and even ordinary people collapsed and he was deposed.

While the king remained at Smolensk, Żółkiewski entered Moscow. He negotiated with the Russian leaders, who were still facing the threat of the second 'Dmitri' and his army of renegades. The deal Żółkiewski struck was that the Russian nobles would elect Zygmunt's son, Władysław, as tsar. Freedom was guaranteed for the Orthodox faith and Poland and Russia would enter into a voluntary union much as Poland and Lithuania had done some two centuries earlier.

This far-sighted approach was immediately frustrated by the king who insisted on being proclaimed tsar himself. Protracted negotiations ensued, but the king refused to budge, inflaming the suspicions of the Orthodox clergy who began to agitate against the Poles. While the siege of Smolensk went on, the second 'Dmitri' ran afoul of his own supporters and was assassinated, removing one threat to Moscow. As the king dithered, public opinion in Moscow turned against Żółkiewski's Polish garrison. In March, April, and May, the city rose up against the garrison. They succeeded only in destroying most of their own city but forced the Poles to barricade themselves inside the Kremlin.

In June, the king's army finally took Smolensk. Zygmunt proclaimed victory and returned to Poland. Meanwhile, the Polish garrison in Kremlin waited for relief, surrounded by a hostile populace and a growing Muscovite army. In October, the king signed a truce with Sweden, bringing the long war to temporary halt. But it was not until the following year that the king managed to organize an expedition to Moscow. The Poles inside the Kremlin had driven back every effort to take the ancient Russian stronghold, but were reduced to cannibalism and eating rats. Zygmunt's army moved at a snail's pace and before it got close to Moscow, word arrived that the garrison had finally surrendered.

The wars with Russia and Sweden continued in a desultory fashion throughout the 1610s, with each of the three countries gaining little advantage before signing 'permanent' peace treaties. Poland retained Smolensk but lost a section of Livonia.

The Turkish War

Although despite all odds Polish arms had proven triumphant on the battlefield, the political results of Zygmunt's adventures were disastrous. Polish military victories had gained almost nothing and the detritus of war afflicted the country in the form of bands of unpaid, hungry soldiers roaming the land, stealing, killing, and pillaging. The king's ability to gain the support of a significant portion of the gentry had been frittered away on his schemes to regain the Swedish throne. Nevertheless, his ability to hatch plans that landed the country in hot water remained intact. For their part, the gentry were highly factionalized and powerful magnates began to make foreign policy for themselves based on personal interest.

The old chancellor Zamoyski and later *hetman* Żółkiewski had worked hard to keep Poland out of any conflicts with the powerful Ottoman Empire to the south. Such a conflict was greatly desired by the pro-Habsburg faction of the gentry – especially by those with estates in the path of Tartar raids – as well as by the king. Apart from

Tartar attacks, Polish and Turkish interests collided only in Moldova and friction there could be limited by careful treaties. War with the Ottomans would greatly benefit the Habsburgs who sought to recover rich lands in Hungary, but would bring little gain to Poland.

Magnates in south-eastern Poland were able to stir up trouble with Turkey in 1617, but cooler heads prevailed and war was avoided. A more difficult problem was the Cossacks who protected Poland's border with the Tartars but whose undisciplined nature meant that they raided freely into Ottoman-controlled areas. These raids increased and Polish efforts to stop them met with only limited success. At the same time, while Zygmunt was forbidden to aid the Habsburgs directly, he managed to raise an army of Polish and Cossack mercenaries out of his own funds and sent them to help the Austrians in their conflicts with Turkey.

In 1618, the Ottomans sent an expedition into Poland to end the Cossack incursions, but were repelled by Żółkiewski's army. The *hetman* then reaffirmed the agreements of the previous year. This truce did not last long and conflict broke out again over Moldova. In September 1620, Żółkiewski faced a hardened Turkish army three times the size of his own. During a seventeen-day battle around Cecora, the Turks managed to break the Polish army and Żółkiewski fell with most of his men. The *hetman*'s head was sent as a prize to the sultan. The following year, Sultan Osman II himself led an army of 100,000 into Poland. The disaster at Cecora, however, galvanized the Poles who organized a force of 45,000 Poles and Cossacks under *Hetman* Chodkiewicz. The *hetman* dug his army into a massive fortified camp at Chocim. For more than a month, Ottoman forces battered away at Chodkiewicz's forces, losing 40,000 men in the process. Exhausted, the two sides entered negotiations and signed a lasting peace treaty.

The Swedes renewed their conflict under a new king, Gustavus Adolphus (1594-1632), in 1617 in alliance with Brandenburg. The Swedish warrior king captured Riga and several Polish coastal cities as the main Polish armies were facing the Turks in the south. At Gniew in 1626, he defeated a Polish army commanded by Zygmunt III who proved no more adept at military command than in the political arena. Polish armies under *Hetman* Stanisław Koniecpolski undertook a more aggressive defence. At Tczew, in 1627 Gustavus was wounded and the Swedes had to retire. In November of that year, Polish privateers from Gdańsk defeated a larger Swedish fleet. What followed thereafter was a war of manoeuvre, with neither side willing to join battle directly. The only major battle occurred at Trzciana in 1629, when Gustavus managed to escape Koniecpolski's hussars only by sacrificing most of his cavalry. The Polish parliament, however, decided to buy the Swedes off with the Treaty of Altmark in which the Swedes received 3.5 per cent of trade revenue from Polish coastal towns. The Swedish king then turned his attention to defending the Protestant cause in Germany, where the experience of his Polish campaigns would help make him one of the most famous generals of his age.

The Wild, Wild East

Poland's experience in the east during the sixteenth and seventeenth centuries has often been likened to America's 'Wild West'. Polish nobles created an inland empire based on peasant labour, carved out of a beautiful though often harsh and lawless land. They reaped vast wealth from the region's rich soil and built castles, palaces and churches to rival any in France or England, places that became oases of European high culture in the east. To generations of Poles, the great fortresses of the Kresy (or 'Borderland') evoked images of swashbuckling heroes battling Turks, Tartars and Cossacks.

Kamieniec Podolski (literally 'the rock of Podolia') was considered Poland's greatest fortress. 'Kamieniec is fortified as if by Providence,' one saying went. Set on a bluff above a tributary of the Dniestr and surrounded by massive walls, Kamieniec protected routes into volatile Moldova and Transylvania and anchored part of the defence of the south-eastern border. In the east stood Kiev, the ancient capital of Ukraine with its golden domed churches and key position on the Dnieper River. Beyond Kiev was the even wilder trans-Dnieper coveted by Cossacks, Tartars, Poles and Russians. In the west was Lwów, or Leopolis, city of the lion. In between were scores of outposts built by Polish and Ruthenian gentry – such as Zbaraż, Bar or Żółkiew – who acted very much as independent princes in their own right, dispensing commands and rough justice often with little reference to king or parliament.

Although Polish nobility were the ruling strata, the Kresy was a land of many peoples. Ruthenian, Polish or Ukrainian peasants were the largest segment of the population, though terms such as 'Polish' or 'Ukrainian' would have had little meaning to them. Tied to the land and working as semi-slaves, their lot was one of hard and almost unending toil. Conditions varied depending on the humanity of their masters and vagaries of the weather. The peasants' outlook was deeply fatalistic. Family and religious faith (whether Orthodox, Eastern-rite Catholic, or Roman Catholic) were the central pillars of their identity. Religious and popular festivals, visits by travelling merchants or mountebanks, and village squabbles provided entertainment.

Jews formed a vital part of life in the Kresy. They had followed the path of Polish settlement and played a vital role in the region's economic development. They were merchants, agents for Polish landlords and craftsmen. There was a rich tradition of learning and scholarship as well, though by no means were all Jews well educated, especially those who lived in remote villages. Urban communities, however, supported a wide range of institutions, including schools and libraries. The Armenians were another group that proved crucial to the economy of the Kresy. Concentrated in larger cities such as Lwów or Kamieniec, Armenians often facilitated long-distance trade with Turkey and Persia. They played a key role in textile production, especially silk weaving and carpet manufacture.

Yet of all the groups in the Kresy, the most pivotal were the Cossacks. Erroneously seen by later commentators as 'Ukrainian', the Cossacks described themselves as a free brotherhood of warriors. Their members came from many nations, though most were Orthodox East Slavs. Polish parliaments and kings encouraged their settlement on the south-eastern border, a region with many escaped serfs and outlaws who proved ready recruits for the Cossack brotherhood. From their fortress of the 'Sich' on islands near the rapids of the Dnieper, they formed an effective barrier against Tartar incursions. As light infantry and cavalry they had little parallel, combining eastern and western tactics. Fighting from fortified wagons or riverboats mounted with light cannon, they were formidable.

Yet the fierceness that made them so feared was also the source of a major problem for Poland. The Cossacks existed outside of the effective control of any entity of the Polish crown or parliament and their raids into the Ottoman sphere of influence constantly threatened Poland with a war that few Polish leaders (aside from the pro-Habsburg faction) wanted. This led to a half-hearted effort to bring the Cossacks under some sort of control.

The solution was to 'register' Cossacks as regular soldiers of the Commonwealth. Registered Cossacks enjoyed a degree of personal liberty, exemption from many taxes and a yearly wage. In essence, Registered Cossacks would become members of the gentry. Naturally, this did not sit well with many existing members of the gentry, especially the magnates who saw Cossacks as merely useful armed peasants who could be just as well employed tilling the land. In addition, giving privileges to so many Cossacks would potentially dilute the political power of the magnates and create a class of gentry whose loyalty might be given to the king. So in the seventeenth century while Cossacks themselves began to press more and more for an expansion of the Cossack Registry, the magnates fought to keep the Registry as small as possible. The more the nobles succeeded in this, the more resentful the Cossacks began to feel.

Władysław IV Wasa (1595–1648) and the Silver Age

Zygmunt III died in 1632. His dreams of ruling a vast dynastic state consisting of Sweden, Russia and Poland had come to nothing. Yet his all-consuming ambition had cost Poland dearly. Great amounts of blood and treasure had been squandered in the king's effort to regain the Swedish throne. The intervention of Gustavus Adolphus in the 1620s had seriously diminished Poland's position on the Baltic Sea. Worse yet, it revived the power of Brandenburg and allowed Prussia to once again loosen its bonds to Poland. The king wasted a golden opportunity to end a major threat from Muscovy for good. Following his abortive effort to take the Russian throne and his disregard for the sensibilities of Orthodox leaders, Mikhail Romanov had taken the throne, beginning the Romanov dynasty that would rule Russia until the twentieth century and which would prove to be Poland's implacable enemy.

Zygmunt's reign had seriously disrupted the political culture of the Commonwealth. His secretive nature and his habit of ignoring consensus and embarking on rash and costly adventures increased the fragmentation of the gentry. It also greatly increased the power of the magnates versus the middle and lower nobility. The magnates increasingly conducted policy that suited their own interests rather than those of the Commonwealth.

Yet, all was not lost. Poland's armies had proven the equal of the best in Europe, fighting the great Gustavus Adolphus to a standstill. The magnate class was still able to produce military leaders of great devotion and skill. And while the Baltic coast region had fallen under Swedish influence, no invader had penetrated the core of the country.

Zygmunt was succeeded by his son, Władysław, who was elected after a short interregnum. Władysław was far better suited to be king than his father. He was more adept at politics and military affairs. His first major test was the defeat of a Muscovite effort to seize Smolensk. Thereafter, with peace treaties in effect with both Russia and Sweden, Polish armies had to contend only with more isolated threats from the Tartars and disgruntled Cossacks. The king, however, kept up diplomatic pressure on Sweden after the death of Gustavus Adolphus and even managed to win the withdrawal of Swedish garrisons from some of the Baltic ports. Nevertheless, by the mid-1640s it was clear that his efforts were going nowhere. Instead, Władysław turned his attention toward Turkey. Here, he could gain the support of many of the gentry and such a war would appease the increasingly restless Cossacks who would be assured of much booty in the conflict. The parliament, however, baulked at the idea of a war with Turkey, especially after the long conflict with Sweden had finally seemed to die away.

During Władysław's reign, Polish culture continued to develop. Permanent theatre, opera and a royal orchestra made their appearance. The king himself was especially fond of the Dutch painter Rubens and even corresponded with Galileo. The king was able to keep the fires of religious conflict at bay, and while Protestantism continued to decline, toleration was the official policy.

THINGS FALL APART

In 1648, the Cossacks of the Sich revolted. The cause of the revolt was essentially the same as the revolts that had occurred periodically over a couple of decades – especially the restriction of the list of Registered Cossacks, the encroachment by Polish nobles on what Cossacks considered their rights, and restrictions on the Cossacks' ability to raid Turkish territory. Ironically, the desire for peace in the Polish parliament helped spark the revolt. The peril of an independent army of warriors without enough wars to fight was now apparent, especially when they were repeatedly promised and then denied improved social and legal standing within the Commonwealth. Yet two things set this revolt apart. First, was the charismatic leadership of Bohdan Khmelnicki, a Ruthenian nobleman who harboured strong resentments against the Polish elites, one of whom was responsible for the death of his son. Khmelnicki was a skilled military leader and politician who did not intend to repeat the mistakes of previous Cossack revolts. What he did intend is a matter of some debate. The notion that he wanted an independent Ukrainian state is anachronistic, since Ukrainian identity is a modern development. It is probable that he sought to carve out a place within the structure of the Commonwealth for himself and his followers similar to that enjoyed by Lithuania. Regardless of what he intended, his revolt would unleash a torrent of bloodshed that would result in destruction and centuries of slavery for Ukraine and bring the Commonwealth to the brink of disaster.

Khmelnicki's first act was to secure an alliance with the Crimean Tartars who were eager to resume raiding into the Commonwealth. With a strong force including Tartars, he advanced toward Kiev. The Polish commander, Mikołaj Potocki, sent part of his army to confront this threat, including a large force of Registered Cossacks. At Złote Wody, the Cossacks deserted to Khmelnicki. The remaining portion of the Polish army was destroyed. Potocki then confronted Khmelnicki at Korsun. The outnumbered Poles were outgeneralled and outfought.

Potocki's army was trapped against a river and then tried to fight its way free, only to be cut to pieces.

Further disaster followed. As the armies were gathering at Korsun, Władysław IV died, leaving the country leaderless. The Cossack victories at Złote Wody and Korsun left the Kresy with no protection. Khmelnicki's forces swelled with recruits and Tartars and masses of armed Cossacks spread out across the countryside killing, raping, and pillaging. As Polish control faltered, local peasants – encouraged by the Cossacks – rose up against their overlords, repaying years of oppression and humiliation with blood.

The rebels targeted Polish and Ruthenian nobles, Catholic clergy, and especially Jews. Entire families were burned alive, hacked to pieces, flayed, hung, or impaled. Children, old people, and pregnant women were subjected to unspeakable tortures. It is likely that at least 100,000 people were massacred, though exact figures are impossible to calculate. According to Jewish sources, 300 communities were destroyed and at least 50,000 Jews lost their lives, a death toll not exceeded until the Nazi Holocaust. Tens of thousands more – including many peasants who supported the Cossacks – were sold into slavery by the Tartars. The household forces of the Polish nobility, where they still existed, turned on the peasants – guilty or innocent – and put many to the sword.

A makeshift Polish army confronted the Cossack horde in October at Pliwice. The royal infantry put up a heroic stand, but the levee of Polish nobility fell apart. The result was another disaster. Khmelnicki advanced on Lwów but was bought off by a ransom from the city fathers. His army moved on to Zamość, but the strong fortress and the coming winter forced him to fall back to winter quarters.

The parliament, meeting under these desperate circumstances, elected the late king's brother, Jan Kazimierz Wasa (1609–1672) as his successor. Jan Kazimierz had the support of those who wanted to prosecute the war as well as those who wanted a negotiated end to the conflict. The king sent a delegation to meet with the Cossack chieftain whose demands for greater power within the Commonwealth were evolving into something like a vision of an independent Cossack state with himself as its ruler. The negotiations broke down and war resumed in June 1649. At the fortress of Zbaraż, the Polish defences held firm against great odds. As royal forces rushed to the relief of the town, they confronted the Cossack and Tartar army at Zborów. A two-day battle ensued, ending only when the Poles induced the Tartars to abandon the field. Khmelnicki was forced to retreat and agreed to a truce and general amnesty. The tentative peace agreement the two sides reached pleased no one and was rejected by the parliament while Khmelnicki had to keep some of its provisions secret from his own followers lest they revolt against his authority.

In 1651, Khmelnicki attempted to force the issue again. With an army of 100,000 Cossacks and Tartars, he advanced toward Lwów, meeting the Polish army at Beresteczko. This time, the Poles were much better led and familiar with Cossack tactics and Khmelnicki was defeated in detail and forced to withdraw. A Lithuanian force recaptured Kiev. Yet, while neither side could win an outright victory, peace at the bargaining table was equally elusive. The Polish magnates sought to crush the rebellion while Khmelnicki's own followers grew increasingly distrustful of his motives. Seeking allies, Khmelnicki then turned to Russia, concluding a treaty that put Ukraine in the hands of the Tsar.

THE DELUGE

The Russian-Cossack alliance was as good as a declaration of war and in 1655, large Russian armies attacked Poland. One Cossack-Russian army was defeated at Ochmatów, but by the summer of that year, Russian armies broke through the Commonwealth's defences and captured Wilno, sacked the city, and put thousands of its inhabitants to the sword. At the same time, urged on by Khmelnicki and by the disaffection of many Polish magnates, Swedish forces under King Charles X invaded western Poland. Levees of noble troops refused to fight. In Lithuania, *Hetman* Janusz Radziwiłł switched sides and joined the Swedes. Swedish armies captured Warsaw and then Kraków. The king fled to Silesia and the armies of Brandenburg joined in, attacking West Prussia. Within less than a year, the Commonwealth had simply collapsed. Cossacks occupied the south-east, Russians the east, Swedes and Brandenburgers central and western Poland. The traitor Radziwiłł controlled part of Lithuania as a vassal of Charles X. Only Gdańsk, Lwów, and a few other towns held out for the king.

If the Commonwealth's collapse had been remarkable, its recovery was even more so. The regionalism that had made the country so hard to govern worked against the invader. Although Charles X had visions of ruling over much of Poland, the actions of his soldiers turned the population against the Swedes. Swedish troops pillaged the country-side, killing, burning, raping and looting. Catholic churches and Catholic clergy were singled out for attack. The Swedes made a fateful mistake of besieging the monastery of Jasna Góra near Częstochowa, a place of pilgrimage for Catholics that housed a sacred image of the Virgin Mary, the famous Black Madonna. The place had no military value but Swedes believed it contained significant wealth donated by the faithful. A small force of soldiers, citizens, and monks held out against the Swedes and stories began to circulate among the faithful that the Virgin was shielding the fort from Swedish cannon balls.

By the beginning of 1656, a full-scale revolt was underway against the Swedes. The return of King Jan Kazimierz caused many Poles to flock once again to the royal standard. In Lithuania Radziwiłł's soldiers began to desert en masse. Bands of Swedish soldiers in rural areas disappeared into the hands of enraged peasants who took revenge for the looting and killing. In the east, the Poles made a truce with the Russians and concentrated their forces against the Swedes and Brandenburgers. Polish cavalry under *Hetman* Stefan Czarneki harried Charles X's army at every turn, trapping them for a time at the confluence of the Rivers San and Vistula. At Warka the Poles crushed the army of Brandenburg. Warsaw changed hands twice after pitched battles. The Swedes redoubled their efforts the following year, enlisting the aid of the Transylvanians and Cossacks to once again retake Warsaw. By then, however, the Swedes had aroused other enemies. The Tartars and Austrians had no interest in seeing a strong Transylvanian state and immediately promised aid to the Poles. Denmark, eager to revenge previous losses to Sweden and prevent their rival from controlling the Baltic trade, struck an alliance with the Poles and declared war on Sweden. Charles X was forced to return home, leaving the Swedish forces in Poland isolated and without a strong leader. The Transyl-

The famous Black Madonna from the monastery of Jasna Góra
near Częstochowa

vanian army was defeated as it tried to return home and its prince lost his throne.

Polish forces and their allies gradually retook most of the major towns. The Austrians, however, proved an unreliable ally and induced the king to give up East Prussia as part of a peace treaty with Brandenburg. Polish forces even went to Denmark to strike at Sweden from the south. In 1660, Charles X died. Because Poland was already engaged in a new fight with Russia, the Swedes were able to achieve a fairly easy peace in which they retained their possessions in Livonia taken thirty years earlier.

In 1657, Khmelnicki died and the Cossack *hetmen* that followed had neither the stature nor the ability to equal his conquests. Russia began to exert more and more control in Cossack lands and many Cossacks who had been intent on slaughtering all Poles and Jews a few years before began to have second thoughts. The main Cossack group switched sides back to Poland and signed the Compact of Hadziacz in 1659, but a Russian-controlled group remained on the east bank of the Dnieper which had effectively become Russian territory.

The Russian response was immediate but ineffective. At Sosnówka a combined Polish-Tartar-Cossack army destroyed a huge Russian-Cossack army. Further dissension within the Cossack ranks prevented a major advance into Russia. Khmelnicki's son George was elected *hetman* and he soon switched sides back to Russia, pledging loyalty to the tsar. In 1660, two Russian armies advancing on Warsaw were defeated. The crown *hetmen* Pawel Sapieha and Stefan Czarneki then routed Khmelnicki's Cossacks and forced his surrender. Then the Poles surrounded the main Russian army in Ukraine at Cudnów and forced its surrender.

With success in sight, the Polish magnates managed to snatch defeat from the jaws of victory. Urged on by his French-born queen, the king proposed a series of reforms that would again strengthen the power of the executive. This brought about a crisis that paralysed the parliament. The infamous *liberum veto* was invoked a number of times to halt legislation, especially against efforts to eliminate the *liberum veto*. Its use resulted in the shutting down of parliament, sometimes without approving the collection of taxes or voting money for the army. In 1667, the crown *Hetman* Jan Sobieski had to repulse a large Tartar and Cossack incursion with only those troops he could raise from his own private funds. The inability of the Commonwealth to speak with a single voice resulted in the unfortunate treaty of Androsovo in 1667 that, despite the drubbing administered to the Russian army, ceded the territory east of the Dniepr to the tsar along with the city of Kiev and the fortress of Smolensk. The conflict between king and parliament resulted in open rebellion led by *Hetman* Jerzy Lubomirski. The rebels defeated the royal army, ending all hope of reform. In 1668, the king resigned the crown, warning of the decay of the Commonwealth.

Although the Deluge ('Potop' in Polish) had ended, Polish power had been fatally diminished. The economy of the country was ruined and the lack of trade and ongoing wars with the Turks further drained available resources. Politically, the spirit of civic virtue that brought the gentry to defend the common good in times of crisis and which had been damaged under Zygmunt Wasa deteriorated further. Magnates in particular put their own interests ahead of the country and foreign governments were able to use factions of the nobility to exert leverage over Polish policies and decision-making.

Jan Sobieski (1624–1696)

In 1668, the parliament elected a native Pole, Michał Wiśniowiecki (r. 1669–73), to the throne with the support of the pro-Habsburg faction and against the opposition which was receiving support from France. The twenty-nine-year-old Wiśniowiecki proved a weak figure with few of the political or military skills then needed. Fortunately for the Commonwealth, it had not yet run short of brilliant generals. *Hetman* Jan Sobieski assumed command of Polish forces in the southeast. In 1671, supported by the Tartars, the Cossacks launched another revolt. With 8,000 men Sobieski conducted a brilliant campaign that turned back the threat. Parliament, however, failed to approve the money for further reinforcements, and Sobieski was unable to follow up on his success. The following year, the Ottoman Empire declared war on Poland. This complicated the position of the pro-French party, since France was allied with Turkey against Austria. Sobieski, who sided with the French faction, however, vigorously prosecuted the war.

In the face of the Turkish threat, parliament was paralyzed with infighting and the border fortresses were not adequately provisioned and the army not equipped. A massive Turkish army took Kamieniec Podolski and marched on Lwów. Sobieski's 3,000 men could not stop the main Turkish advance, so the *hetman* raided deep in enemy territory, marching hundreds of miles, defeating Tartar forces totalling 20,000, disrupting the enemy's supplies and freeing some 40,000 prisoners. Yet, again parliament sought to buy off the Turks, ceding Podolia and promising the sultan an annual tribute.

This humiliating turn of events galvanized the majority of the nobility who rebelled against the magnates and the peace party, demanding that the king be replaced. A compromise was reached and the war with Turkey resumed. In 1673, Sobieski led the combined army of the Commonwealth to destroy a Turkish army of 30,000 at Chocim. Days before the victory, King Michał died (possibly of stomach cancer). As parliament convened to choose a successor, Sobieski's victory was foremost in everyone's mind. His proven military skills and the lack of a compelling Habsburg-backed candidate resulted in the election of Jan Sobieski in May 1674. The new king's wife, the French noblewoman Marysieńka, played an important role in the election. Shrewd, ambitious and deeply devoted to her husband, she worked behind the scenes to galvanize support for Sobieski.

Sobieski's major task was to repel continued Turkish attacks on the Commonwealth's southern border, which he did successfully. Yet, as previous kings had discovered, parliament's unwillingness to supply adequate funds for the costly ventures hampered his ability to reap the fruits of victory. The king's efforts at internal reform were also hampered by parliamentary rivalry, especially by his opponents who were concerned lest the popular monarch grow too powerful. Early on, Sobieski made some effort to appoint men of ability and merit to high office from the middle and lower gentry, but political realities eventually led him back to the practice of selling offices to wealthy magnates. The Sobieski family grew extremely wealthy and the king and queen apparently considered this a step toward creating a strong hereditary monarchy. Instead, it merely hardened the opposition of the king's enemies, increased the fear of absolutism and fuelled internal corruption.

VIENNA

Sobieski had begun his reign as a friend of France. He spoke French fluently and he and his wife wrote each other long affectionate letters in French. However, growing conflicts with Turkey increasingly drew Poland closer to Austria. French support for Sweden and Brandenburg further alienated Poland. In 1683, Poland entered an alliance with Austria, Venice and the Papacy against a resurgent Ottoman Empire bent on the conquest of central Europe and the expansion of Islam. In the summer of that year a massive Ottoman army of 115,000 led by Grand Vizier Kara Mustafa advanced into Austria and surrounded the imperial capital of Vienna. Sobieski mobilized Polish forces and marched on Vienna. His reputation as the 'Scourge of the Turk' made him the natural choice for overall command of the allied forces. Leading a combined army of about 75,000 (about a third of whom were Poles), Sobieski sent the Germans, the Austrians and the Polish infantry to engage the main body of Kara Mustafa's army while his heavy hussars struck the Turkish flank. As Sobieski's plan developed, the Turks fell back to avoid encirclement but the Polish cavalry charge turned the retreat into a rout. The Turkish camp, baggage and much weaponry fell into Sobieski's hands. The Polish king entered Vienna in triumph, much to the chagrin of Emperor Leopold I who had earlier fled his capital and played no role in its relief.

Sobieski pursued the Ottoman army into Hungary. After a setback at Parkany, Sobieski trapped the Turkish army along the banks of the Danube and destroyed it. The Ottoman commander was ordered to commit suicide and the Turkish drive into Europe was halted for good.

Sobieski's remaining years were spent in political frustration. He conducted minor campaigns against the Turks and Tartars, who wisely avoided battle whenever possible. Poland remained allied to Austria, but the French regained some of their influence thanks to the queen. The parliament became increasingly unworkable and unable to achieve consensus on anything. Yet, during his reign, the country remained largely at peace and its people were able to reconstruct some of what had been wrecked during the disastrous years of the Deluge. The Sobieski family palace of Wilanów near Warsaw is emblematic of the brief flowering of Polish culture that took place during his reign. Built in the Baroque style, Wilanów was contemporary with Versailles and bears traces of French influence. Unlike Versailles, however, Wilanów was meant as the home of a warm and loving family rather than as a grandiose statement of royal power. This palace would be the place where Sobieski spent his final years. The last years of the king's life were plagued with illnesses, some picked up during his long years of military campaigning. In 1696 Jan III Sobieski died.

The Saxon Kings

In 1697, the royal election featured the late king's son, Jakub Sobieski, as the Austrian candidate pitted against a French prince. When neither candidate was able to achieve success, a dark horse candidate emerged: Augustus the Strong, Elector of Saxony (1670–1733). With the support of the Russian tsar and some timely bribes, Augustus was elected king. Though he ruled a modest-sized German territory, Augustus II the Strong (August Mocny) was one of the wonders of his age who managed to father some 300 children by wives and scores of mistresses and lovers. He was a great patron of the arts and his cultural legacy in his capital at Dresden was immense. Many of the great works of art in that famous city were purchased with Polish money.

In the political realm, Augustus tried to be a good king and use his position in Saxony and Poland to isolate the growing power of the Prussian state. His major ally was Tsar Peter the Great of Russia, which from the point of view of Poland was disastrous. Having helped destroy Polish power half a century earlier, Sweden now faced Russia and two countries squared off over control of the Baltic. In 1700, Augustus tried to improve his position and help Peter's cause by winning back the city of Riga. The effort failed and it triggered a Swedish invasion of Poland. The Swedish king, Charles XII, defeated Polish and Saxon forces at Kliszów in 1702 and Pułtusk in 1703. Soon the Swedes occupied much of the country and a pro-Swedish confederation of Polish nobles formed to back an alternative candidate to the throne, Stanisław Leszczyński. As it had during the Deluge, Lithuania switched to the Swedish side, thanks to her disloyal magnates. In 1706, Charles XII invaded Saxony and forced Augustus to sue for peace. The Swedes then turned their forces on Russia. In the meantime, strong opposition had arisen to Swedish rule, especially among the peasants and the nobility of Małopolska, who harassed Swedish supply lines. The Russian armies defeated the Swedes first at Lesnaya and then at the decisive battle of Poltava in 1709. The war dragged on for another ten years, but at its conclusion Swedish power in the Baltic Sea was broken forever. The three-sided struggle for control of the Baltic that had begun with the Russian invasion of Livonia in the mid-1500s had come to an end. Poland and Sweden had lost and Russia would become the dominant power in the region.

For Augustus the Strong, the Russian victory meant restoration of his Polish crown, the dispossession of Leszczyński and the opportunity to once again pursue the beautiful wives and daughters of the Polish gentry. The country itself was devastated by various armies and by the costs of trying to sustain even a shadow of an army. Peter the Great's Russians had systematically looted the country, and the tsar personally plundered the estates of wealthy Poles to enrich his own rather paltry art collection.

By the end of the Great Northern War, the Saxon king was immensely unpopular in Poland and a confederation of gentry sought to expel Augustus for good. This was something that Peter the Great, prosecuting the final stages of his war against Sweden, could not permit. The tsar decided to impose a political solution on both countries. He forced the Saxon army to withdraw from Poland, kept Augustus on the throne and dictated the budget of the Polish crown and the size of its army. To ratify this, in 1717 the tsar surrounded the Polish parliament with Russian soldiers and forced through approval of his dictates. No delegate dared to object and the parliament went down in history as the Silent *Sejm*.

The Silent *Sejm* marked the beginning of the end for the Commonwealth. It ended the possibility of gradual reform from within. The status quo in Poland suited the interests of powerful neighbours like Russia and Prussia, making them natural allies of those members of the gentry who had for over a century put personal power and wealth above the interests of the nation. Members of the gentry who sought to save Poland and restore its prestige lacked the power and the resources to overcome this opposition. Members of the lower gentry suffered ever-greater impoverishment and their political voice was all but silenced. The economic condition of the country deteriorated. The Northern War undid the beneficial effects of Sobieski's reign. Although Augustus the Strong was not incompetent, he was severely constrained by Russian interests and spent much of his energy on Saxony. Real authority at the regional level existed largely with half a dozen magnate clans such as Radziwiłł, Potocki, Lubomirski, Sapieha, Wiśniowiecki, or Czetwertyński, and a second group of slightly less influential families. These magnates existed as a state within a state with their own armies, officials, and courts. National institutions withered along with royal authority and with them the glue that had held the Commonwealth together began to come undone.

In 1733, Augustus II died and was succeeded as Elector of Saxony by one of his legitimate sons, Friedrich-Augustus. However, in Warsaw his candidacy ran afoul of a more independent-minded delegates and French influence. Parliament elected the pro-French candidate Stanisław Leszczyński (1677–1766) who had previously challenged Friedrich-Augustus' father for the Polish throne. This effort to restore a modicum of independence via legal means sparked the War of Polish Succession. Russia, Saxony, and Austria faced off against France, Spain, and the pro-French party in Poland. During the reign of Augustus II, the Polish army had dwindled to less than 20,000 effective men and while swelled by volunteers, it was no match for the massive forces of Russia and Austria. The Russian capture of Gdańsk in 1734 ended serious fighting in Poland, though resistance continued into 1736. Leszczyński fled to France, which enjoyed greater success in Western Europe than it did in supporting its Polish allies. The Russians organized a new election with a hand-picked electorate surrounded by Russian troops that placed Friedrich-Augustus on the throne as Augustus III.

Augustus III (1696–1763)

Augustus III's reign was an age of decay of Poland. The new king simply used his Polish possessions as a source of money. Russian armies were quartered in Poland or marched through to prosecute campaigns elsewhere and largely did as they pleased. Parliament withered and only local legislatures bothered to meet. Royal administration ground almost to a halt. Prussian armies under Friedrich the Great marched across northern Poland at will. Poland's magnates, however, partied hearty. 'Under the Saxon king, eat, drink, and loosen your belt' was a common refrain. With wealth to spare, the magnates could afford to be generous patrons of art, music and theatre. The rest of the country fell into poverty and hunger.

At the same time, many members of the gentry and the clergy began to seriously consider what radical reform of the system would entail. French Enlightenment writing had a great impact on literate Poles. Individual magnates had the wherewithal to promote Enlightenment schemes in their own lands. Among the most radical was Andrzej Zamoyski who abolished serfdom on his own estates, an example few of his peers followed. Europe's first public library was established in Warsaw in 1748 by nobleman and educator Stanisław Konarski and Bishop Józef Andrzej.

Stanisław August Poniatowski (1732–1798)

In 1763, Augustus III died and the Saxon era in Polish history came to an end. At this juncture, Poland had little actual control over its own destiny. The mechanisms of government were either non-existent, too weak to matter or in the control of Russia (usually through Polish proxies). The new king was installed with Russian backing. His name was Stanisław August Poniatowski, a scion of the wealthy and pro-Russian Czartoryski family. While in Russia as Polish ambassador (1755–58), the future king had been one of Empress Catherine the Great's many lovers. In 1764 he was meant to serve the empress' pleasure in another capacity. Catherine's goal was to tie Poland as closely and permanently as possible to Russia, which required a government that was both effective and pliant.

Stanisław August was indeed a weak and vacillating man with many faults. However, unlike Augustus III, he sought, to the surprise of many, to act like a king and a leader. Moreover, as a literate and cultured man, he had real ideas about how Poland could be reformed and better governed. His early attempt to establish a customs service was blocked by the Prussians who simply threatened to sink Polish boats on the Vistula if the plan was realized. He did manage to establish a 'Cadet Corps' to serve as a modern training school of military officers. In 1773, he created Europe's first ministry of education with the idea of providing universal basic education to all citizens. The king's early plan to end the *Liberum Veto,* however, was halted in the parliament.

In 1767, as opposition to Russian rule began to get better organized and ideas of serious change circulated more widely, the Russian viceroy in Poland, Prince Nikolay Repnin, organized a series of fictitious 'confederations' (or revolts of the nobility) and then used them as a pretext for arresting the four leading opposition figures, including the bishops of Kraków and Kiev and sending them in chains back to Russia. The Russians played effectively on the notion that they were the protectors of the rights of the nobility and defenders of Christian religious minorities, especially the Orthodox, and manipulated these groups to their advantage whenever possible.

Although this put the pro-Russian party firmly in control of the king and the government, it sparked widespread outrage and led to revolts across the country. Moreover, the presence of Russian troops in Poland threatened Turkey, which declared war on Russia. The most effective revolt was the Confederation of Bar. The staunchly Catholic confederates sought removal of Russian influence and the creation of a modern governmental system. They carried on a highly effective partisan campaign against the Russians. Among its leaders were Jan Michał Pac and Kazimierz Pułaski. It took the Russians four years to defeat the Confederates of Bar. At the same time, Ukraine was convulsed with a major peasant revolt. The Orthodox peasants massacred tens of thousands of Jews and Poles under the slogan 'Pole, Jew, Dog: All the same faith.' Many of the victims were herded into their synagogues and Catholic churches respectively and burned alive.

In 1772, at Prussian instigation and with the alleged aim of bringing

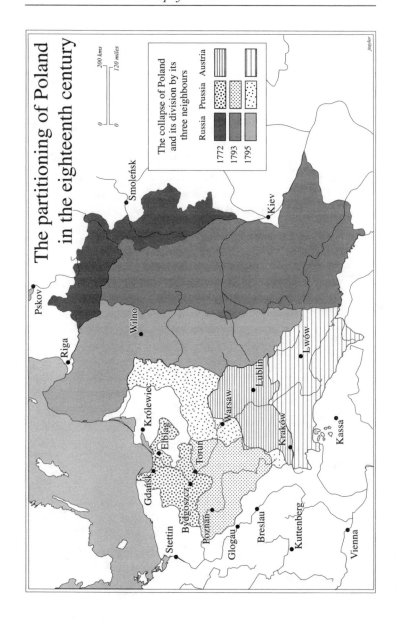

The partitioning of Poland in the eighteenth century

The collapse of Poland and its division by its three neighbours

Russia Prussia Austria

1772
1793
1795

peace to the region, Poland's three powerful neighbours staged the first partition of Poland. Prussia seized West Prussia and Warmia, reuniting her western and eastern portions and bringing home to roost the folly of Zygmunt Stary's failure to fully incorporate Prussia into Poland in 1525. Gdańsk, which had a long tradition of governing its own affairs, remained a free island isolated from Poland by Prussian territory. Austria seized a huge portion of Małopolska, including the ancient city of Lwów and the entire Carpathian region. Russia took relatively modest lands in the east. The partition took away almost a third of Polish territory. This act of aggression was couched in a specious legal framework and presented to the parliament where Russian troops ensured its ratification. Only a few delegates dared to raise their voices in protest. One of the delegates threw himself on the floor of the chamber screaming 'Kill me! Stamp on me! But do not kill the Fatherland!'

3rd MAY, 1791

It was now abundantly clear that Poland had lost its independence in all but name. Many Poles preferred exile. Among them were one of the military leaders of the Confederation of Bar, Kazimierz Pułaski, who in 1775 made his way to Britain's American colonies where he organized the Continental Army's first real cavalry unit. Another Pole who made his way to the colonies was a young military engineer Tadeusz Kościuszko, who would play a crucial role in the American victory at Saratoga, design North America's mightiest fortress at West Point on the Hudson River and strike up a close friendship with a Virginia rebel leader named Thomas Jefferson.

Back in Poland, the king continued to act as if matters were somehow different than they truly were. In 1787, with Russia again facing war with the Ottoman Empire, he proposed a Russo-Polish alliance against Turkey to the empress and with it an expansion of the Polish army. In anticipation of her acceptance, the king convened the parliament to pass necessary enabling legislation. Catherine refused, naturally having little need to make an alliance with a country she already controlled.

Small events often have unexpected results. When the parliament gathered in 1788, it had nothing on its agenda thanks to Catherine's rejection of the king's proposal. So it began to debate the question of political reform and it did so for nearly four years and was henceforth called the Four Years' *Sejm*. A remarkable group of thinkers and politicians led the charge for reform. In a Poland filled with magnates willing to sell out their country to a foreign power, they stood out as men who would give birth to a new idea of Poland. Among them were Bishop Ignacy Krasiński, poet, translator, and satirist. Then there was Fr. Hugo Kołłątaj who reformed the Jagiellonian University and played a major role in the Four Years' *Sejm*. Fr. Stanisław Staszic, a writer and translator, denounced social ills and promoted schemes for economic and cultural advancement. Playwright Julian Ursyn Niemcewicz mocked the self-importance and corruption of the magnates.

To avoid the scrutiny of the Russians, the reform party worked in secret and prepared a document that would change everything. Waiting for a day when most of the delegates were away on a holiday the reformers gathered. The creation of the American Constitution in 1789 was in their minds as was the less happy example of the French Revolution. On 3 May, 1791, with the king presiding, the parliament ratified the new Polish Constitution. Its preamble read:

> In the name of God, One in the Holy Trinity, [I] Stanislaw August, by the grace of God and the will of the people King of Poland and Grand Duke of Lithuania ... together with the confederated estates in dual number representing the Polish people: Recognizing that our destiny depends solely on the establishment and perfection of a national constitution, having by long experience learned the inveterate faults of our government, and desiring to take advantage of the season in which Europe finds itself and of this dying moment that has restored us to ourselves, free of the ignominious dictates of foreign coercion, holding dearer than life, than personal happiness, the political existence, external independence and internal liberty of the people whose destiny is entrusted to our hands, desiring as well to merit the blessing and gratitude of contemporary and future generations, despite obstacles that may cause passion in us, do for the general welfare, for the establishment of liberty, for the preservation of our country and its borders, with the utmost constancy of spirit ordain the present constitution and declare it to be entirely sacred and inviolable until the people, at the time by law prescribe, by their clear will recognize a need to alter it in any of its articles.

The Constitution, while recognizing the leading role of the nobility, gave political rights to Polish towns and cities and provided protection for the peasants and laid at least the groundwork for emancipation. Catholicism was declared the dominant faith, but full freedom of conscience was granted to all citizens. Parliament was the supreme legal authority, and the king the chief executive, and independent judiciary established. Foreign candidates to the throne were discouraged.

The Constitution, with its dangerous American and French ideas, was a slap in the face to the Russians who responded with force. In 1792, a group of compliant Polish magnates formed the Confederation of Targowica to oppose the Constitution and restore 'liberty'. This 'liberty' was to be reinforced with Russian bayonets. The new Polish army, led now by Tadeusz Kościuszko, returned from his American sojourn, resisted. At this moment, King Stanisław August lost heart. Fearing bloodshed, he ordered the army to lay down its arms. The reformers fled or were arrested and the Constitution overthrown.

To punish the Poles and to make sure that Poland had no ability to engage in future experiments in ordered freedom, Russia and Prussia organized the second partition of Poland in 1792. Prussia absorbed Gdańsk (renamed Danzig) and all of Wielkopolska, including the ancient cities of Poznań and Toruń, land that had been part of the Polish crown since the origins of the Polish state. Russia took more than a quarter of a million square kilometres, including all of Ukraine and much of Belarus.

Tadeusz Kościuszko

Despite its forceful measures and its direct takeover of a large piece of Polish territory, Russia's control over the Poles was slipping. The execution of Louis XVI and Europe's revolutionary ferment set the tone for all of Europe and Poland was no exception. Anti-Russian feeling spread and Poles abandoned the puppet government. In early 1794, the Russians sought to disband the Polish army and incorporate it into the Russian army. Polish commanders refused the order.

On 24 March, 1794 the revolt began. Kościuszko returned to

Kraków and publicly read 'The Act of Insurrection' in the city's main market square and pledged faithfully to defend the nation and uphold its laws and the liberties granted by the Constitution of 1791. Kościuszko marched on Warsaw with some 2,500 soldiers. He recruited another 2,000 peasants, promising their freedom if they fought for the nation. Kościuszko's experience in America had convinced him that only a popular rising of the whole nation could defeat the Russian. The peasants were armed only with long scythes.

At Racławice, on the march to Warsaw, the Poles were confronted by a much larger Russian force backed by artillery. The Polish regulars engaged the Russians in a desperate struggle. The battle hung in the balance until Kościuszko led a unit of peasant scythemen on a direct attack against the Russian gun batteries. One peasant, Wojciech Bartos, reached the Russian guns first and dropped his cap over the touch hole of a loaded cannon, preventing the surprised gunner from firing it. The Russian forces fled from the 'reapers of death' and Kościuszko scored a huge moral victory.

On 17 April, as news of the battle reached Warsaw, the population rose up in revolt, led by a cobbler, Jan Kliński. The Russian garrison and Russian officials were set upon by angry mobs and killed. Anyone associated with the Russian administration – nobles, clergy or merchants – faced mob justice. Days later, a similar revolt broke out in Wilno. A new revolutionary government, led by Kościuszko and with the blessing of the king, formed and declared the country free. A regiment of five hundred Jewish volunteers joined Kościuszko's army – the first organized Jewish military unit since Biblical times. On 7 May, Kościuszko issued the Manifesto of Połaniec eliminating many of the duties of serfdom. He ennobled the peasant Bartos for his courage at Racławice and gave him the surname Głowacki.

But the insurrection's success was not to last. Prussian and Russian forces converged on the Poles. The first Russian attack on Warsaw was repelled but two large armies advanced on central Poland. At Maciejowice on 10 October, Kościuszko tried to prevent them from linking up. The Poles inflicted heavy casualties on the Russians but Russian superiority in numbers was too great to overcome. Kościuszko was wounded three times and captured. The Scottish poet Thomas

Campbell would later write: 'Hope for a season bade the earth farewell, And freedom shrieked when Kościuszko fell.'

Russian and Prussian forces proceeded to systematically destroy the remaining resistance, brutally killing, looting and raping as they went. In Warsaw, Cossacks slaughtered the entire population of the Praga district. The king was sent into exile and those associated with the revolt rounded up and sent to Russian prisons.

In 1795, Russia and Prussia agreed to the third partition, and to mollify Vienna, Austria was also given a share. Warsaw and Mazovia were given to Prussia. Lublin, Kraków and the area south of Warsaw went to Austria. Wilno, Lithuania, Livonia and eastern Poland went to Russia.

The Polish state which had existed in some form since the tenth century ceased to exist. The two major causes were the weakness of the country's internal structure and the excessive rapaciousness of its neighbours. Debating the root causes of the partitions has long been a popular pastime among Poles – historians and non-historians alike. Identifying the exact point where the Commonwealth, a political experiment unlike anything known before or since, became broken beyond the point of fixing is hard to assess and there is no single cause for the disaster that befell Poland. The reign of Zygmunt Wasa and the Deluge played a major role in the decline of the Polish system, but symptoms were visible much earlier. At the same time, the Commonwealth had proven highly resilient and had recovered from major losses. Its armies defeated powerful enemies like Sweden, Russia and Turkey time and again. Yet, it was the decline of the magnate class and the corruption of the gentry as a whole that ultimately doomed Poland. Regionalism and the willingness to conflate personal interests with those of the country as a whole, ever the temptation of the powerful, made it much easier for Russia and Prussia to destroy the Commonwealth. The loss of freedom was a bitter curse and would henceforth mark the Polish character in ways unforeseen. From a political standpoint, it placed the Poles in a position of weakness that would bring generations of tragedy to central Europe. From a cultural standpoint, Poland was eclipsed. Once a vital part of Western Civilization, Polish contributions to art and learning would be ignored, forgotten or attributed to others.

Yet, while the Polish state disappeared from the map of Europe, the Polish nation did not. To the contrary, the loss of independence forced the Poles to think much more deeply about what it meant to Polish, what role they would play in history, and why such a fate had befallen them.

CHAPTER SIX

The Long Nineteenth Century,
1795–1914

For Poland the nineteenth century would last 123 years. The partitions would sweep away much that had come before yet leave other things intact, so that even the memory of the age of Poland's greatness would seem dim and strange. Countless Poles would devote themselves to what was called 'the Polish cause' which meant the restoration of Polish independence. Yet, there was no consensus on what sort of Poland was to be restored or what independence would mean. There was even less agreement on how to go about such a task. What was clear, though, was that as long as there were Poles, Poland would still exist. From a physical country, Poland would become a country of the mind and the heart. The first line of the national anthem would be 'Poland is not yet lost while we yet live.'

The 123 years from the loss of independence in 1795 to its rebirth at the end of the First World War would be, in many ways, a lost century for Poland. The nation would largely disappear from the consciousness of enlightened Europe and would be remembered with contempt only for its failures. At the same time, the crucible of national servitude would transform Polish culture and national consciousness unlike any other event before or since.

Poland in the Age of Napoleon

The failure of Poland's effort to regain an independent government was set against the backdrop of a Europe bracing for war. Poland's three partitioners, especially Russia and Austria, were in the forefront of the coalition building against France. The rise of Napoleon kindled Polish hopes that the French might restore the nation's independence. Napoleon himself encouraged this thinking. Polish volunteers and exiles in France and elsewhere formed the first Polish Legion in 1797 to fight alongside the French in the battles for Italy. Hopes for an early liberation of Poland were frustrated by the peace of 1801, but soon Napoleon was on the march in central Europe, crushing Prussian armies in 1806 and then defeating Russia in 1807 during what he sometimes referred to as the 'Polish War'.

Napoleon's victory brought about the French creation of the Duchy of Warsaw, which consisted of the central Polish territories taken by Russia in 1795 and the regions of Warsaw and Poznań taken by Prussia. The duchy was ruled by the king of Saxony, a French vassal, and it had no real independence. Poles staffed the middle and lower levels of the duchy's government, but had little decision-making power.

Tens of thousands of Poles volunteered for French service and were the largest and most loyal of his foreign contingents. At the Battle of Borodino in 1812 Poles made up about one in six of Napoleon's troops. Polish cavalry were particularly significant, but Polish infantry units also served. The most famous unit was the Vistula Legion, formed in the Duchy of Warsaw in 1807. It fought in numerous campaigns.

Despite the heroism of the Poles, their service did almost nothing for Poland and many Polish leaders distanced themselves from the French emperor as he grew more and more power hungry. Tadeusz Kościuszko, after his release from a Russian prison, refused Napoleon's offer of a general's rank in the French army, telling fellow Poles that the French leader was simply a tyrant who would never be a true friend of Polish liberty.

Moreover, Polish troops were often used in the most disagreeable circumstances. They were sent to Spain to help put down Spanish partisans who fought French domination. In 1801, a unit of Poles was sent to Haiti to help put down a revolt by black Haitians who refused to return to slavery after being freed in the early years of the Revolution. Most of the Poles sent there died of yellow fever, but a few deserted to the Haitian rebels where their military expertise was welcomed. The Poles themselves got little from Napoleon. Armies marched back and forth across Poland, often looting and burning as they went. Yet, many

Poles retained a strong affection for Napoleon and for France in general based on the misguided notion that the emperor and his country had been true champions of Poland's freedom.

If Napoleon's victories had little impact on the Polish cause, his defeat was more significant. At the Congress of Vienna in 1815 Russia gained an even larger share of Polish land, including Warsaw and Mazovia. Kraków was made an independent city under the protection of Austria. After heated negotiations, the three partitioning powers reached an understanding that all efforts were to be made to discourage the idea of Polish independence.

'FOR YOUR FREEDOM AND OURS'

The example set by Pułaski and Kościuszko in the American Revolution and the role played by the Polish legions in the Napoleonic wars provided an example for generations of Poles who took up arms for the independence of countries around the world under the slogan 'For Your Freedom and Ours.' By bringing liberation to others, they felt they were bringing closer the day when Poland would be free. At the same time, a generation of men had grown up knowing little but war although travelling to the far-flung corners of the world at least provided the chance for employment and perhaps even advancement. Poles became known as the 'scourge of tyrants' or to use Otto von Bismarck's phrase, 'the general staff of world revolution.'

In addition to the Poles' distinguished service in the American Revolution and their rather more futile efforts on behalf of Napoleon, Polish volunteers fought alongside Simon Bólivar in Latin America and with Garibaldi in Italy. Polish volunteers were especially prominent in the United States. In the US Civil War, Polish officers and enlisted men served on both sides. At the Battle of Chancellorsville in 1863, Poles in 58th New York Volunteers trying to hold off a Confederate onslaught were attacked by the Louisiana Polish Legion. The Poles on both sides travelled halfway around the world to shoot each other down in a Virginia field. Poles volunteered to fight against Russia in the Crimea and fought in distant Paraguay in the War of the Triple Alliance. In 1848, Poles fought to free Hungary and Polish General Józef Bem remains a national hero in Hungary.

Romantics and Positivists

From the nineteenth century onward, two major intellectual trends would dominate Polish thought, Romanticism and Positivism. Romanticism took a strong hold on the Polish consciousness following the Napoleonic wars. With little political or military power, Polish intellectuals emphasized Poland's spiritual force as the key to freeing the nation. The Commonwealth had been lost not due to internal weakness, but because of powerful and rapacious enemies who feared and envied her freedom and goodness. In the writings and thoughts of many Poles, Poland was – as poet Juliusz Słowacki (1809–41) put it – the Christ among Nations. Poland suffered for the sins of Europe and her freedom would mean freedom for all. Hence, Polish idealists who fought for other nations under the slogan of 'For Your Freedom and Ours' were participating in the liberation of Poland. Just like Christ, Poland would indeed rise again. The mystical Słowacki even made the outlandish prediction that a Slavic pope would come forth and lead Poland and other nations to freedom.

The foremost writer of the Romantic period, however, was Adam Mickiewicz (1798–1855). Inspired by Byron, Mickiewicz, along with Aleksandr Pushkin and Taras Shevchenko, was one of the triumvirate of great Slavic romantic authors. His play *Dziady* (Forefathers' Eve, 1823–32) dealt with themes of loss, martyrdom, and suffering – both of individuals and of Poland as a whole. His epic poem *Pan Tadeusz* (1834) evokes the life and landscapes of Polish gentry life in Lithuania. Writers such as Mickiewicz created a modern Polish literary language as well as a heroic vocabulary through which to describe the fate of the nation.

On the musical scene, the score for the tragic heroism of the Polish Romantics was written by Fryderyk Chopin (1810–49). Just as Mickiewicz and Słowacki created a Polish literary voice, Chopin used the sounds and rhythms of the Polish countryside to develop a distinctly Polish musical style. The Polonaise, once a courtly dance of the Polish gentry, became the basis for many of his greatest works, as did the more humble regional dance, the Mazurka.

The Romantic impulse also helped to determine political choices. If

The Romantic composer, Fryderyk Chopin

Poland had lost its freedom merely due to external foes, then reversing the partitions had to be the goal. A sudden blow that would overthrow foreign occupation would restore what had been lost. Thus, revolution was the preferred tool of the Romantics – a bold, heroic act that would rouse the spirit of the nation and bring liberation. The failure of insurrections in 1831 and 1864 resulted in many Romantics going into exile rather than compromising with the foreign occupiers. Paris developed a large expatriot community with luminaries such as Chopin and Mickiewicz. As a result, French Enlightenment thought and modern French artistic tastes had a disproportionate impact on Poland, despite its traditional rural conservatism and religiosity.

Alternating with Romanticism was Polish Positivism, which emerged in its strongest form in the late nineteenth century in the aftermath of the January Insurrection. Positivists believed Poland had fallen due to its own failings and weaknesses. Poles were simply not ready for freedom. What was needed, the Positivists believed, was to build up the nation's internal resources – moral, educational, economic, social and scientific. This programme was broadly termed 'organic work'. Only through reform and hard work would Poland be free. Positivists reacted strongly against the carnage brought about by Poland's failed insurrections. Bravery alone in the face of the military might of the partitioning powers would never succeed.

Just as Romantic writers had dominated the literary scene in the first half of the century, Positivist writers predominated in the second half of the nineteenth century. Among the greatest was Bolesław Prus (1847–1912) (the pen name of Aleksander Głowacki), who eschewed the epic poetry of the earlier generation for the novel. His best known works were *Lalka* (The Doll), a novel of bourgeois manners set in Warsaw, and *Faron* (Pharaoh), a novel of high politics set in ancient Egypt that criticized the emptiness of power without knowledge.

Many Positivist authors sought to educate or inspire their audience. Although written in a style reminiscent of Alexandre Dumas, the novels of Henryk Sienkiewicz were written from a Positivist perspective to draw lessons from the triumphs and failings of the Polish past. Sienkiewicz's great Trilogy (*With Fire and Sword, The Deluge*, and *Pan Michael*) were set during the years of the Cossack rebellion and the Swedish invasion. Although best known for his novel of early Christians in Rome, *Quo Vadis?*, it was the Trilogy that won the nation's first Nobel prize winner for literature in 1905. Strong historical themes also pervaded the visual arts. Jan Matejko's paintings featured many of the moments of triumph from the Polish past, such as the victory at Grunwald, but also chronicled moments of national shame, such as the parliament of 1772 that ratified the first partition.

Russian Poland

Following the defeat of Napoleon, the largest share of the Polish lands fell under Russian rule. Lithuania and Ukraine were directly incorporated into the empire. Central Poland, including the Warsaw region, was placed into a quasi-autonomous entity called the Congress Kingdom of Poland. Its king was the tsar and its autonomy was limited. While under tight Russian control it had a separate administration, army, and customs service. A rump parliament also existed, with the senate appointed by the tsar and the lower house consisting of select landowners. Polish was the official language of the kingdom. This autonomy was possible under the relatively enlightened rule of Tsar Alexander I.

This situation existed for about ten years, until the death of Alexander and the accession of Nicholas I in 1825. The new tsar opposed reforms and his reign began with the crushing of the Decembrist revolt in Russia. Tsarist police soon discovered links between the Decembrists and Polish secret societies. The new tsar made tentative moves to restrict the limited power of the kingdom's administrative structure, and political repression and censorship increased. Russia had also acquired the largest proportion of Polish Jews and it eliminated the tolerant laws of the old Commonwealth and replaced them with highly restrictive statutes.

In 1830, revolts broke out in Paris and Belgium and the Russians began to mobilize forces to intervene, forces that included the army of the Congress Kingdom. On the night of 29 November, 1830 a band of army cadets attempted to seize the Russian governor of Poland, Grand Duke Constantine, and overthrow the government. Inspired by revolutionary ideals that emphasized bold, inspirational action, the cadets had given little thought to forming a government. The Grand Duke fled, but the action created chaos on the streets of the city as large sections of the populace took to the streets to oppose Russian rule. The moderate Poles in the government found themselves caught between the revolutionaries and the tsarist authorities. General Józef Chłopicki (1771–1854) declared himself dictator and took leadership of the movement. As a sound military man Chłopicki felt that the Congress Kingdom could never resist the might of the Russian army and so attempted to open negotiations with the tsar. When these failed and the tsar demanded absolute subjugation, Chłopicki was overthrown. A junta-style government took the dictator's place and the parliament, under the pressure of the revolutionary mood, officially dethroned Nicholas I as king of Poland. While the radicals applauded the move, support was not universal. Although few Poles supported the tsar, many distrusted the radical tendencies of the new government. The most experienced generals were among those least enthusiastic about the cause, which was particularly harmful to military operations.

The Congress Kingdom was woefully unprepared for war with

Russia, but managed to raise an army of about 85,000 by March 1831. A guerilla revolt in Lithuania and other border provinces that had large Polish populations helped the cause by complicating Russian operations. In February, the Russians moved toward the capital, but were defeated at the Battle of Białołęka. In April, the Poles won a series of victories over the Russians and advanced into Lithuania, but failed to capture Wilno. The Russians gradually crushed the revolt in Lithuania and counterattacked. On 26 May, the Poles were beaten at Ostrołeka. The insurrection began to fall apart as radicals rioted in Warsaw, claiming that influential conservatives were guilty of treason. In September Russian forces retook Warsaw. Although a large Polish army remained intact, it had little left to fight for. The government collapsed and the army disbanded.

Following the November Insurrection, the Russians imposed a draconian regime of repression on the country. The tsarist police cast a wide net to catch anyone even suspected of involvement in the revolt. Those who had not been killed or driven into exile were rounded up, chained together and marched to Siberia along with their families. Most would never return. Landowners involved in the insurrection lost their property which was often given to Russian officials. Polish schools and institutions were closed down or severely restricted. The Russians sought to crush all aspects of Polish identity, built a massive fortress in the heart of Warsaw and began official discrimination toward the Catholic Church. The Eastern-rite Catholic Church suffered especially severe repression and many of its members were forcibly 'converted' to Russian Orthodoxy.

Polish society responded to the failure of the insurrection with efforts at internal reform on the local level. Movements emphasizing temperance and economic self-reliance became popular. At the same time, the Russian campaign to stamp out Polish identity backfired. Repression of the Catholic Church gradually stimulated feelings of national identity on the part of the peasantry. Minority groups such as the Jews found themselves betwixt and between. In the eastern marches, where fewer Poles resided, Jews increasingly saw themselves as Russian rather than Polish and after Yiddish, Russian not Polish became the preferred language. In central Poland, most educated and

– increasingly – assimilated Jews were sympathetic to the Polish cause. Jewish community leaders, too, often stood in solidarity with Poles against the Russian authorities who threatened both communities. This solidarity reached its height during the patriotic demonstrations of the early 1860s. When Russian authorities closed Catholic churches in Warsaw, the Jewish community closed its synagogues in sympathy and the city's chief rabbi was arrested by the authorities. During the 1850s and early 1860s, leading Polish writers and activists increasingly saw Jews as brothers in a common struggle against tsarism and the idea of full Jewish assimilation into Polish society was viewed as a real possibility. At the local level, relations between Jews and gentiles remained largely unchanged – a mix of co-operation, suspicion and mutual stereotypes. Russian authorities maintained severe restrictions on Jewish occupations and travel until the 1860s.

By the 1860s, a reform movement again took hold in Russia and Poles began to organize and sought great autonomy and freedom. Russian authorities, however, were unprepared to grant much of anything to the Poles and tried to crack down on Polish organizations seeking reform. On 8 April, 1861 Russian troops opened fire on a peaceful demonstration, killing men, women and children. As political activism increased, the Russians responded with greater repression and placed most of Poland and Lithuania under martial law. With peaceful means cut off, support grew for armed action and a large conspiratorial organization emerged. (Among the leaders was the father of the novelist Joseph Conrad-Korzeniowski.) To break this movement, the tsarist authorities tried to impose military conscription, hoping to draft a majority of able-bodied young men into the army and send them to remote parts of the empire. To ensure that the most radical elements were overrepresented, landowners and farm workers were exempted from the draft.

On 22 January, 1863 the underground National Central Committee declared armed insurrection and constituted itself as a shadow national government. Among other things, it declared emancipation for the peasants and removal of all restrictions on Jews. Unlike the November Insurrection, the January Insurrection was well organized and the Polish underground infrastructure was highly efficient and secretive. It had cells throughout the country that operated under orders of the secret central authorities. On the military side, Polish forces, while ill-equipped, commenced guerilla operations against the Russian army, forcing it to abandon large swathes of the countryside. The insurrection quickly spread to Lithuania and Belarus. Russian authorities, however, were ruthless, hanging and imprisoning the innocent as well as the guilty. Despite the support of a panoply of European radicals, the great powers refused to intervene and Russian liberals saw the entire insurrection as a plot to overthrow the tsar. Gradually, the insurgents' infrastructure was destroyed and the last chief of the armed resistance, Romuald Traugutt, was captured and executed in the autumn of 1864.

Once again, Russian reaction was extreme, with executions, imprisonment, and mass deportations. Churches and social institutions were closed and education beyond the primary level in Polish was almost abolished. Yet, repressive measures again backfired as Poles took to secret self-education and the strength of patriotism grew. One young girl, Maria Skłodowska (1867–1934), remembered how her teacher would instruct the students in forbidden Polish subjects while the school janitor kept watch for Russian inspectors. When the authorities approached, students hid their Polish books and continued their lessons in Russian. One time the inspectors entered the class and demanded a recitation of a lesson. The teacher called on the young girl and Skłodowska recited the lesson in Russian without error. The satisfied inspectors went away and the young girl would soon complete her studies and later travel to Paris to attend university where, with her future husband, Pierre Curie, she would discover the secrets of radiation and win two Nobel Prizes.

In economic terms, while Poland was one of the most advanced sectors of the Russian empire, it was among the most backward parts too. Only in the last decades of the nineteenth century did Russian authorities allow some limited economic freedom. The rural population remained mired in poverty. Only in border regions where the possibility existed of emigration or seasonal migrant labour in other countries was there any sort of economic advancement.

Prussian Poland

The Prussian or German controlled sector of Poland was the smallest of the three partitions. It was in many ways the most effectively repressed but also the most economically advanced. Prussian state authorities sought effective and efficient exploitation of the Polish areas under their control. The process of peasant and Jewish emancipation began even before the end of the Napoleonic wars and as a result agriculture was more modern and the majority of the Jewish population migrated to the larger cities in search of economic opportunity.

In 1848, a revolt occurred in Poznań in concert with revolutions that occurred in cities across Europe, but the rebellion faltered and Prussian authorities quickly reasserted control. In 1863, volunteers from Wielkopolska crossed the border to aid their compatriots in fighting the Russian army, but in general the Prussians kept tight control over the region. Until German unification, Poles in this region had limited opportunities for national expression but were not as severely oppressed as in the Russian partition. Poles served in the Prussian army and many Polish grenadiers performed heroically during the Franco-Prussian war. After 1870, however, the situation began to change. Ethnic Germans had been leaving western Poland for the cities of America and Germany for a number of decades and while some Poles also migrated, higher birthrates meant a growing Polish population that in an age of nationalism was seen as a threat to the unity of an organically German empire. That Poles were concentrated on the frontier with Russia only made matters worse from the perspective of German leaders such as Otto von Bismarck.

To stamp out any potential fifth column Bismarck initiated the *Kulturkampf* (or culture struggle) aimed at repressing the Catholic Church and at Germanizing the Polish population in the western reaches of Germany. In addition, in the 1890s, the German government tried to encourage resettlement of ethnic Germans in Polish areas and made strenuous efforts to take land away from Poles and to restrict land sales to Poles. These efforts backfired badly. From a reasonably loyal population, the German moves greatly strengthened Polish nationalism. Intellectuals, clergy, members of the gentry, independent farmers and the urban middle class banded together to resist German influence and to undertake education and 'organic work'. The German colonization effort had only limited success as few Germans were interested. Beginning in 1901, authorities attempted to force all religion classes to be taught in German. When Polish schoolchildren refused, they were whipped and their parents jailed. Beginning in 1906, many Poles fought back by refusing to send their children to school until the authorities relented. German authorities also tried to stop Poles from building new houses on their own property. One farmer, Michał Drzymała, in a highly publicized protest, brought a circus wagon to his property and proceeded to live in it. As a result of government repression, by the start of the First World War, Poles in western Poland were among the best organized in all of the partitions.

Austrian Poland

The Austrian empire was the weakest of the three partitioning powers. The region of southern Poland that it ruled over was termed Galicia and included most of eastern and western Małopolska. From 1815 to 1846, the city of Kraków had the status of a free city, though under Austrian protection. Economic conditions in Galicia were among the least advanced in all of Poland and the social stratification among the most severe. While the Russian authorities would eventually permit some industrialization in their sector of Poland in the 1890s, in Galicia, except for an early oil boom in the 1850s there was virtually no industry. Wags joked that the province's official name 'Galicia and Lodomeria' should be '*Golicia* and *Głodmeria*' (i.e., barren and hungry).

Although economically backward, culturally and politically, Galicia was the freest of the partition sectors. The only significant revolt occurred in the city of Kraków in 1846 and was quickly put down by Austrian troops. At the same time, the authorities encouraged a local peasant revolt which resulted in the deaths of some 2,000 members of the gentry and their families. Such events, however, were the exception.

Following the great compromise of 1867 which turned the Austrian empire into the Austro-Hungarian Empire and established the dual monarchy, Polish nobles were given a degree of local autonomy. Polish officials staffed the local administration and Polish was widely used. Polish deputies in the imperial parliament were drawn largely from the old aristocracy. They supported Emperor Franz-Josef's conservative policies and could be counted on to oppose any excesses of republicanism. As a result, Poles played an important role in Vienna and Galicia served as the empire's 'Polish' province, which did not sit well with Ukrainians living in the eastern regions of Galicia. Kraków with its Jagiellonian University became a major centre for Polish art, learning and culture. Polish national celebrations could be held there. Censorship of books and periodicals was light and infrequent.

THE END OF SERFDOM

By the middle of the nineteenth century, it was increasingly understood that serfdom was a major obstacle to the modernization of agriculture. Moreover, as radicals sought to win the loyalty of peasants in their schemes for revolution, conservatives and moderates sought to secure the support of the peasantry by gradual emancipation. Prussia began the process of emancipating its peasants in 1807. Austria declared emancipation in 1848 and Russia in 1863.

Although several variations were tried, the most common sort of emancipation was to convert the peasants' labour obligations and in-kind taxes into cash rents. In return, the peasants would receive a small plot of land. As one scholar put it, this scheme took the shackles off the peasants' feet but took away their shoes as well. Prior to emancipation, cash was not common in the countryside. After emancipation, it was necessary for peasants to come up with cash. Their small parcels of land were rarely sufficient to generate the money needed for their rents. Moreover, common lands and property, such as forests, pastures, mills and streams were usually kept by the landlord who, instead of allowing the peasants to use them in return for labour, charged them for it. Local courts in the latter nineteenth century were filled with cases of peasants suing to get possession or use of such facilities. To make matters worse for the peasants, the tradition of dividing up inheritable property evenly among the surviving heirs resulted in ever-smaller parcels in each generation.

The usual result of these changes was that peasants were rarely able to pay cash rents, forcing them to find jobs that paid a wage. Commonly, the peasants simply worked for their local landlord. Nevertheless, as time went on peasants began to go further afield in search of jobs. Sometimes a family would send its grown children to work as migrant labourers. Groups of Polish peasants – usually young men or women – followed harvests of sugarbeets or potatoes from Prussia to Denmark or Sweden. Soon this migration took on a more significant characteristic as peasants who earned wages in this way could provide the money needed for rents and even provide a surplus.

The Great Diaspora

Beginning in the 1850s in western Poland – Silesia, Kaszubia, western Pomerania and Wielkopolska – rural people began to migrate in search of jobs and opportunity. Many learned about opportunities for work through German neighbours. Although the first migration occurred within the region, the need for more and better farmland soon drew many to the western hemisphere. Small groups of Polish exiles had settled in North and South America since the 1830s, but they had not formed any significant communities. In 1854, a shipload of Silesian immigrants landed on the Texas gulf coast and established the community of Panna Maria. Within fifteen years scores of small settlements had sprung up in the American Midwest. Although early communities were agricultural, wages in the United States were generally higher than in Europe and America's industrial expansion created an almost limitless demand for new workers from all over Poland. Cities like Chicago, Milwaukee, Detroit, Cleveland, Buffalo and Pittsburgh developed large Polish immigrant communities. In the late 1880s and 1890s, many Poles also migrated to southern Brazil, to the states such as Santa Caterina or Rio Grande do Sul. By the 1890s, the trickle of Polish immigration had become a flood and in the decade before the First World War the flood became a torrent. As many as three million Poles came to the New World. Nor was this movement confined to Polish gentiles. Massive numbers of Polish Jews also left for the United States, greatly swelling America's small Jewish community.

The diaspora had a major impact on the Polish countryside. In many communities, remittances sent by immigrants and money brought by returning immigrants fuelled an economic expansion. (About one third of all Polish immigrants returned home permanently.) The sojourners in America also injected new ideas into the villages. In the New World, Polish immigrants played an important part in the struggle for unionization and the rights of workers. They joined mass organizations, voted and were exposed to politics and newspapers. For the first time, immigrants attended celebrations of national holidays such as 3 May (Constitution Day) or 29 November (the start of the November Insurrection) that had been banned in their homeland. They were exposed to the writing of Mickiewicz and Sienkiewicz and perhaps even the music of Chopin. In Poland, churches had been endowed only by the nobility, but in America the sons and daughters of peasants built magnificent neo-Gothic edifices and contracted architects and artists. They created hundreds of organizations, almost all governed by democratic principles with a written constitution, by-laws and regular elections. All of these new trends stimulated the national consciousness of rural Poles and helped to create a ferment of new ideas and, increasingly, demands for change.

INDUSTRIALIZATION

As migrants began to leave for America to take up industrial work, the stirrings of industrialization began to reach Poland. In western Poland, the German government did little to promote industry and Poles tended to migrate to the factories and mines of the Ruhr to take industrial jobs. The one major exception to this was Silesia, which had begun to industrialize in the late 1700s under Prussian rule. Silesia developed a significant metallurgical industry and became one of Europe's largest coal-producing regions. Austrian Galicia remained virtually free of significant industry. The oil fields south and west of Lwów discovered in the 1850s and the ancient salt mines of Wieliczka were the major exceptions. In both partition areas, the policies and economic logic of the governing empires worked against industrial development. Both the German and Austria partitions were among the most agrarian in their respective empires and both bordered Russia, a potential military threat that made significant investment unlikely.

The Russian-controlled sector of Poland, however, was the most advanced region of the empire and close to European markets. The first significant industry emerged in Łódź, southwest of Warsaw. Local entrepreneurs built the first textile plant in 1822 and the city grew rapidly to produce cotton and linen goods for the Russian market. Much of the capital investment came from Germany, but Jewish entrepreneurs, such as the Poznański family, were also very successful. The city – known as the Polish Manchester – attracted an ethnically diverse workforce consisting of Germans, Jews and Poles. Tariff barriers between the Congress Kingdom and Russia proper introduced to punish the Poles after the November Insurrection harmed Łódź's position in the Russian market. This led in turn to the development of Poland's 'little Manchester' – the city of Białystok. Lying just outside the boundaries of the Congress Kingdom, Białystok's modest textile industry expanded rapidly in the 1830s. Just to the east of Białystok, the town of Grodno also benefited from the Congress Kingdom's misfortune in the 1830s to become a significant maker of woollen goods.

Investment in infrastructure was limited. Significant railway development did not exist until the 1880s and the railway network in the German-controlled regions of western Poland was far more extensive than in the other two partitions. The lack of investment and inconsistent economic policies kept most industries and businesses small. Due to the policies of the partitioning powers and the general poverty of the region, the largest enterprises tended to be in the hands of foreign investors or members of the German or Jewish minorities.

Politics, Society, and the Rise of National Identity

The end of serfdom, the changes brought about by mass emigration, industrialization and the shifting policies of the partitioning powers brought about a major disruption in the patterns of life for the majority of Poles. Among the most significant of these changes was the growth of national identity among the Poles as well as among minority groups. The aftermath of the January Insurrection brought disillusionment, especially in the prospect of a modern, multi-ethnic Polish identity. The new ideas that flooded into Poland created a wide variety of political and social movements that divided communities in new ways.

Among Catholics there was a tremendous increase in lay involvement in religious life, often in the social and charitable realm. Mirroring the secular concept of organic work, some of this involvement resulted in the establishment of new religious orders. After Vatican I, the Church council of 1869-70 which was called in response to the changing political status of the papacy in relation to the newly-unified Italy, but which also dealt with a host of other issues including redefining the relationship of the Church to the secular state, new devotional forms began to appear as well. Some of these changes resulted in heresies such as the Mariavite movement that began in the 1890s. Followers of the mystic Felicja Kozłowska, the Mariavites considered the Virgin Mary to be the equal of Jesus and after the foundress' death one branch of the movement would eventually develop a female priesthood and consider Kozłowska herself divine.

Two major political groupings emerged in late nineteenth century Poland, both led by forceful and charismatic leaders who would offer competing visions for Poland's future. Both parties emerged during a period of intensifying nationalism during which the very concept of what it meant to be a Pole was increasingly debated and contested. Would a broader, more expansive definition of Polishness serve as the right catalyst to mobilize people to regain independence? Would a narrow vision of Polishness create problems with ethnic minorities? How were the claims of Polishness coming from assimilated Jews to be judged? What role would religion play in Polish identity? All of these questions bubbled beneath the surface of late nineteenth century Poland and different political factions attempted to come up with new answers.

The Polish Socialist Party (PPS), founded in 1893 in Wilno, combined socialist economics with nationalism. Its best known leader was Józef Piłsudski (1867–1935), the scion of a minor gentry family in Lithuania which had a long history of conspiratorial activity. (The elder brothers of Piłsudski and V. I. Lenin were executed together on the same scaffold following a plot against the tsar.) The PPS sought Polish independence and social liberation for workers and peasants. It envisioned a secular, multi-ethnic Poland in which Jews, Lithuanians and Ukrainians would join together under Polish leadership in the spirit of the old Commonwealth. While Lithuanian and Ukrainian membership was not significant, the PPS did have a strong Jewish section. The PPS was deeply influenced by Romanticism and under Piłsudski's leadership developed a strong conspiratorial movement with secret fighting squads. Piłsudski himself once led a band of PPS gunmen in hijacking a tsarist payroll train to finance his party's activities. To avoid the Russian police, Piłsudski moved his base of operations to Austrian Galicia where he created the paramilitary Polish Fighting Organization that became the basis for a Polish Legion under an Austrian aegis during World War I. Piłsudski saw Russia as the major obstacle to Polish independence and was willing to work with Austria to thwart Russia.

The other major political grouping was the National Democratic Party (or Endeks), founded by Roman Dmowski (1864–1939) in 1897. For Dmowski and the National Democrats, Polishness was based on shared ancestry and faith. A Pole was to be Catholic and Slavic. Unlike Piłsudski, Dmowski lobbied for a smaller, more compact and ethnically homogeneous Poland. Poland's weakness, according to Dmowski, was that the middle class was dominated by too many Jews and Germans. Dmowski saw economics as a zero-sum game in which one group won at the expense of another. The National Democrats were influenced by Positivism – Dmowski sought to work within existing power structures rather than overthrow them – and emphasized education and self-help over armed action. Dmowski was very hostile to Germans and unlike Piłsudski came to see Russia as Poland's possible ally in the face of German aggression.

The rise of the National Democratic Party followed the introduction of new racial ideas into the Polish discourse, including the concept of racial anti-Semitism. Although there had always been some level of discrimination against Jews which varied according to the economic and political situation, this prejudice was based on religious characteristics. This anti-Jewish prejudice could turn nasty and even violent. Catholic clergy at times encouraged anti-Jewish prejudice based on erroneous interpretations of Church teaching though simultaneously discouraging violence. At other times, clergy preached against Jew-hatred. Religious prejudice, however, existed as long as Jews remained practising Jews, and such sentiment did not attach to Jewish converts to Catholicism. By contrast, the new racial anti-Semitism of the 1890s saw Jews as a race with immutable racial characteristics that existed regardless of religion or socio-economic status. In this view, Poles, Jews, Germans or Russians were separate and even opposing races that were destined for conflict. This ideology – while not dominant – added a new level of tension to Poland's ethnic mix. Ethnic divisions were exacerbated by economic conflicts. The country's economic back-wardness during the partitions, the devastation brought about by wars and uprisings, and the 'state capitalism' later pursued by the Polish Second Republic, limited possibilities for economic advancement. Poland's middle class, its small business people, craftsmen and pro-fessionals, were heavily Jewish. Middle and working class Poles who were in direct competition with Jewish neighbours in a limited economy were among those most likely to join parties like the Endeks.

In addition to the PPS and the Endeks, other parties emerged as well. A Christian Democratic Party was founded after the turn of the century as a more moderate alternative to the Endeks. A significant Peasant Party also came into being in the 1890s and 1900s. Although some factions of the peasant movement were more closely aligned with the socialists, the majority of the movement was best described as con-servative agrarian populism. Its main goal was to protect the livelihoods of the rural majority from exploitation, especially at the hands of the state or the large landowners. Although poorly organized prior to the First World War, the Peasant Party encouraged self-help in the form of co-operatives as well as land reform. On the far left were small radical groups linked to the Communist International. The internationalist wing of the Polish socialists produced the infamous Rosa Luxemburg (1871–1919), born in Zamość, but since they denied the need for Polish self-determination they had no widespread support.

If ethnic Poles were divided over new concepts of identity, so too were the nation's minority communities, especially the Jews. Jewish divisions in some ways ran even deeper than those among the Poles, who at least generally agreed on the need for an independent Poland.

The infamous Rosa Luxemburg, born in Zamość

In the eighteenth century, two new movements had arisen among Poland's Jews. The first was Hasidism, which emphasized the ability of individual Jews to grow closer to God via everything that they do, say or think without veering from a commitment to the Torah. Its mystical and exuberant style was in contrast to the more intellectual style of the mainstream Jewish leaders of the day and their emphasis on the primacy of Torah study. The second movement was the Haskalah, or Jewish Enlightenment, an intellectual movement that lasted from the 1770s to the 1880s. It encouraged Jews to study secular subjects, to learn both the European and Hebrew languages, and to enter fields such as agriculture, crafts, the arts and science. The movement had strong assimiliationist tendencies, encouraging the end of distinctive Jewish dress and loyalty to the ruling state. It strongly discouraged the use of Yiddish in favour of Hebrew.

Both movements resulted in significant splits within Polish Judaism, although the majority of Jews remained strongly traditional in belief and custom. By the late nineteenth century, however, even isolated *shtetls* felt the winds of change. This was not made easier by Russian state authorities who periodically tried to enforce draconian measures on Jews, such a restricting Jewish education or mass conscription of Jewish youth into the army. Emigration to America or Western Europe was an attractive option for millions of Jews. The conservative majority within the communities was also challenged by socialism and Zionism. Socialism provided a vision of a society based on equality and free of ethnic prejudice and had a special appeal for young Jews in response to both external government repression and the strictures of their own community. Zionism emerged as the Jewish response to European nationalism and sought a Jewish homeland and a national identity. Zionists themselves were divided between right and left as well as over means and methods for achieving their goals. Jewish traditionalists looked on both movements with disdain if not horror. To further complicate matters, in the late nineteenth century a backlash began to emerge against the move away from Yiddish. A new generation of writers began to compose stories and poems in Yiddish as the language of the people.

YOUNG POLAND

The social and political ferment of late nineteenth and early twentieth century Poland provided fertile ground for the flowering of a Polish modernist movement called Young Poland. The movement was particularly strong in literature, the visual arts, music and theatre, though echoing the Arts and Crafts movement in England and the United States, many of its leading figures also dabbled in photography, typography and interior design. Influenced by Neo-Romanticism and art nouveau styles, the Young Poland movement sought to create a distinctive modern Polish style. Many of its artists holidayed regularly in the mountain town of Zakopane and the town's distinctive folk culture made a strong impression on the artists and writers while they in turn helped to popularize the town as a holiday destination. The Young Poland movement was the first major Polish artistic movement to include a significant contribution from women as artists in their own right. In literature, among its best known figures were Stefan Żeromski, Gabriela Zapolska and Władysław Reymont. Reymont's 1901 novel *The Peasants*, the first great novel of Polish rural life, won the Nobel

Prize in 1924. In music, Karol Szymanowski and Grzegorz Fitelberg were among the leading composers. In the visual arts, Jacek Malczewski, Olga Boznańska and Józef Mehoffer were prominent.

Young Poland's greatest genius, however, was Stanisław Wyspiański (1869–1907), known as the 'Polish Da Vinci'. As a playwright, his allegory *Wesele* (*The Wedding*) marked the genesis of modern Polish drama and explored the tragedies and divisions of Polish history. As an artist, Wyspiański created haunting and sensitive portraits of children and ordinary people and places, especially in his beloved Kraków. He also designed stained glass windows, furniture, costumes and stages for the theatre, and was an illustrator and typographer who designed and printed his own works and those of fellow artists and writers. Tragically, Wyspiański died of tuberculosis in 1907 at the age of thirty-eight, cutting short the career of one of Poland's most brilliant artists.

1905

In 1904, Russia went to war against Japan and suffered a crushing defeat. The war caused great excitement among Poles who hoped it would bring about significant changes in the Russian imperial system. Piłsudski travelled to Japan seeking aid in provoking a revolution

A staircase balustrade designed by the 'Polish da Vinci' Stanisław Wyspiański in 1905

against Russia in Poland. Dmowski followed him to persuade the Japanese against such a move. The outbreak of the 1905 Revolution in Russia had strong echoes in Poland. As the grip of the tsarist government weakened, Polish demands for greater freedom and autonomy grew bolder. Massive strikes occurred among workers and students. PPS fighting squads attacked Russian police patrols and officials in a campaign of targeted terror. In return, the police summarily executed PPS activists. In the countryside, lawlessness increased and banditry proliferated.

When the tsarist authorities agreed to empire-wide elections to a new Russian parliament, Dmowski's Endeks participated while the left boycotted the proceedings. Dmowski's party gained over fifty seats, but this had little practical effect as tsarist authorities effectively blocked efforts at national reform and gradually reasserted control over the Polish provinces. While the events of 1905–1908 resulted in deeper splits between right and left and between and within ethnic communities, they also whetted appetites of reform and cracked the façade of Russian imperial power. Although the authorities reasserted themselves through sheer force, it would take only one good shock to bring the system down.

CHAPTER SEVEN

Rebirth,
1914–39

In the early months of 1914 floods ravaged parts of Galicia, killing many and displacing tens of thousands from their homes. It was as if nature was providing a foretaste of what was to come.

Ideological conflicts swirled in all three partitions. Ideas ranged from the reactionary to the very radical. Each ethnic and religious community had its own spectrum of debate so that not only were they divided from one another, but each community had its own internal fault lines. While the dreams of freedom and self-determination remained as alive as ever, the chance that these dreams would be realized was no closer than it had been a hundred or fifty years earlier.

That spring, life went on as usual. Urbanites strolled the Planty in Kraków and Saxon Gardens in Warsaw, while in the countryside, storks marked the return of warmer weather and peasants went about the task of preparing fields for their seed. The sabre-rattling of the Great Powers, which had gone on for several years, was worrying but few paid it much heed.

On 28 June, a radical Serb nationalist assassinated the heir to the thrones of the dual monarchy of Austria-Hungary, Franz Ferdinand and his wife. The murder created a political crisis between Austria and Serbia. Austrian demands were rejected by Serbia, which called on Russia for support. Austria called on its German ally, while the Russians called on the French and the French on the British. By the end of July, armies were mobilizing across the continent.

Brothers killing Brothers

In the east, Russia faced Germany and Austria. Almost all the major armies stood in historically Polish lands. Soon almost two million Poles would be mobilized, many to face each other across a hostile battlefield. Nearly half a million would die. The armies marched in August 1914 and Polish villages went up in flames, peasants fled marauding troops and indiscriminate shelling. Within months hundreds of thousands were refugees.

Russian forces crashed into East Prussia. The Russians proved tough and courageous but were outgeneralled by the Germans. At Tannenburg, the Germans smashed the Russian invasion in a victory so complete that Germans accounted it as revenge for the humiliation of Grunwald. The Germans counterattacked and took Łódź by November. In the south, the Russians met with greater success against the poorly prepared Austrians, seizing much of Galicia. The spring of 1915 opened with a major German-Austrian offensive which broke Russian defences in central Poland and Lithuania. Warsaw fell, then Wilno and Kowno. In the south, the Austrians drove Russian armies out of Galicia. By the end of the year, most ethnically Polish regions were in the hands of the Central Powers. The following year a Russian offensive against Austria met with only limited success. Both sides reached a point of stalemate. In the west, Germany was being bled white in trench warfare, while the Austrians faced determined Serbian resistance and war with Italy. The armies of the dual monarchy had a mixed record, but those of Russia were falling apart. Tsarist forces suffered massive losses, compounded by supply problems and poor leadership.

On a human level, the war was a tragedy for Poles. Brother killed brother. As one poem of the day noted:

> We're kept apart, my brother,
> By a fate we can't deny
> From our opposing dug outs
> We're staring death in the eye....
> So when you catch me in your sights
> I beg you, play your part,

And sink your Muscovite bullet
Deep in my Polish heart.
Now I see the vision clearly,
Caring not that we'll both be dead;
For *that which has not perished*
Shall rise from the blood we shed.

Tragedy also brought opportunity. As the three partitioning powers
lost more and more men, their need for new sources of recruits grew.
All three empires sought to mobilize the Poles against their enemies.
Each one promised national unification under the sceptre of one
emperor or another. In 1916 Germany announced the creation of a
new kingdom of Poland from territory taken from Russia. The kingdom was a rump state controlled by German military authorities in
Warsaw and one of its main goals was the raising of a *Polnische Wehrmacht* to serve as cannon fodder against Germany's foes. Nevertheless,
for the first time in a century, the issue of Poland was back on the
agenda of the great powers.

Polish leaders, especially in the Austrian partition, had not been idle.
In August 1914, Józef Piłsudski's Polish Legion had staged a march on
Kielce without Austrian consent. The act was something of a comedy
and the legion was forced to withdraw. The legion was then officially
subordinated to Austrian command where it served with distinction.
Meanwhile, centrist leaders in Kraków formed the Supreme National
Committee to unite all independence movements under Austrian
control. Nationalist leader Roman Dmowski's Polish National Committee sought Polish autonomy within the Russian empire. Dmowski's
group moved to St Petersburg after the fall of Warsaw and later to
Switzerland where it developed support among Poles in exile, among
them the world-famous pianist Ignacy Jan Paderewski (1860–1941).
Meanwhile, Polish immigrants in the United States began to mobilize
to support Polish relief and the cause of Poland's self-determination.
Though the US was not officially at war, the Polish community tended
to be strongly anti-German and so found an ally in the pro-Allied
Dmowski. Paderewski made a point of encouraging the mobilization of
Polish Americans and tried to use the growing political awareness of the

The world famous pianist Ignacy Jan Paderewski

community to influence American President Woodrow Wilson to back Polish independence.

In 1917, the rhetorical struggle over Poland heated up yet further, with all sides attempting to simultaneously encourage and control the momentum of Polish aspirations. In April, America entered the war and a Polish army made up largely of Polish Americans, trained in Canada and commanded by former Austrian general Józef Haller, would take to the trenches in France by the following year. President Wilson proclaimed his support for a free Poland with access to the sea in his famous Fourteen Points. Meanwhile in Russia, the Revolution in February had overthrown the monarchy. It established a provisional government which put Polish independence on the agenda, though little was done.

The Central Powers had the advantage of controlling most of the territory in Europe with an ethnic Polish population. However, Austria, the power potentially most sympathetic to the Poles, grew ever weaker and Germany increasingly determined the common policy in central Europe. German occupation of the former Russian partition areas was harsh. As the fatherland grew increasing bankrupt, German officials systematically stripped occupied Polish territories of food, timber, and finished goods. Factories were dismantled and cannibalized for spare parts to keep industry going inside the Reich. Worse yet from the Polish perspective, the Germans demanded that the Polish Legion under Austrian command be incorporated in the *Polnische Wehrmacht*. Austria agreed, but Piłsudski and many of his legionnaires refused to swear allegiance to the Kaiser. Piłsudski was imprisoned and the rank and file of the legions were incorporated.

The Bolshevik Revolution of November 1917 brought an end to Russian participation in the war and a peace treaty with Germany in 1918 left most of the Polish lands firmly in German hands. The German authorities had tried to put a damper on Polish national aspirations, but as Germany's military fortunes declined in the summer and autumn of 1918, the situation in Poland grew more and more fluid. By November, Germany was facing collapse and opened armistice talks with Entente Powers. Revolutions broke out in Kiel and other German cities and the Kaiser abdicated the throne and fled to Holland. On 10 November, Piłsudski was released from prison.

Rebirth

By 11 November, 1918 German military authorities had lost complete control of central Poland. Soldiers began to form revolutionary 'soviets' and refused to obey orders. Citizens began to disarm German soldiers, whose main desire was to return home. Bases, weapons and equipment were peacefully abandoned. Into this power vacuum came Piłsudski. As the only figure with any real stature, he was able to form a Provisional Government on 11 November, the same day as the armistice, which would forever be remembered as Polish Independence Day. Piłsudski convinced the Germans to simply leave the city and hand over all their weapons. Within days, German forces had quietly abandoned most of the former Russian Congress Kingdom and returned home. In the south, Austrian power had also collapsed and local authorities in Kraków assumed control and threw in their lot with Piłsudski's provisional government.

For the first time in 123 years, Poland returned to the map of Europe, though securing independence would take longer.

The most immediate problem was the formation of a Polish army. Fortunately, there were plenty of weapons lying around and a significant number of Poles who had served in the German or Austrian forces were prepared to join. They would later be joined by Poles from the former Russian army and the Polish forces raised in the west fighting under French command. Integrating all of these into a coherent fighting force was another matter. Polish forces were armed with a wide variety of Russian, German, Austrian, British, French, American, Italian and Mexican equipment captured, given or purchased. In the meantime, however, these troops provided Piłsudski and his nascent government with the backing they needed to avoid destruction.

The most immediate issue was the fate of Lwów. Like the Poles, the Ukrainians had long thirsted for freedom and their opportunity also came in 1918. Ukrainian nationalists in the ethnically mixed region of eastern Galicia considered the city to be an integral part of any future Ukraine. In early November, Ukrainian militia tried to seize the city. Polish residents formed their own militia, including units of boys and girls as young as thirteen or fourteen, called 'Eaglets'. Though outnumbered, the Poles managed to hold a significant part of the city. A relief force of 1,400 men made a forced march from Przemyśl to reach the city and drive out the Ukrainians. Nevertheless, the city remained isolated for several months with the Ukrainians in control of the surrounding area.

In December 1918, following a visit by the famous Paderewski, one of the world's most famous concert pianists and after Artur Rubenstein perhaps the most famous interpreter of Chopin, Poles in the Poznań region rose up in revolt and declared for Poland. In fierce fighting with local Germans, the Poles managed to secure the city and most of the surrounding countryside by February. In January, Czech forces seized border areas from Poland; a brief clash ensued, leaving the Czechs in control of the Cieszyn (Teschen) region.

Border disputes with both Germany and the new Czechoslovakia were handled by treaties imposed by the Western Powers at Versailles.

Poland was represented by Dmowski and Paderewski, but the major players were the British, French and Americans. The French and Americans supported a larger Poland, each for their own reasons. The British reverted to their traditional stance of attempting to create a 'balance of power' on the Continent and were opposed to strengthening any potential French allies such as Poland. Moreover, British leader Lloyd George was ferociously anti-Polish, infamously remarking 'I would no sooner give a clock to a monkey than give Silesia to Poland.' The final treaty borders gave Poland the old province of Royal Prussia, or Pomerania, as well as Poznań. Silesia, East Prussia and Cieszyn were to be subject to plebiscites in which the local population was supposed to vote on which neighbouring state it wished to join.

As Poland's access to the sea had been a major point of Wilson's initiative on Poland this meant having a port. As a result, the largely German-speaking city of Danzig (Gdańsk) ended up in an odd position. It was declared a Free City under the protection of the League of Nations. Poland would have access to its port and Polish officials would regulate its customs. Although the city was not militarized, the Poles were allowed to garrison a small force on a peninsula in the harbour called Westerplatte, which was reserved for Polish military shipments. This attempt at reasonable compromise between Polish and German interests would have fateful consequences.

THE POLISH-SOVIET WAR

In the east, Poland faced a fluid situation and there was little effort by the Western powers to delineate the country's eastern boundaries. German forces in north-eastern Poland, Belarus and Lithuania had not suffered the same collapse as their counterparts in central Poland. In February 1919, they withdrew in an orderly fashion toward East Prussia. The Belarusans were the least organized of all the groups in the region and had only barely begun to develop a sense of national identity. Efforts to form an independent Belarus, led by a relatively small circle of intellectuals, were stillborn. Bolshevik forces took control of the eastern reaches of the country and Poles and Lithuanians claimed the west and north respectively. Poles and Lithuanians clashed over the city of Wilno. Although the city and its immediate environs were largely Polish it was the historic capital of Lithuania and its capture was seen as crucial to national aspirations. In the Lwów region, various Ukrainian forces remained in control of swathes of the countryside.

Poland's eastern borderlands were again the scene of great disorder and violence. Banditry and lawlessness were rampant. Irregular partisans of one side or another were common and were often little distinguishable from the poorly trained regular armies of the new nations. Ethnic tensions led to bloodshed and acts committed by individuals of a particular group were often attributed to the whole group and collective responsibility and collective punishment became the order of the day. Bolshevik sympathizers sought to spread 'revolutionary' disorder by attacking estates, houses of worship, clergy, merchants and anyone allegedly associated with the 'ruling class'.

Jewish communities were particularly vulnerable. Jews had a higher proportion of merchants and artisans who were prime targets for robbers. In addition to being targeted by common bandits and criminals, Jewish communities also fell under suspicion from elements of both the left and right. To some leftists – including some younger radical Jews – the Jewish merchants and wealthier artisans were seen as 'bourgeois' exploiters of the proletariat and peasantry while some local nationalists viewed them as supporters of Bolshevism and Russification. While some elements of the Jewish community supported one cause or another, most, like their gentile neighbours, simply sought to survive. Attacks on Jews occurred in a number of cities, including Wilno and Pińsk, and among the offenders were units of the Polish army or local militia.

Reports of massive pogroms in which hundreds of thousands of Jews died began to circulate in the Western press, sparking outrage against the new Polish government. Since no photos were available, newspapers like *The Times* of London reprinted photos of dead victims from the 1903 Kishinev pogroms in Moldova with new captions to reflect the reports. Investigation by American and British officials, however, determined that most of the reports had emerged from a single German news agency. Individuals reported dead were found alive and well at home. Investigations by official US and British commissions found little support for these lurid claims. Although documented attacks on Jews had occurred, the government had acted to stop them when it had the power to do so. Nevertheless, the stories did immense damage to Poland's international reputation that it was never able to live down. Zionist activists in Europe and America saw these reports as confirmation of the need for a separate Jewish homeland in Palestine. Radical elements among both Poles and Jews seized on the incidents as fodder for their agendas. Polish anti-Semites pointed to the reports and the Jewish response as evidence of 'Jewish ingratitude' toward a Poland which had a tradition of being hospitable to minorities. Some Jewish leaders saw this as evidence of implacable Polish hostility toward Jews. Over time, this theme would come to dominate discussion of Polish-Jewish relations, crowding out the more complex reality.

Yet the major problem was Bolshevik Russia under the dictatorship of Lenin and its reorganized Red Army. Faced with early defeats at the hands of the White forces in the ongoing civil war, the Bolsheviks turned reform of the army over to Leon Trotsky who turned the army into an effective fighting force. One by one, the White armies were gradually defeated along with various independent armies and local 'Green' forces made up of peasants who supported neither the Reds nor the Whites.

The Soviets had recognized Polish independence at the outset, even though Red forces sought to seize Polish territory and armed clashes between Polish and Bolshevik forces were common in 1919, especially in Lithuania and Belarus. Although an alliance with the White forces might have made sense and was even urged on Poland by Western diplomats, such an effort was made impossible by the refusal of the White generals to acknowledge Polish independence. Instead, they in effect insisted that the Poles were just as much rebels against the tsar as the Bolsheviks.

By early 1920, the Red Army had defeated most of the organized White forces in Ukraine and southern Russia. The Soviets had assumed control over much of eastern and central Ukraine, also eliminating free Ukrainian forces. Only a small independent force remained under Simeon Petlura in western Ukraine, though Petlura claimed leadership of the Ukrainian national movement.

Freed from facing off against the White forces, the Soviets began to mass their armies for a reckoning with Poland. In addition to eliminating Poland as a potential threat, Lenin's goal was to provide direct support for communist forces in Germany and other parts of Europe. 'Over the corpse of White Poland lies the road to world-wide conflagration!' read one order of the day to Soviet forces. Nearly a quarter of a million Red Army troops were massed in Belarus and a huge force of Red cavalry, mainly Cossacks, was poised to move on Ukraine.

Piłsudski, however, decided to strike first. After signing an alliance with Petlura's rump Ukrainian state, he sent Polish forces barrelling into Ukraine. Although the Soviets held the edge in manpower, neither side possessed sufficient forces to create a continuous frontline across the whole of the vast border region. The result would be a highly fluid war of manoeuvre in which cavalry, motorized units, and aircraft would play crucial roles. The war would be less like the trench warfare of World War I than a preview of blitzkrieg.

Polish forces in Ukraine drove the Soviets back hundreds of miles within weeks. The Poles seized the ancient city of Kiev which came under Polish control for the first time in nearly 250 years. It was not to last long.

The Ukrainians, exhausted by years of bloody warfare, showed little enthusiasm for Petlura's vision of a free Ukraine and even less for Polish troops. Worse yet, while the Poles had driven the Reds back, they had largely failed to destroy Bolshevik forces in Ukraine. As Polish momentum slowed, the Poles found themselves far from their bases of supply, amid an indifferent populace, facing a resurgent Bolshevik army that was being rapidly reinforced by a giant force of Red Cossacks. At the same time, the main Red Army strike force in Belarus under the command of the brilliant young general Mikhail Tukhachevsky broke Polish defences and advanced west.

By July 1920, Piłsudski faced a major strategic problem. Two huge Soviet spearheads were converging on central Poland from the northeast and southeast. From Belarus came Tukhachevsky and his 700,000-strong army. From Ukraine came the Cossacks of the First Red Cavalry Army under the command of Simeon Budyonny and his political commissar, Josef Stalin. Polish forces in Ukraine were falling back, trying to avoid being cut off. On both fronts, the Poles fought rear-guard actions, desperately trying to stem the Bolshevik onslaught. In the southeast, determined Polish resistance was aided by superior airpower. Although tiny by later standards, the new Polish air force, supplemented by a group of American volunteers, successfully harassed the advancing Reds and provided crucial intelligence on their movements, allowing the much smaller Polish forces to block their advances and escape encirclement time and again.

Tukhachevsky, however, was advancing relentlessly on Warsaw. By early August, Red forces were almost at the gates of the city and it seemed as if the infant Polish state would be strangled in the cradle. The Western powers were of little help. A French military mission in Warsaw provided plenty of impractical suggestions and was for the most part ignored. Britain refused to provide any assistance. Meanwhile, socialist and radical elements throughout western Europe launched a major public relations campaign in support of the Bolshevik regime. Socialist railway and dock workers blocked ships and trains going to Poland, whether they carried military supplies or humanitarian aid.

Tukhachevsky's battle plan was to strike Warsaw directly from the northeast while sending a second pincer to cross the Vistula north of the city and envelop Polish defences from the west. To counter this, Piłsudski placed a line of troops under the command of General Józef Haller around Warsaw, supplemented by citizen volunteers. Haller strengthened his line with trenches, machine-gun nests and barbed wire. Meanwhile, Piłsudski's able lieutenant, General Kazimierz Sosnkowski, had undertaken a daring reorganization of the army, shifting forces away from Tukhachevsky's pincer movement north of the city to the open land south of Warsaw.

On 13 August, the Red Army attacked Warsaw's defences. Fighting was fierce and bloody. Some Polish units broke and fled from their positions, only to be severely disciplined with summary executions of deserters. To the west of Warsaw, the undersized Polish Fifth Army, under Poland's future leader Władysław Sikorski, used a small force of armoured vehicles to put up a pugnacious defence that kept the main Soviet advance off balance. Units of students and workers fought in the trenches alongside soldiers. Priests led counter-attacks armed only with crucifixes held high to ward off the atheist foe. Warsaw's defences held and Tukhachevsky tried to shift the axis of his attack to the west. His forces would never get their chance to complete the manoeuvre.

On 16 August, Piłsudski's strike force – secretly assembled by Sosnkowski southeast of Warsaw – slammed into Tukhachevsky's southern flank. The Bolshevik attack collapsed and turned into a full-scale retreat. The Polish advance pushed toward the East Prussian border, cutting off Tukhachevsky's spearhead. Over 40,000 Soviet troops fled into German territory and were disarmed and 100,000 surrendered to the Poles.

In the south, despite delaying actions, the Red cavalry approached the lightly defended city of Lwów. On 17 August, a massive force of Bolshevik cavalry attacked a single Polish battalion at the village of Zadwórze on the approach to the city. The doomed Poles mounted a Thermopylae-like defence, repulsing repeated cavalry charges with heavy losses. Of the entire 330-man force, only twelve survived but the battle halted the Soviet advance and allowed Lwów's protectors time to organize an effective defence of the city. By the end of August, Polish forces counterattacked. At Komarów, near Zamość, Budyonny's Red Cossacks narrowly avoided complete destruction in the largest cavalry battle in modern European history. By early September Soviet forces in Ukraine were in full retreat.

On 15 September, as the battered Tukhachevsky tried to reorganize his forces on the Nieman River, the Poles struck again, shattering Soviet lines with a combination of motorized troops, cavalry, infantry, and aircraft. Tukhachevsky's army began to disintegrate. His troops mutinied and began looting local villages and attacking Jews.

At this point Lenin was forced to sue for peace. The Poles accepted and although some wanted to march on Moscow, the Polish army did not have the strength or resources to destroy Soviet power. By early 1921, the two sides hammered out the Treaty of Riga which demarcated the Polish-Soviet frontier. A large swathe of modern-day Belarus and Ukraine were added to Poland, including the historic cities of Lwów, Tarnopol, Pińsk, and Sarny.

The Polish-Soviet War would prove to be a foretaste of things to come. While most military thinkers looked to more and more massive fortifications, Władysław Sikorski, who had led Polish mechanized forces during the conflict, wrote a treatise on mobile warfare that was published in French. It was largely ignored by most generals in the West, though it was read avidly by a young French officer who had participated in the French military mission to Poland. This officer, named Charles de Gaulle, wrote his own contribution to the subject. Although neither book was popular, both were read with interest in Germany and would help pioneer a new way of thinking about warfare that would have disastrous consequences for Europe.

In the aftermath of the war, Piłsudski sought to settle scores with the Lithuanians who had supported the Soviets and occupied the city of Wilno after the Soviets took it from the Poles. In October 1920, Polish forces seized the city and the surrounding area under the flimsy pretext of being a mutinous army unit. Although this high-handed act was largely ignored by the rest of the world, it poisoned relations with Lithuania for the next seventy years.

An equally messy situation arose in Upper Silesia, where the local Polish majority rose up in revolt three times under the leadership of Wojciech Korfanty in an attempt to be united with Poland. The Poles clashed with members of the German *Freikorps*, a force made up of former soldiers bent on protecting Germany from threats inside and out. In 1921, Upper Silesia was partitioned between Germany and Poland, with the Poles receiving a lesser share of the territory but more of the industrial and mining facilities.

Of the two main competing visions of Poland, neither was realized. Dmowski's vision of a smaller, ethnically homogeneous state was frustrated by the acquisition of large eastern territories with significant minority populations, especially Jews and Ukrainians. At the same time, Piłsudski's vision of a Polish-led multi-ethnic federation with Lithuanians and Ukrainians was frustrated by the bad blood that resulted from the wars of 1919–20. Poland acquired just enough territory from Ukraine and Lithuania to stimulate the resentments of nationalists in both camps but not enough to claim significant power over either group as Polish subjects.

Problems of a New Nation

Poland had regained its independence, but little else. Nearly six years of war and occupation had wrecked much of the economy. Basic infrastructure was a shambles. So many farms had been looted or destroyed that the country could not feed itself. Although American food aid, administered by future US President Herbert Hoover, saved millions from starvation, malnutrition was one of the leading causes of death especially among children and the elderly. Diseases such as typhoid and cholera reached epidemic proportions. Banditry and lawlessness were common in many parts of the country as authorities struggled to provide basic services.

Structural problems were even more serious and almost every facet of public life had to be rebuilt from scratch. The economic legacy of the Partitions meant that each zone was oriented toward markets that either no longer existed or were closed to Polish exports. The textile factories of Łódź and Białystok had produced cloth for the Russian marketplace. The farmers of Wielkopolska had shipped their produce to Berlin and the German market. Both of these markets were now gone. Several different currencies were in circulation from the three partitioning powers and money printed for the occupation zones. All of these had to be recalled and reorganized. Three different legal systems were in place. The Russian partition even used a different rail gauge so all the railroad lines had to be converted to a standard gauge.

Since in the Russian and German zones of partitioned Poland, Poles had been kept out of most administrative positions, the only cadre of experienced civil servants was found in Austrian Galicia. So officials with a modicum of administrative experience were those whose outlook was shaped by the sclerotic Austrian bureaucracy, whose major contribution to civilization had been to inspire the work of Czech author Franz Kafka.

The place of minorities in the new nation also presented a major problem. A third of Poland's population was not ethnically Polish. After 123 years of foreign rule, Poles were eager to express national pride and relatively unconcerned over the effect of such displays on minorities, such as Ukrainians, who had lost their own bid for national independence. Although each minority group had a different relationship to the new Poland, in each group there were elements that were hostile as well as those who sought accommodation and acceptance. Most minorities simply wanted to get on with their lives and took a cautious approach to any extremes.

Five million Ukrainians constituted the largest single minority in Poland and in many ways it was the most difficult to handle. They were heavily concentrated in the southeast where they made up a majority of the rural population in many areas. The bad blood between Poles and Ukrainians was fuelled by economic conflicts between Polish landowners and Ukrainian peasants and resentment over the loss of Lwów in 1918–19. This would be further exacerbated by the government's policy of giving farms to Polish army veterans in eastern Poland amid large Ukrainian and Belarusan populations. Unlike areas of central and eastern Ukraine where national feeling was not well developed, the region of western Ukraine, formerly ruled by Austria and now by Poland, was a hotbed of militant Ukrainian nationalism.

Belarusans and other smaller east Slavic groups (Lemkos, Bojkos and Hutsuls) had a far less developed sense of national identity. As late as 1931, the census recorded that over a quarter million people in eastern Poland expressed no national identity at all and were simply listed as *tutejszy* or locals (literally, 'the people from here'). Most were Ortho- dox or Eastern-rite Catholics and their primary loyalty remained to family, church and village. While they lacked the simmering resent- ment of a group denied full self-determination, Belarusans were also largely apathetic toward the Polish state, neither despising it nor feeling strong loyalty.

The same could not be said for Germans. Following Polish inde- pendence, many Germans preferred emigration to life in Poland. Yet, about 750,000 ethnic Germans remained in Poland (outside of the Free City of Danzig), the majority in western Poland. Unlike other mino- rities, the Germans had a powerful, self-appointed protector in the next-door German state. Although many Germans would ultimately remain loyal to their new country a significant proportion were later seduced by Nazi propaganda.

THE JEWISH COMMUNITY

Of all the minorities in Poland, the one that has attracted the most attention has been the Jewish community. By 1939, over 3.3 million Jews lived in Poland, constituting ten per cent of the population. This percentage was much higher in cities, especially in eastern Poland. Warsaw had the largest Jewish community, with forty per cent of the city being Jewish. Pińsk in the eastern marches was eighty per cent Jewish. Significant numbers of Jews also resided in rural towns and villages. The *shtetls* in these communities ranged from a few hundred inhabitants to a few thousands. Some were prosperous and supported a variety of community institutions, others too poor or too small to even support a synagogue.

Although Zionism and socialism had made significant inroads, the majority of Jews remained traditional and culturally conservative. While Hebrew was increasingly common among the Jewish elite, Yiddish was still the primary language of everyday life. Although most Jews knew at least some Polish, the majority did not speak it well and some did not speak it at all. About a tenth of the Jewish population, however, was highly assimilated into the Polish mainstream, preferred to speak Polish, and was well represented in the Polish cultural, academic and professional elite. Jews made up nearly half of the country's doctors and lawyers.

Jews could be found in every socio-economic category from the richest to the poorest. On average, Jews were slightly better off than Poles, Belarusins and Ukrainians, the majority of whom remained peasant farmers. Most Jews remained small merchants or craftsmen, but this ran the gamut from prosperous store owners to peddlers and tinkers who eked out a living selling small items to peasants.

Jewish cultural life flourished. There were about thirty dailies and over 130 Jewish periodicals in circulation prior to the outbreak of the war in 1939, not counting many smaller local publications. Assimilated Polish Jews made major contributions to a shared Polish and Jewish literature. Aphorist Stanisław Jerzy Lec, Julian Tuwim, leader of the Skamander group of experimental poets, and the brilliant writer and illustrator Bruno Schulz were well known and highly regarded among both the Jewish and Christian intellectual elite. Author and children's welfare expert Janusz Korczak, pioneered new ideas of child care. He was also the author of *King Matt the First*, one of the most widely read children's books in pre-war Poland. Yiddish-language theatre, music and film were widespread in pre-war Poland, forming a large 'niche' market.

The great problem of pre-war Jewish life could be found in the contradictory impulses of wanting to be included in Polish life and yet wishing to remain wholly separate. Polish Christian society, itself deeply divided on the place and role of minorities, experienced similar contradictions of wishing for assimilation and seeking to keep Jews at arms' length. Economic hardships, especially those brought on by the Depression, heightened tensions and increased anti-Semitism. Polish nationalists attempted to stage periodic local boycotts of Jewish-owned businesses and campaigns to 'buy Polish'. All of these efforts failed and much of local trade, particularly in eastern Poland, remained in Jewish hands. Yet the threat of boycotts and the generally poor economic conditions ensured that Jewish small businesses usually struggled to survive.

Education was another flashpoint and groups of Jewish and Christian students had frequent scuffles that sometimes resulted in more serious violence. In 1930, Jewish students in Wilno killed a nationalist student, sparking an anti-Jewish riot. With space in universities limited, in the late 1930s some nationalists made efforts to place quotas on Jewish students and to restrict Jews who did get in to special 'ghetto benches' in the back of the classroom. At schools where such measures were implemented, Jewish students refused to sit and were joined by sympathetic Polish students in standing throughout the lectures.

Feelings of antagonism went both ways, as some Jews felt nothing but contempt for Poles and the notion of going to Palestine to build a possible future Jewish state grew more attractive. At the same time, there were numerous examples of good relations and friendships that went across ethnic and religious lines. Politics also made for alliances. The Jewish Bund worked with the PPS. The right-wing Zionist Revisionists trained with the Polish army and joined with nationalist paramilitary groups in battling left-wing opponents. The majority of Poles and Jews, however, remained indifferent to one another, interacting only in limited circumstances. This was not so much a result of antagonism but of a profound sense of difference. Each community lived in a self-contained world of its own and rarely if ever needed to interact with the other.

The situation of Jews in Poland was by no means the worst in Europe and was clearly superior to the situation in most neighbouring countries. It is possible that over time, Poles and Jews would have worked out better mutual relations, muddling their way through good times and bad side by side. Both communities and the country as a whole lacked leaders of stature and vision who could have made this possible. Tragically, neither Poles nor Jews would have the time to resolve their differences.

The Crisis of Politics

The effort to create a new nation was first and foremost a political contest. Although Poland had ancient democratic traditions on which to draw, its leaders were formed under the painful times of the partitions in which political freedom was either non-existent or severely curtailed. Many, like Piłsudski, came with a conspiratorial mindset. Party structures were weak and leaders inexperienced. Parties of the right were dominated by Dmowski's National Democrats (or Endeks), which was the largest single party in the country. More traditional parties representing the old aristocracy were largely sidelined and found little common cause with the Endeks, especially on economic and social issues. The most robust party on the left was Piłsudski's Polish Socialist Party (PPS). Poland's communist party never presented a serious challenge since its unwavering goal of extinguishing Polish independence and uniting Poland with the Soviet Union guaranteed universal dislike. Poland's Peasant Party was deeply divided between a smaller leftist faction and a larger centre-right grouping. A wide array of small parties and those fielded by national minorities played a secondary or supporting role.

Because of the personal popularity of Piłsudski as a military leader, his rightist opponents worked hard to limit the power of the executive branch. As a result, the Polish Constitutions of 1919 and 1921 vested the strongest power in the parliament or *sejm*. As a result of this, Piłsudski declined to stand for the presidency in the 1922 elections and retired temporarily from public life the following year. The *sejm* and the country were deeply divided by party and regional rivalries. Neither the constitution nor the actions of the earlier governments enjoyed the full trust and support of the electorate. Corruption and political gamesmanship seemed to dominate public life. In 1922, the *sejm* elected Gabriel Narutowicz as the first president of Poland. Shortly after his election, the new president was shot and killed by a deranged rightist who believed Narutowicz was a tool of the Jews.

Although this crime shocked Polish society, it did nothing to halt the political infighting in Warsaw. Although some economic reforms were started, the currency (the *złoty*) stabilized, and the basic form of the civil service was laid down, conflicts and changes of government hamstrung efforts to put Poland back together. Eighty parties vied for power and fourteen governments rose and fell in less than seven years. Politicking was also rife within the army, the one major institution that had the unquestioned admiration of most sectors of Polish society. In addition to party and regional divisions, army officers were divided into a majority who favoured Piłsudski and felt he had not been treated with due gratitude and those who felt he was too powerful. In 1926, the appointment of an anti-Piłsudskite general as war minister sparked a chain of events that would lead to a dramatic change in government.

THE MAN ON A WHITE HORSE

Piłsudski was a complex man who did not reveal his intentions in public. Although rarely seeking glory for himself, he was also convinced that he had a particular mission to save Poland. In interwar Europe, he was a rare combination of a convinced socialist and an

Józef Piłsudski

ardent nationalist whose concept of nation had little to do with race or ethnicity. He was capable both of great subtlety and harsh violence. Though intensely political, he despised the normal give and take of democratic politics but never offered any kind of clear alternative to that system.

The political crisis of 1926 seems to have brought to a head two major issues for Piłsudski: first, the possibility that his own supporters would be purged from the leadership of the armed forces; and second, his disgust with the corruption and infighting of Polish politics which he saw as harkening back to the days of the *liberum veto*, when parliamentary politics tore Old Poland apart and led to the partitions. Piłsudski noted 'Poland is the victim of her Parliamentary system. The Government loses nine-tenths of its force from pacts made with party groups.' The *sejm* was 'a sterile, jabbering, howling thing that engenders such boredom as makes the very flies die of sheer disgust.'

In May 1926, backed by three regiments of the army, Piłsudski launched a coup and marched on Warsaw. Sympathetic socialist railwaymen halted loyalist forces from reaching the city. After three days of fighting, the government abdicated, leaving Piłsudski the virtual dictator of Poland.

Piłsudski's first concern was to legitimize his actions. He had his sympathizers in parliament elect him president of Poland. Then he declined the post, claiming that it required a man of a temperament very different from his. A chemist from Lwów, Ignacy Mościcki (1867–1946), was elected president in his stead. Piłsudski took the positions of prime minister, minister of war, and inspector general of the armed forces. From these posts, he would rule the country often from behind the scenes, through the actions of subordinates.

Although originally supported by the Polish Socialist Party, he failed to create a fully socialist regime and soon lost their support. In its place he created a non-party governmental bloc, a sort of anti-party. Aside from supporting Piłsudski, the platform of the new political organization was rather vague – it supported efficient government and a disinterest in politics for its own sake. The coup restored economic confidence in country, but did little to resolve the political crisis.

In 1928, using a mix of pressure and cajoling, Piłsudski's non-party bloc won the largest number of seats in the parliament, but was insufficient to form a strong government. A series of Piłsudskite governments rose and fell. The parties of the centre and left banded together to oppose Piłsudski and demanded an end to the dictatorship. At one rally in Kraków, 30,000 demonstrators turned out to support their call. In 1930, Piłsudski dissolved parliament and called new elections in which direct pressure and ballot stuffing helped to ensure a victory for his non-party bloc. Thereafter, Marshal Piłsudski would be ruler of Poland in all but name.

UNDER THE MARSHAL'S BATON

Piłsudski ruled Poland for nine years until his death from cancer in 1935. This period was one of significant achievement and weakness for the new Poland. The country was able to re-integrate its economic, legal, transportation, and administrative systems. After 123 years of division this was no small achievement.

The armed forces were likewise integrated from disparate parts. The army in particular enjoyed high prestige. Poland also created its first modern navy, which, although modest in size, was designed to counter the Soviet naval presence in the Baltic Sea. The Polish air force was significantly ahead of its time – by the early 1930s Poland had the world's only all-metal air force. At the same time, Piłsudski's idiosyncrasies left the armed forces with significant structural problems. Bored by detail, Piłsudski created a two-track system in which peacetime administration of the armed forces was handled by the ministry of war, while wartime command was the task of the inspector general of the armed forces. This retarded the creation of a modern, effective general staff and weakened command and control. Moreover, for political reasons, many talented officers, such as Władysław Sikorski, were sidelined. As in political life, Piłsudski surrounded himself with yes-men. While some of them were quite talented, none of them had the breadth of vision necessary to lead the country effectively.

Piłsudski was most effective in the realm of foreign policy. He guided a careful middle path between Poland's two main threats – the Soviet Union and a resurgent Germany. Poland's alliance with France proved increasingly fraught with problems as French politics entered a time of fragmentation and frequent shifts in government left the French alliance system in central and eastern Europe in disarray. With the French proving increasingly untrustworthy, Poland strengthened traditional alliances with Rumania and Hungary.

In the 1920s, Poland's border with the Soviet Union was the scene of significant problems. The Soviets sought constantly to disrupt life in the border regions and sent groups of guerillas into Poland to stir up trouble among ethnic minorities, undermine government services and gather intelligence. In response, Poland developed a fortified zone on its eastern frontier and created the Border Defence Corps, a 30,000-man force trained in 'unconventional warfare' – diversion, intelligence and counterintelligence, surveillance and halting cross-border incursions. To help counter the Soviet threat, Poland developed closer relations with Japan and often shared intelligence on Soviet activities with their Asian counterparts.

Faced with large, hostile enemies and few friends, Poland also created an extremely effective intelligence service. In the late 1920s and early 1930s, a group of young mathematicians from the university of Poznań cracked supposed unbreakable German military codes. They had equal success deciphering Soviet codes.

Diplomacy was not neglected either. In 1932, Poland signed a non-aggression pact with the Soviet Union that helped normalize relations and reduced the tensions and the armed incidents along the border. Adolf Hitler's rise to power in Germany in 1933 was viewed with great alarm. Nazi rhetoric was extremely anti-Polish and one of Hitler's major goals was to regain 'lost' German territory in Poland and to create additional 'living space' for Germany. Piłsudski correctly foresaw the potential threat this posed and secretly proposed a joint Polish-French military operation to remove Hitler from power. French leaders rejected the Polish idea as mad warmongering. Faced with France's unwillingness to confront the aggressive new Nazi regime, Piłsudski sought to buy time for Poland and negotiated a non-aggression pact with Germany in 1934 that helped to reduce tensions and normalize trade.

The country's experience during the Polish-Soviet War had convinced Polish leaders that while they had some control over the port of the Free City of Danzig (Gdańsk), real access to the sea would only be accomplished with a port entirely under Polish control. In 1927, the fishing village of Gdynia along the small strip of Polish coastline north of Gdańsk was chosen as the site for a new port. A new city sprang up overnight. Engineers designed the most modern facilities for loading and unloading ships. By the late 1930s, Gdynia had 100,000 inhabitants and had surpassed Gdańsk as the busiest port on the Baltic Sea.

On the economic front, Piłsudski-led governments had a mixed record. Economic stability in the late 1920s caused a quick expansion of the economy and brought a certain degree of prosperity to Poland. But the Depression of the 1930s hit Poland very hard. The government's conservative monetary policy kept public debt low but provided little public spending that would help jumpstart the economy. Poland practised a form of 'state capitalism' in which the government held monopolies in key sectors (alcohol, tobacco, matches, salt, and lottery) and owned a wide variety of other industrial concerns in the areas of armaments, iron, coal, chemicals, and metallurgy to name a few. On the one hand, this helped to foster the growth of industries that were considered vital to the national interest or which had a direct impact on daily life. On the other hand, although firms were usually managed by businesspeople rather than bureaucrats, the system encouraged inefficiency and corruption. Private businesses often had difficulty competing directly with state-owned firms, especially for public contracts.

Conditions for Polish workers were quite good considering the country's general underdevelopment. Piłsudski and many of his associates had a strong socialist bent and enacted very advanced ideas for pensions and social insurance. The problem was that this increased labour costs for fledgling companies and took away one of Poland's potential assets – a cheap workforce. Agriculture continued to have serious problems. Land reform plans were only marginally effective in putting farms into the hands of peasants and pressure on rural areas from an expanding population increased social tensions. Poland's population grew dramatically as it had before World War I. Unlike the pre-independence period, however, emigration provided no safety valve. In 1924, the United States cut off immigration of 'racially undesirable' peoples from central and eastern Europe. German hostility also ended the tradition of working in the industrial regions of the Ruhr. Other countries such as France, Canada, and Australia accepted some Polish immigrants, but never enough to make a significant difference. Polish authorities sought additional destinations for immigration, including exotic locales such as Peru. Jewish emigrants were encouraged to go to Palestine even at the risk of British displeasure. Some Poles even considered the fantastical possibility of gaining the former German colony of Cameroon in central Africa. Nevertheless, these schemes made little difference to the country's demographic problem. Rural populations were expanding and the industrial sector simply could not absorb the excess fast enough.

Piłsudski did little to create a political system to deal with these underlying issues. Opposition figures were sometimes arrested or sent into exile, although police repression of political activists was haphazard and farcical in comparison to Stalin's USSR or Hitler's Germany. Political relations were largely frozen in place. City and provincial elections took place on a regular basis and there was less interference by the government in local politics.

Minority rights were generally respected under Piłsudski. Mainstream minority parties tended to support his non-party bloc. The biggest of these was the conservative Jewish party, Agudat Israel. In general, Piłsudski was friendly toward Jews and promoted Jews in the ranks of the military. The same could not be said for Ukrainians. Poland took an assimilationist approach to the Ukrainians in southeastern Poland and colonized areas with Polish settlers. Throughout the 1920s and early 1930s the radical and violent Ukrainian Military Organization, supported by Germany and Czechoslovakia, carried out terror attacks against Polish estates, government buildings, Polish officials, and fellow Ukrainians viewed as too accommodating toward the government. In response, Piłsudski unleashed the army in a so-called pacification campaign. The pacification attacked the guilty along with the innocent. More often than not, Polish soldiers sacked Ukrainian libraries and schools rather than seeking real terrorists. While the campaign resulted in little loss of life, it did irreparable damage to efforts to turn the Ukrainian minority into loyal citizens of Poland.

CULTURE AND THE ARTS

Like many newly independent countries, Poland put a major emphasis on education. Basic literacy rates grew dramatically and higher education, while still rare by today's standards, was strengthened and opportunities expanded across the board. Newspaper and book publishing expanded greatly, not merely in Polish, but also in Yiddish, Hebrew and German.

After more than a century of division and partition, Polish artists often strove for a more integrated style. The Art Deco movement, whose arrival in Poland almost coincided with independence, had a significant impact on Polish arts and blended seamlessly with a growing interest in Polish folk arts – especially in the 'Zakopane style' – and in the art of the everyday. These Polish achievements came to the notice of European contemporaries. At the 1925 L'Exposition des Arts Decoratifs et Industriels Modernes held in Paris, Poles won the largest number of prizes for their original work and designs. The interwar years were also the 'time of the avant-garde', which appeared most clearly in the works of the Polish Formist group whose members adapted features of Futurism, Cubism and Expressionism. Stanisław Ignacy Witkiewicz (known as 'Witkacy') and Leon Chwistek were its leading figures. Polish film also had it first flowering. Filmmakers produced both historical epics and avant-garde works (many of which did not survive the war).

Polish scholarship and science had an opportunity to develop relatively unfettered during the period of independence. Polish mathematics was particularly significant. The young mathematicians from the university of Poznań who cracked the 'unbreakable' German military codes were perhaps the best known. Equally important, however, was Jan Łukasiewicz, a specialist in mathematical logic who developed a three-valued propositional calculus (true/false/don't know). This resulted in the idea of a 'truth table' by which all the possible inputs and outputs of a logic system can be tabulated. Another major contribution was his development of 'Polish Notation' which simplifies the expression of logical and arithmetic relationships by eliminating parentheses and other unnecessary symbols. Also important was Stefan Banach who pioneered functional analysis.

The Regime of the Clerks

On 12 May, 1935, Marshal Józef Piłsudski died of cancer. His passing brought forth an outpouring of genuine grief. The old marshal had saved the country from destruction in 1920 and while many deeply opposed his handling of the political opposition, he had symbolized the nation's rebirth.

His successors were a group of his former associates – principally, President Ignacy Mościcki, General Eduard Śmigły-Rydz, and Foreign Minister Józef Beck. Collectively, they were known as the 'regime of the colonels' as several held that rank. Each had done well in a role subordinate to Piłsudski but none had the ability, vision, or the personal authority to fill the old marshal's shoes. Of these three, Śmigły-Rydz as commander of the armed forces was acknowledged as the 'first person' of the republic. Piłsudski had chosen him based on the impression that of all the generals he was the least political. This proved a mistaken assumption.

Piłsudski left no real political legacy. There was no 'Piłsudskism.' The old marshal had improvised, changed course, and acted as the situation merited, but there was no coherent philosophy behind his actions other than what he perceived to be the good of the Polish state. As a life-long conspirator he had often worked by misdirection and kept his motives as secret as possible. The limited men who followed him had no template to follow, and there were left to guess what the marshal would have done in this situation or that. Historian Jan Karski likened it to an office where the boss suddenly dies without leaving instructions. The clerks continue to show up for work every day and open the office, but they lack any sort of direction. Hence, they were more like the 'regime of the clerks.'

The regime of the clerks inherited the pro-government adherents of the Sanacja regime, but lacking the marshal's presence, they needed to broaden their base, especially as the opposition began to get better organized. They made a decision to appeal to the rightist parties, especially the National Democrats. To do this, the regime began to emphasize anti-Semitism, proposing a law to ban ritual slaughter (which was later dropped without a vote being cast) and attempted other measures of a similar nature. Government leaders spoke with open contempt about the Jewish community and encouraged immigration to Palestine and elsewhere. This effort backfired. The Polish right had bitterly opposed Piłsudski and his henchmen and it would take more than a few anti-Semitic actions to convince them otherwise. Fresh in the minds of many on the right were incidents of violence directed at right-wing political rallies where police beat and even killed demonstrators. At the same time, this overt anti-Semitism alienated many of the regime's supporters or potential supporters, including Jewish minority parties and many moderates. These disparate forces would band together in the 1938 local elections to hand the ruling clique a series of defeats at the ballot box.

Nor were the Jews the only group deeply dissatisfied with the regime. The peasants were increasingly restive over the poor economic conditions and lack of meaningful land reform. The demonstrations of 1936–37 were well organized and though they faced a severe police response, the peasant demonstrators remained remarkably cohesive.

The regime's effort to turn toward more authoritarian rule proved a mistake as it had neither the resources nor the support to institute a real regime of repression. The press, for example, freely published accounts of police abuse and excoriated the mistakes of the government. At the same time, the new leaders squandered any opportunity to win the trust of the majority of the population by building on the affection felt for their former leader. It is likely that the regime would have fallen had international events not intervened.

The Road to War

The Munich crisis of 1938 proved a major turning point for Poland. The Czechs and the Poles had long been at loggerheads over issues dating back to 1918. However, facing the Nazi threat, the two countries took steps to mend fences and create a united front against Germany. The proposed alliance would have returned Cieszyn to Polish control and given Poland part ownership of the Skoda defence works. In return, the Poles would agree to intervene against Germany in case of an attack on Czechoslovakia. This promising development might have at least forced Hitler to delay his plans for conquest given the relative weakness of the German army at that time, but it was never to be realized. French and British leaders instead decided to buy Hitler off with a piece of Czech territory that included nearly all of the country's fortifications in return for guarantees of peace from Hitler.

Frozen out of the Munich Pact, the Polish government moved to secure the Cieszyn region and keep its vital road and rail links out of German hands. While the region had been seized by the Czechs by force at the end of World War I, the move made it appear that the Poles were helping promote the destruction of Czechoslovakia. As Hitler prepared to gobble up the rest of the Czechoslovakia, the Poles also supported the Hungarian move to take control of the trans-Carpathian region of far eastern Czechoslovakia. This area had a strong Ukrainian presence and its leaders looked to Germany for support. In 1939, they attempted to create an independent Ukrainian state under German influence. Polish and Hungarian special forces disrupted this move and allowed the Hungarian authorities to assert their control. This created a common border with friendly Hungary.

Prior to 1938, the Czechs had believed that Hitler would strike first at Poland, while the Poles believed he would move against Czechoslovakia. The Polish assessment proved correct. The Poles also assumed it would take the Germans a few years to fully absorb the Czech state before moving on to other conquests. This proved a serious mistake. In the spring of 1939, after Hitler violated the Munich Accords by occupying all of Czechoslovakia, the Germans began to issue threats to Poland, demanding the Free City of Danzig and even the 'Polish Corridor'. Unlike the Czechs, however, the Poles had no intention of knuckling under. Shocked by Hitler's violation of Munich, the British now entertained the idea of giving Poland security guarantees and the Anglo-French alliance at last began to close ranks as Hitler's threats escalated.

At home, the population rallied around the government in the face of the German threat. Anti-Semitic rhetoric – associated with the Germans – faded from the public scene as Poles of all nationalities drew closer in the face of the coming storm.

CHAPTER EIGHT

War, Occupation and the Holocaust,
1939–46

In late August 1939, wheat and rye were ripening fast under the Polish sun and the world was moving toward war. Hitler's ultimatums to Poland had been refused and German armies were massing on Poland's border. On 23 August, Nazi Germany and the Soviet Union, long in secret contact despite their apparent hostility, signed a non-aggression pact aimed at Poland. A hidden provision of the pact called for a partition of Poland by the forces of Stalin and Hitler. After the fiasco of Munich, however, the British and French gave guarantees that they would defend Poland. Nevertheless, Poland's allies bullied her into halting full mobilization to avoid 'provoking' Hitler. Although Polish intelligence had identified the location and disposition of eighty per cent of the German army, the failure to mobilize fully thanks to Allied pressure would prove fatal.

The Polish high command understood what it was up against. Poland could not stop Germany's industrial might alone. Despite heroic sacrifices by Polish society to modernize the military, the budget of the German air force alone was ten times greater than the entire Polish defence budget. Poland's main goal was to force France and Britain into the war and this meant preventing Hitler from scoring a quick victory or taking a piece of Polish territory and declaring the war over. Poland's strategy was to fight on the borders, engage the German army immediately, and then gradually withdraw to southeastern Poland, where substantial stockpiles of supplies had been placed in reserve. With the friendly Rumanian border close by, Polish forces could be resupplied by British and French ships docking at the Black Sea port of Constanţa.

Just prior to the start of hostilities, the leaders of Polish military intelligence invited their French and British counterparts to a meeting outside of Warsaw. To their stunned colleagues, the Poles unveiled the secret that would ultimately help win the war against Hitler. Polish codebreakers had cracked the Nazis' supposedly unbreakable 'Enigma' military code. The Poles provided the Allies with full details and working models of the German machine and their decryption device, a protocomputer called the *bomba*. During the war, the Polish device was refined further by British codebreakers, and would provide the Allies with vital information on German military operations.

Hitler's strategy was to win within a week to ten days. With the help of a Soviet invasion from the east, the Nazi plan was to inflict terror on the population and break Poland's will to resist. As he gathered his generals, he ordered them to 'kill without pity or mercy all men, women, and children of Polish descent or language ... only in this way can we achieve the living space we need.' Mobile killing squads would follow the main body of troops, shooting prisoners and any Poles who might organize resistance. On the night of 31 August, Nazi agents staged a mock Polish attack on a German radio station in Silesia, dressing concentration camp prisoners in Polish uniforms and then shooting them. Hitler declared that Germany would respond to 'Polish aggression.'

Black September

The war began at 4.45 a.m. The battleship *Schleswig-Holstein* was moored at the port of the Free City of Danzig on a 'courtesy visit' near the Polish transit station of Westerplatte. The station was on a sandy, narrow peninsula in the harbour, garrisoned by a small force of 182 men. At 4.45 a.m. on 1 September, 1939, the giant guns of the battleship opened up on the Polish outpost at point-blank range. As dawn broke, Danzig SS men advanced on Westerplatte expecting to find only the pulverized remains of the Polish garrison. Instead, they found the defenders very much alive. In moments the German attack was cut to pieces. Further attacks followed. The Polish defenders duelled the mighty battleship with a small field gun. At the Polish Post

Office, postal workers and Polish boy scouts held off Nazi forces for most of the day before surrendering. The post office defenders were summarily executed. A similar fate awaited Polish railway workers south of Gdańsk after they foiled an attempt to use an armoured train to seize a bridge over the Vistula.

German forces and their Danzig and Slovak allies attacked Poland across most sectors of the border. In the north, they attacked the Polish Corridor. In southern and central Poland, Nazi armoured spearheads attacked toward Łódź and Kraków. In the skies, German planes commenced terror bombing of cities and villages. Everywhere were scenes of unbelievable fighting and carnage. Polish forces defending the borders gave a good account of themselves. At Mokra, near Często-chowa, the Nazi 4th Panzer Division attacked two cavalry regiments. The Polish defenders drew the Germans into a tank trap and destroyed over fifty tanks and armoured cars.

Where the Poles were in position, they usually got the better of the fight, but due to the delay in mobilization, their forces were too few to defend all sectors. The effectiveness of German mechanized forces proved to be their ability to bypass Polish strong points, cutting them off and isolating them. By 3 September, although the country was cheered by the news that France and Britain had declared war on Germany, the Poles were unable to contain the Nazi breakthroughs. Army Łódź, despite heroic resistance, was pushed back and lost contact with its neighbouring units. German tanks drove through the gap directly toward Warsaw. In the Polish Corridor, Polish forces tried to stage a fighting withdrawal but suffered heavy losses to German tanks and divebombers. In the air, the outnumbered Polish fighter command fought with skill and courage, especially around Warsaw. Nevertheless, Nazi aircraft systematically targeted Polish civilians, especially refugees. Bombing and shelling sent tens of thousands of people fleeing for their lives, crowding the roads, hindering military traffic.

On 5 September, the Polish High Command, fearing Warsaw was threatened, decided to relocate to southeastern Poland. This proved a huge mistake as the commanders soon lost contact with their major field armies. Warsaw itself was thrown into panic at the news.

Although the situation was grim, it was not yet hopeless. Following the High Command's departure, the mayor of Warsaw Stefan Starzyński and General Walerian Czuma rallied the city's defenders. Citizen volunteers built barricades and trenches. An initial German attack on the city's outskirts was repulsed.

The German advance took little account of Army Poznań which had been bypassed on the Nazi's quick drive toward Warsaw. On 8–9 September, Army Poznań counterattacked against the flank of the German forces moving on Warsaw. The Nazi advance halted in the face of the initial Polish success on the River Bzura. The Nazis' superiority in tanks and aircraft, however, allowed them to regroup and stop Army Poznań's southward push. The counterattack turned into a battle of encirclement. Although some forces managed to escape to Warsaw, by 13 September the Battle of Bzura was over. The delay, however, had allowed Warsaw to marshal its defences, turning the perimeter of the city into a series of makeshift forts. In the south, German forces had captured Kraków early in the campaign but their advance slowed down as they approached Lwów. The defenders of Westerplatte had surrendered after seven days of fighting against overwhelming odds, but the city of Gdynia and the Hel Peninsula still held as Polish coastal batteries kept German warships at bay.

By the middle of September, Polish losses had been severe and the German advance had captured half of the country. The high command's fateful decision to leave Warsaw had resulted in more than a week of confusion, rescued only by the courage of Army Poznań's doomed counterattack. By the middle of September, however, Polish defences were stiffening. Local commanders and army-level generals now directed troops around the key bastions of Warsaw, the seacoast, and Lwów. German losses began to rise. Small Polish units isolated by the rapid advance regrouped and struck at vulnerable rear-area forces.

This thin ray of hope, however, was extinguished on 17 September when Red Army forces crossed Poland's eastern border as Stalin moved to assist his Nazi ally and to seize his share of Polish territory. Nearly all Polish troops had been withdrawn from the eastern border to fight the Nazi onslaught. Only a few units of the Border Defence Corps aided by local volunteers stood in the way of Stalin's might. Although often outnumbered 100 to 1, these forces refused to surrender.

One such force commanded by Lt. Jan Bolbot was attacked by tens of thousands of Red Army troops in their bunkers near Sarny. Bolbot's men cut down thousands of Soviet attackers. Finally, the communists piled debris around the bunkers and set them on fire. The lieutenant telephoned to his commander to report that his bunker was on fire and filled with thick smoke but that all his men were still at their posts and shooting back. Then the line went dead. The entire Sarny garrison fought to the last man.

Polish defences in the southeast fell apart as formations were ordered to fall back across the relatively friendly Rumanian and Hungarian borders to avoid capture. Fighting raged around Warsaw, the fortress of Modlin and around the seacoast. On 28 September, Warsaw capitulated. Polish forces on the Hel Peninsula staved off surrender until 1 October. In the marshes of east central Poland, Group Polesie continued to mount effective resistance until 5 October. When this final organized force gave up, its ammunition was gone and its active duty soldiers were outnumbered by the prisoners it had taken.

Throughout the first two and half weeks of September 1939, Germany threw its entire air force, all panzer forces, and all of its frontline infantry and artillery against Poland. Its border with France was held by a relatively thin force of second and third string divisions. The French army, from its secure base behind the Maginot Line, had overwhelming superiority in men, tanks, aircraft, and artillery. A concerted push into western Germany would have resulted in disaster for Hitler. Yet the French stood aside and did nothing. The British were equally inactive, sending their bombers to drop propaganda leaflets over a few German cities. Had the Allies acted, the bloodiest and most terrible war in human history could have been averted.

THE BEGINNING OF THE OCCUPATION

The campaign against Poland was conducted with a savagery previously unknown in modern European warfare. The scale and extent of the brutality practised in occupied Poland far exceeded anything experienced in other occupied countries of western Europe. Polish civilians and prisoners of war were systematically shot by German and Soviet forces. Although the Nazi SS and *Einsatzgruppen* (or Special Action

Units) and the Soviet NKVD committed the worst crimes, regular army and air forces of both totalitarian states were full and willing participants in the slaughter. The German use of Einsatzgruppen in Poland was a test run. Later these same units would play an even more terrible part in the Holocaust of European Jewry.

Poland's eastern third was taken by the Soviets, while the central and western parts of the country were under Nazi occupation. Western Poland, Silesia, and the Polish Corridor were to be directly incorporated into the Reich. Its Polish and Jewish population were to be killed, deported, or, in the case of some Poles, Germanized. Central Poland was organized into the 'General Government' ruled by a Nazi functionary in Kraków.

Those members of the Polish elite that the Nazis arrested but did not kill were shipped to concentration camps. For example, many of the clergy seized in western Poland were shipped to Stutthof near the Baltic Sea or to Dachau in Germany. It was soon apparent to the Nazi leadership that the scale of their plans would overwhelm their existing systems of prison and concentration camps, so a series of new camps was created. The most infamous of these was located near Kraków in the town of Oświęcim, known by its German name, Auschwitz. The Auschwitz camp was designed to house Polish political prisoners and a workforce of inmates built the initial camp. As in Dachau and Stutthof, the camp guards at Auschwitz spent much of their time torturing and

The gates of Auschwitz extermination camp

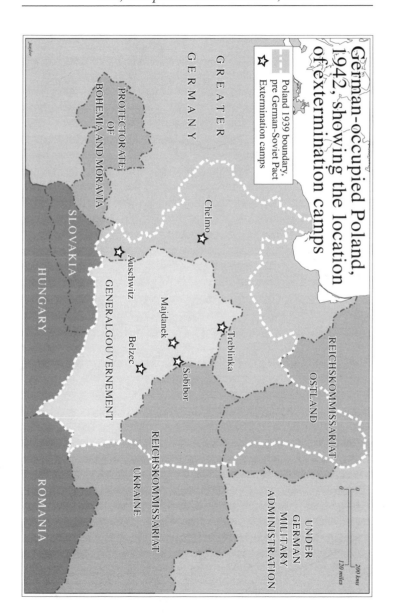

German-occupied Poland, 1942, showing the location of extermination camps

abusing prisoners in sadistic ways. Camps were also supposed to add to the Reich's economy. As the war went on and the need for labour grew, prison industries expanded. German businessmen and Nazi officials seeking to make a quick Reichsmark were eager to exploit the free labour of prisoners. Over the course of its existence, Auschwitz alone spawned a score of subcamps located in and around the original camp site.

Nazi theory put Jews at the bottom of the racial ladder with Roma (gypsies) and Poles just slightly above. At the beginning of the occupation, German plans were relatively incoherent, and interpretations of Nazi philosophy and the orders of the top leadership differed within the bureaucracy. Certainly, there was a general plan to kill the leadership of both Jews and Poles and deport and/or enslave the remainder of the population. Depopulated areas would be resettled with ethnic Germans. Poles believed to have a sufficient quantity of German blood might be 're-Germanized'. How all this was to be done was unclear at first.

From the start, Nazi forces paid special attention to Poland's Jews, burning or desecrating synagogues, killing individual Jews, and abusing and humiliating others. The first task for Hitler's minions, though, was to eliminate any Poles who could be considered leaders. By October, German authorities in western Poland, often aided by local ethnic Germans, rounded up government officials, teachers, clergy, and business people. Victims were either killed or sent to concentration camps. A young priest from Rypin, Stanislaus Grabowski, recalled what happened after his arrest:

> It was 9 p.m.... We heard laughing, footsteps, and suddenly very heavy strikes with whips. At the same time a man cried out loudly 'Jesus, Mary, Joseph.' Looking through the opening in our provisional door, we recognized, lying spread out on the floor, the administrator of an estate, a man well known to us. He was a man of good health, strongly built, about fifty years old. He was flat on the cement floor. Local German boys stood around him, hitting him repeatedly, flogging him mercilessly, beating him to death. Some got tired, others took their place. The murderous flogging continued.... Then there was silence, deadly quiet. They grabbed his legs and pulled the body outside.... I counted the blows, one hundred, two hun-

dred, four hundred. So many blows were needed to complete the painful tragedy. Then another man, and then the next, and the next, and so on.... In the silence of the night and the seclusion of a basement people were dying, people we knew and respected. I can still hear that cry of helplessness: 'Jesus, Mary, Joseph.'... Around 3 p.m. [the next day] Fr. Gajewski, a woman school inspector, and several principals were taken away in an open truck to the woods at Skrwilno and shot. Their bodies were placed in a grave where over 10,000 members of the Polish intelligentsia were buried. The Germans planted trees and bushes over the grave to try to hide their crime.

Similar scenes occurred across Poland. Most of the professors of the famous Jagiellonian University were rounded up and sent to concentration camps. Politicians, writers, scientists, doctors, artists, teachers, Olympic athletes – none were to be spared. All Polish schools above the grammar school level were closed. 'The Poles,' Nazi governor Hans Frank proclaimed, 'do not need universities or secondary schools; the Polish lands are to be changed into an intellectual desert.' In keeping with this ideology, Polish libraries and archives were burned and the country's art treasures systematically looted. Jews were a special target of Nazi robbery. In Rypin, for example, German authorities set fire to the local synagogue and prevented the fire brigade from dousing the flames. Afterward, they blamed the Jewish community for setting the fire and fined the Jews 30,000 *złoty*.

In addition to taking money and works of art, both Nazi and Soviet occupiers treated Poland like an economic colony. Peasants were required to give up a large portion of their produce. Special taxes were instituted. Factories, shops and banks were appropriated by the occupiers. Young, able-bodied men and women were taken to Germany for slave labour on farms and in factories.

A particularly ominous development was the effort to isolate the Jewish population. Jewish freedom of movement was officially restricted and Jews were to be concentrated into specific districts within cities and towns. Later, Jews would be made to wear yellow stars and eventually forced into physically isolated Jewish ghettos. At the beginning of the occupation, however, most ghettos were open and Jews were able to mix freely with the rest of the population. Few Jews made an effort to escape, as there was no particular sense that something much, much worse was coming. Repression among the Polish population was also severe and it was not clear that things would be better anywhere else.

Those Jews best able to blend into the local population were the assimilated, secular minority who spoke good Polish and had personal contacts among Christian Poles. For the majority of Jews, however, such a course of action was rarely considered until later in the war. Few spoke good Polish. Most were unfamiliar with the habits of gentile society – particularly little things such as turns of phrase or gestures. The Nazis exploited differences between Jews and Christians and played up resentments among both groups. Christians were enticed with Jewish property while living in a ghetto was portrayed as a measure that would protect Jews from hostile or avaricious neighbours. German authorities appointed Jewish community leaders within the ghettos and then used those leaders to divide and exploit the Jews.

In the Soviet-controlled sector, matters were just as bad. At the start of the Soviet invasion, local Ukrainian nationalists were encouraged to attack Poles, resulting in sporadic killings that would presage greater atrocities to come. Captured Polish officers were often executed on the spot by the NKVD. The Soviet authorities' first goal was to destroy the local Polish leadership. As in the German-occupied areas, round-ups, arrests, executions and deportation to the gulag were all used. Simultaneously, the Soviets moved again the economic elites, especially anyone engaged in private enterprise. Ethnic and class tensions were exploited to the fullest. Young Jews and Ukrainians were enticed with promises of a future without Polish overlordship, anti-Semitism or poverty. Local collaborators were used against the Soviets' enemies then the collaborators themselves were sometimes arrested and sent to the camps.

In February 1940, the NKVD began its second phase of occupation, the mass deportation of almost all Poles from the Soviet occupation zone. Over the course of the next fifteen months, over 1.5 million Polish men, women, and children were packed into unheated cattle railway wagons and sent to the gulags where many died of hunger, disease, overwork, or were executed. They were soon joined by many

Jews, Ukrainians, and Belarusans. Polish POWs who had fallen into Soviet hands met an even worse fate. Approximately 20,000 Polish officers, mostly well-educated reservists, were executed on Stalin's orders. The most notorious massacre site was at Katyń in Belarus, but there were many others. Living conditions became so bad in the Soviet occupation zone that many refugees who had fled the German invasion, including some Jews, petitioned to return to the Nazi-run part of Poland.

As heinous as these acts were, however, much worse was to come.

RESISTANCE, ACCOMMODATION AND COLLABORATION

From September 1939, Polish society faced an assault on its fundamental existence that was unprecedented in human history. This assault would push Polish society to breaking point. Although inter-war Poland had been an imperfect country at best, its citizenry somehow found the inner resources to survive and even resist the power of the two most murderous totalitarian regimes in history.

People had three major alternatives: to collaborate, to accommodate, or to resist. A small minority chose to collaborate with either occupier. The most likely to collaborate were the dregs of society, especially criminals, but collaborators were found among all classes, professions, and ethnicities. Most collaboration occurred out of greed. Living conditions were terrible and collaboration offered a way to make money or get access to scarce goods. Sometimes, people collaborated out of fear of being killed or threats to family. The Gestapo was sometimes able to turn members of the resistance into double agents through various forms of torture or pressure. In general, however, few collaborated for ideological reasons. There had been no Polish equivalent of the Nazi party. Parties of the extreme Right in Poland were implacably anti-German. Likewise, communist support in Poland was very low, even among members of disaffected minorities such as Jews or Ukrainians. The Nazis in particular had little desire for formal collaboration. Their goal was to crush Poland and there was no interest in creating a puppet government as existed in France and Norway. The Soviets were successful in enlisting the support of some members of the

Jewish, Belarusan, and Ukrainian communities who were used as a weapon against local Poles. Some of these individuals were true believers, but most were opportunists and they frequently harmed their own communities as well.

Criminal activity became a major scourge in occupied Poland. As the war went on and conditions got worse and worse, more people turned to some form of criminal activity. Blackmailers did horrible damage to the lives of people in hiding, particularly Jews. Although the number of blackmailers was small, they made life extremely difficult for Jews in hiding and their rescuers. Even worse were organized gangs of bandits who prowled the countryside, especially in eastern Poland, robbing, killing, and raping.

The majority of people in Poland simply tried to survive, avoiding both heroism and collaboration. Sometimes, they passively resisted Nazi decrees, at other times they complied because they had no choice. Peasants actively sought to hide grain and livestock from the occupiers and even from partisans lest it be taken and their families left to starve. People who saw resistance activity kept silent and got out of the way. No one wanted to be on the bad side of the occupiers, nor did they want to cross the resistance.

Resistance to the occupiers never really ceased. From September 1939, small bands of Polish soldiers kept on the fighting from the cover of forests and mountains. Among the most famous was the legendary 'Major Hubal,' the pseudonym of Major Henryk Dobrzański. Major Hubal and his band of seventy to a hundred men waged unrelenting guerilla warfare on both occupiers until they were cornered by German forces in April 1940 and wiped out. Hubal's body was burned by the Germans and buried in secret so he would not become a martyr, but others soon took his place.

Early resistance cells were frequently organized around political parties and among groups of people who knew each other from before the war. Many of the early local efforts were infiltrated and destroyed by the Gestapo. Efforts to form a central resistance movement began by the end of September 1939. In December 1939, the Union of Armed Struggle was created, combining elements from the parties of the centre, left, and Sanacja. In 1942, it was renamed the Home Army, or

Armia Krajowa (AK). The right-wing National Democratic Party created the National Military Organization, a powerful resistance force that battled both Nazis and communists. It merged with the AK in 1942 though a separate element, the National Armed Forces, remained outside the AK umbrella until 1944. The Peasant Party formed the Peasant Battalions that were active in rural areas. This force combined with the AK in 1943. The communists formed their own resistance force after the Nazi-Soviet divorce in 1941 called the People's Guard (later People's Army), but this force was minuscule and relied on Soviet operatives parachuted in from Moscow. Because it was entirely a creature of the Soviets it never joined the mainstream of the Polish resistance.

The AK, which eventually came to encompass almost all Polish resistance activities, was a kind of virtual or secret state. It had a chain of command, military formations, intelligence, education, courts, publishing, manufacturing, radio and a host of other branches. Early on it became clear that because the occupation was an assault on all levels of society, the response needed to be equally comprehensive. If the enemy tried to destroy Polish culture, the AK sought to preserve it. If the Nazis shut down schools, the AK organized secret courses of study.

The Polish underground infiltrated many aspects of the Nazi occupation regime. In central Poland, there were not enough Germans to operate the administration so the Nazis had to employ Poles, especially in low-level positions. These individuals provided valuable information on German activities, as well as scarce commodities such as blank forms or documents.

To counter German propaganda, the underground developed a vast number of clandestine publications: flyers, news bulletins and regular newspapers. Teams of boy scouts and girl guides distributed the secret publications while a special unit of scouts called the Grey Ranks painted anti-Nazi graffiti by night. To outwit German radio detection, the AK broadcast coded news to England where it was rebroadcast back to Poland using a powerful transmitter. Information was extremely accurate and up-to-date.

Because so many Poles spoke and wrote excellent German, the AK created a highly effective black propaganda operation. Stolen letterheads provided the medium to send false orders and reports to German officials all over the Reich. A series of anti-Nazi 'German resistance' publications was also produced. These appeared to originate within Germany and were mailed to Nazi party members. Each mailing resulted in costly Gestapo investigations of organizations that did not exist. Similar publications were sent to German soldiers at the front to undermine morale.

In its military activities, the AK's first goal was build up its resources. Large-scale attacks against the occupiers were discouraged as they tended to bring massive retribution down on innocent civilians. For every German killed, the Nazis would execute as many as a hundred Poles. Instead, the AK planned a massive uprising when the Germans were at their weakest.

Army in Exile

After the defeat in September 1939, the Polish high command, which had largely escaped to Rumania, lost all credibility. A new government was quickly formed that included a much heavier representation of former opposition figures. The most important among these was Władysław Sikorski (1881–1943) who as a brilliant young officer in 1920 had envisioned the future of mechanized warfare. Sikorski was named commander-in-chief. Around him a complete government formed in Paris.

Many soldiers who had escaped across the Hungarian and Rumanian borders made their way to France. Although both countries were theoretically under German influence, both turned a blind eye to the many Polish 'tourists' exiting the country despite Berlin's protests. Polish embassies remained open but even when soldiers did not have passports, many managed to bluff their way across Europe or hopped on French or neutral vessels heading to the Middle East. These refugees were supplemented by recruits from the Polish diaspora in western Europe and the Americas. By the spring of 1940, Polish soldiers were again ready for combat. Ships of the Polish navy had slipped out of the Baltic and made it to England. By late September 1939, Polish destroyers were cruising the North Sea in search of Nazi U-boats.

Władysław Sikorski, commander-in-chief

Yet, the Allies had little use for these forces. The Poles' first-hand experience in facing the Nazi blitzkrieg was dismissed by Allied leaders. Their own forces would deal with Hitler in due time and they needed no advice from the defeated Poles. Experienced Polish troops in France were assigned to guard rear areas. The only ray of hope was that some Polish troops were considered for an expedition to aid Finland which was bravely resisting Soviet aggression.

In April 1940, German forces struck Denmark and Norway. To relieve the Norwegians, a joint British-French-Polish expedition landed in Narvik in early May. On 10 May, the Nazi blitzkrieg struck Holland, Belgium, Luxembourg and France. Having completely ignored the lessons of the Polish Campaign, the Allies were unprepared for what happened next. By contrast, the Germans had learned from their mistakes in clashes against the Poles and had further refined their tactics. Although the Allies had superiority in men, tanks and aircraft and had to defend only a single, heavily fortified border, the result was a disaster. Allied forces were cut to pieces in Belgium and forced to retreat to

Dunkirk. Vastly larger Allied forces were able to put up only slightly more resistance than had the outnumbered and surrounded Poles the previous September. Polish forces in France were used piecemeal and often sacrificed to save French units. In one incident a Polish mechanized unit saved a French division from encirclement only to watch the French surrender. As Allied resistance collapse, Sikorski ordered Polish soldiers throughout France to make their way to Great Britain.

After France's surrender, the Polish army in exile was the only major allied force the British could count on. Polish troops evacuated from France and Norway stiffened British land defences, but the greatest threat to Britain came from the air as the Luftwaffe sought to pound England into submission throughout the summer of 1940. Polish pilots who had served with great distinction in September 1939 were at first viewed with suspicion by the Royal Air Force (RAF) which assigned them to training units. As England's situation grew more desperate, however, the Poles were pressed into service. The first unit to see action was the RAF 303 Kosciuszko Squadron. Rejecting the RAF's timid approach, the Poles used shock tactics to break up Nazi bomber formations, leaving them easy prey for fighters. RAF 303 had an immediate impact. On 7 September, the height of the Luftwaffe's assault, 303 defended the humble working-class district of the East End of London from waves of Nazi bombers, shooting down fourteen enemy aircraft, a single-day record that was exceeded only by the squadron's performance on 15 September when it downed fifteen. According to author Adam Zamoyski, many RAF officers felt the Poles were exaggerating their scores and one, Group Captain S. F. Vincent, decided to check up on 303:

> The next time 303 was scrambled, he took a plane up and followed them. The squadron met a large enemy formation over the London docks. Two Hurricanes immediately climbed high above, while the rest hung back, with Vincent behind them. Then the two lone planes dived almost vertically onto the Germans, spitting fire and making to collide with them, which forced the bombers to break formation. 'The Poles behind jumped in on the scattered individuals and suddenly the air was full of burning aircraft, parachutes and pieces of disintegrating wings,' records Vincent. 'It was all so rapid that it was staggering.'

Squadron 303 was soon joined by other Polish units and individual Polish pilots were drafted into regular British squadrons. Throughout the critical month of September, Poles made up sometimes as many as a quarter of fighter pilots defending southeast England. Their squadrons had the highest ratio of enemy planes destroyed to losses incurred of any RAF squadrons.

A network of Polish agents all over the world actively aided the Allied cause. In Greece a one-man army named Jerzy Iwanów-Szajnowicz sunk a German destroyer and a submarine and sabotaged an aircraft factory, causing dozens of German pilots to suffer crash landings. After these incredible exploits he was captured and killed while trying to escape. For his service in neutralizing Axis influence in distant Afghanistan, Bronisław Telatycki would be awarded the Order of the British Empire. In 1944, Home Army intelligence captured a complete rocket engine from Hitler's V-2 'wonder weapon' and samples of the highly secret fuel, which they transferred to England even before the weapon was operational.

Holocaust

In the spring of 1941 Polish underground intelligence documented a massive build-up of German forces near the Soviet border and reported this to London. Although the Soviets were forewarned of Hitler's intentions, Stalin refused to believe that his ally would betray him. For almost two years, the Soviets had supplied the Germans with food, oil, and other vital raw materials. On 22 June, 1941, however, Hitler's armies swarmed into the Soviet-controlled sector of eastern Poland. The ill-prepared Red Army was routed.

In preparing for the attack on the USSR, Nazi officials had realized that gaining control of eastern Poland, Ukraine, and Belarus would greatly increase the number of Jews under their control. Plans to deport the large Jewish populations in the ghettos of central Poland to some unspecified place – such as Madagascar – had proved impossible. Nazi leaders agreed on their desire to get rid of Jews but the exact means were unclear. The ghettos in occupied Poland were being gradually isolated but the new Jewish populations that would be acquired in the east totalled over four million. So Nazi authorities used a concept they had originally tried out in September 1939 – the mobile killing units or *Einsatzgruppen*.

As the German armies drove the Soviets back, *Einsatzgruppen* poured into eastern Poland. They systematically rounded up local Jews in every town or village and shot them – men, women, and children. These actions often happened so quickly that the victims had little time to escape, though a few always did. The first victims were Jews living in smaller villages and towns. Larger Jewish communities in cities were quickly isolated in ghettos.

It is impossible to generalize about the reaction of the non-Jewish population to this unprecedented barbarity and there was little the unarmed peasants could have done to stop it. The period of Soviet occupation had greatly exacerbated tensions among Jews, Poles, Ukrainians, and Belarusans. Many local gentiles saw Jews as Soviet collaborators and could always point to examples and make gross generalizations about all Jews. In some cases, local Christians assisted the Germans in locating or even killing Jews, though such outright collaboration was the exception rather than the rule. It was also common for impoverished villagers to steal the property of those who were taken away to be killed (regardless of the victim's ethnicity). Most people were too terrified and paralyzed by the brutal killing and violence to take any action whatsoever. Jews who escaped were usually hidden for periods of time by local villagers. In occupied Poland, unlike Western Europe, the penalty for hiding Jews was always death, not only for the person who hid the Jews but their family and sometimes the whole village.

Although the mobile killing operations were extremely effective, German officials were concerned about the psychological impact that killing women, children, babies, and the elderly would have on their soldiers. As a result, they attempted to develop a method of slaughter that would be less stressful for the murderers. The end result was the gas chamber in which prisoners were sealed inside and poison gas pumped in. The first trials of this system occurred in the summer of 1942 at the Birkenau subcamp of Auschwitz, the first victims being Poles and Soviet POWs. Soon, however, the gas chambers were in use at

Auschwitz, Birkenau, Majdanek (near Lublin), Belzec, Sobibor, and Treblinka (east of Warsaw). Within months, the killing operations were going constantly. Jews were deported by train from urban ghettos, shipped to the killing sites, gassed, and their bodies dumped in mass graves, covered in quicklime, or burned in special crematoria. Polish Jews were the first to die, but soon the Germans began to ship in Jews from other countries as well. Hundreds of thousands of Roma were also murdered, along with Soviet POWs and any political opponents seized by Nazi authorities.

In addition to the horror of the gas chambers, prisoners were shot, worked to death, starved, or victimized by inhuman medical experiments. Many of the Polish clergy sent to Dachau and the Polish women sent to the women's camp at Ravensbrück were subject to such experiments. Tens of thousands of other prisoners were felled by contagious diseases that ran rampant in the camps.

As the killing process got underway, word of these crimes quickly began to leak out. Polish underground authorities began to collect evidence on the camps early on. A young underground courier, Jan Karski, was smuggled into one of the transit camps to get a first-hand glimpse of the carnage. Karski was then ordered to get to London to report what he saw. On his first attempt, he was captured by the Gestapo and brutally tortured. Clandestine operatives of the underground rescued Karski and after he recovered, he made his way successfully to the West. Karski spent much of the rest of the war trying to get Allied leaders to pay attention to the slaughter of the Jews, but the effort to win the war took priority over the saving of civilians. The Polish government in exile issued a public report on the slaughter of its Jewish citizens in 1943, calling on Allied and neutral powers to pressure the Nazis into halting the massacres. Practically speaking there was little else the exiled government could do.

In the major ghettos, such as Warsaw, life got more and more desperate. A few Jews got wealthy off the suffering of their neighbours by selling food on the black market. Others acted as agents for the Gestapo to catch Jews who tried to escape. The Ghetto Police assisted the Germans in selecting Jews for deportation. Polish gentile blackmailers were an equally dangerous threat. The majority of Jews, however, sought only survival. Many tried to flee the ghetto and some 28,000 would be hidden outside the ghetto walls. An informal network of Christians aided these escapees. There was no rhyme or reason to which Poles chose actively to aid Jews and which ones refused to help their brethren in need. Some Poles who had been close to Jews before the war closed their doors to their former friends or stole property given to them for safekeeping. Some notorious anti-Semites risked their lives to save Jews. Most of the rescuers were simply ordinary people who years later could never fully explain why they had risked their lives to save others.

Polish nuns hid thousands of Jewish children in orphanages and clergy provided many Jews with baptismal certificates to help them pass as Christians. Underground activist Irena Sendler personally saved the lives of over 2,000 Jewish children. Even after being captured by the Nazis and tortured, she did not give up a single one. In September 1942, Polish and Jewish underground activists created the Zegota organization dedicated to assisting Jews in hiding which was the only such organization in all of occupied Europe.

Most Jews had neither the time nor the resources to mount serious resistance to the German killing operations. In most cases it happened too quickly. But in the larger ghettos, such as Warsaw, small groups of Jews began organizing resistance cells with the goal of fighting back. The most extensive network of cells arose in Warsaw. The best-known of these was the Jewish Fighting Organization (or ŻOB, its Polish acronym). Its teenage activists were largely untrained and were not trusted by Polish underground authorities due to the fact that some of its leaders held strong pro-Soviet views. The socialist Bund also had an effective fighting unit. The least known was the Jewish Military Union (ZWŻ), formed by the right-wing Zionist Revisionist movement. Many of its leaders had served in the Polish army and had good links to the Polish underground.

As the deportations to the death camps continued in early 1943, these small resistance units began to mobilize. The Polish underground had no way to provide the Jews with the heavy weapons needed to fight the Germans effectively and therefore provided aid in the form of money, so arms could be purchased on the black market. In addition, it provided some small caches of arms. (Decades later, this decision and the Polish underground's goal of waiting for a national uprising when Germany was on the verge of defeat would be the subject of bitter criticism by many Western writers.) Jewish resistance cells began to target collaborators and leaders of the infamous Ghetto Police.

As conditions in the Warsaw Ghetto worsened, deportations increased. By April 1943, only 70,000 Jews remained in the ghetto. The Germans prepared for the final push to 'liquidate' the ghetto. In the early morning of 19 April, police troops of the Waffen SS supported by a tank entered the ghetto, but this time the 'helpless' Jews fought back, putting the tank out of action and driving the SS men out of the ghetto. At dawn, the people of Warsaw were electrified to see the blue and white flag of a future Israel and the Polish red and white flag flying over the ghetto. Additional forays into the ghetto were repulsed as well. For the 'master race', this was a humiliating comedown. The Germans then attacked the ghetto in force, using incendiaries and artillery to set buildings on fire, but still they met furious resistance. The fiercest struggles occurred on 22 and 23 April. Fighters of the Jewish socialist Bund mounted heroic resistance in the Brushmaker's Area, many of their leaders perishing at their posts. At Muranów Square, the right-wing Revisionists – the Betarim – assisted by members of the Polish Home Army, held off the Nazis for four days. The German commander conceded: 'The stiffest resistance was offered by a rebel group ... at 7 Muranowska Street. This position held out longer than any other ... The rebels were able to obtain a constant supply of ammunition furnished them by a Polish resistance group. The attacks launched by our forces on this position were repeatedly repelled.'

By the fourth day of the uprising, large sections of the ghetto were on fire. Many fighters and civilians perished in the flames and the collapsing buildings. Fighting became sporadic, though German patrols continued to take losses even into early May. Some fighters and civilians managed to escape the ghetto and find shelter outside. On 16 May, the Germans declared victory by blowing up the ghetto's remaining synagogue. They officially admitted less than a hundred casualties, though Polish underground sources estimated Nazi losses at closer to a thousand. Jewish losses were approximately six thousand along with fifty-five fighters of the AK. This heroic, doomed resistance, however, had demonstrated the tenacity of the Jewish people and the utter depravity of the Nazi regime. It would be remembered as one of the bravest struggles ever undertaken by a people faced with destruction.

The majority of Poles, caught up in their own struggles to survive, had little time to spare for their Jewish compatriots. Some were indifferent, others sympathized with them but felt there was little they could do. Decades of separation, furthered by Nazi policies, meant that most Poles and Jews had little contact with each other and viewed one another as alien. Although Polish gentiles could not have prevented the Holocaust, the mutual alienation of the two groups made the situation worse and contributed to the worsening of relations.

THE GATES OF HELL

In the final years of Nazi occupation it seemed as if the very gates of hell had opened in Poland. The Germans increasingly resorted to terror and punishment on the grounds of collective responsibility. Their control in the countryside grew less and less certain and depended more on overwhelming force. Chaos and violence rather than order and control marked the final stages of Nazi rule.

Beginning in 1942, the Polish resistance had stepped up attacks on German military targets. Supply lines for the eastern front all ran through Poland, and the Poles worked to hasten Germany's defeat through sabotaging communications and supplies. The AK's diversion and sabotage section blew up military transports, derailed trains, wrecked bridges and burned warehouses. Agents within railway repair shops delayed or damaged trains and railroad cars. By 1944, there were ten attacks on the railways every day. German transports and rail installations required additional guards, tying down tens of thousands of additional police and troops. German efforts to seize food in the countryside also came in for sabotage. Food quota offices were attacked and burned and efforts to collect the quota met growing resistance.

The Nazi response was overwhelmingly brutal. More than 115 villages were wiped out for hiding Jews or helping partisans. Villages were surrounded and the inhabitants either shot on the spot or transported to death camps where they shared the fate of the Jews. Areas of partisan activity were surrounded and turned into free-fire zones as German police and military forces, sometimes aided by auxiliaries recruited in Ukraine or among former Soviet soldiers, went on the rampage.

In late 1942 Nazi racial theorists sought to clear part of the region around Zamość of Poles and bring in ethnic Germans to create a German colony. Whole villages were rounded up, inhabitants executed, sent to concentration camps or slave labour. Over 110,000 people were displaced from their homes. A similar attempt on a smaller scale occurred in Białystok where some 40,000 were displaced. Polish partisans launched fierce attacks on Nazi forces as well as on German colonists. Attacks on the hapless and mostly unarmed German colonists enraged top Nazi leaders and brought further reprisals. By the summer of 1943 as the fortunes of war began to turn decisively against Germany, further colonization efforts were abandoned.

As horrific as the situation in central Poland was, it paled in comparison to what occurred in eastern Poland. These lands had been captured by the Soviets at the start of the war and the communists had systematically exploited ethnic tensions. When the Germans pushed out the Soviets in 1941, many, especially ethnic Ukrainians, welcomed the new arrivals. The Soviets had committed genocide against the Ukrainians in the 1930s and the bitter fruit of Polish-Ukrainian rivalry in the 1920s and 1930s allowed the Nazis to recruit Ukrainians into police and auxiliary units that were often used to carry out the dirty work of killing. As the war began to turn against the Germans, however, Ukrainians took matters into their own hands. Many Ukrainian auxiliaries began to operate in a semi-independent fashion and used their weapons to further the goals of the most extreme nationalist faction among Ukrainians, the Ukrainian Partisan Army (UPA). With the Jews mostly wiped out, the Ukrainians turned on the Poles, especially in provinces like Volhynia (Wołyn).

Elements of the UPA descended on Polish villages across southeast Poland, killing the inhabitants in the most brutal ways possible. Villagers were forced into their churches and burned alive. Killings were often carried out with axes, knives, saws, pitchforks, scythes, and swords. Men were castrated, sawn in half, burned alive. Women were raped, sexually mutilated, hacked apart. The UPA spared no one, not even children. An estimated 60,000 Poles lost their lives, the largest number in Volhynia where the worst violence occurred. While the killings raged, many courageous Ukrainians risked their lives to save Polish neighbours. Ukrainians who were viewed by the UPA as too favourable toward Poles, or who were caught sheltering Poles, shared their fate. Local Nazi forces had no orders and mostly stood aside while the killings occurring, sometimes sheltering Poles, sometimes aiding the UPA killers.

Polish resistance forces organized self-defence units to fight off these attacks and also launch reprisals against Ukrainian villages, guilty Ukrainians were killed along with the innocent. Collective reprisal and the logic of ethnic cleansing took hold. In early 1944, Poles organized the 27th Home Army Division in Volhynia. In the spring and summer of 1944, this unit, accompanied by a long train of civilian refugees fought its way out of Volhynia, battling Germans and Ukrainians every step of the way before surrendering to the Red Army in the summer of 1944.

In the forests of northeastern Poland, large-scale Soviet partisan units were active by 1943. Made up of a combination of deserters, local recruits, and troops parachuted or inserted by the Soviet command, these forces began to carry out operations against the Germans but also to rob and despoil local peasants. Young Jews hiding in the forests were also sometimes recruited. Jews who were not able to fight were often left to their fate or even killed by the Soviets. These Jewish refugees had been survivors of the massacres of the Nazi *Einsatzgruppen* who had hidden in the forests and survived mostly by begging food from local peasants. As the economic situation grew worse and the peasants had less food to give, relations grew strained, and the Jews sometimes took what they needed by force. The peasants also faced depredations by common criminals in gangs sometimes made up of deserters from various armies or police units. The arrival of the Soviets further complicated matters. Polish resistance had remained relatively quiet and was based on part-time soldiers who lived among the local population. Unlike the Soviets, the Poles depended much more on the goodwill and support of the locals. By 1943, however, they too were organizing active partisan units.

In the beginning, Polish and Soviet units worked together or observed neutrality and did not interfere with each other. In the autumn of 1943, however, following the revelations of the Katyń massacre and the breakdown in official Polish-Soviet relations, Soviet partisans, on orders from Moscow, began an all-out effort to destroy free Polish forces. Leaders of Polish units were invited to parley and then captured, tortured and killed. Lower-level partisans were conscripted into Soviet units or killed. Sometimes, the Soviets betrayed Polish partisans to the Nazis. This began a war of all against all. Poles fought the Germans and sometimes their Lithuanian or Belarusin auxiliaries and the Soviets and Soviet-allied Jewish units. The Soviets fought the Nazis and the Poles. Bandits preyed on the innocent, sometimes pretending to be partisans of one side or another. All fell victim: Jews trying to survive in the forest, local peasants – Polish, Lithuanian or Belarusin – civilians and partisans alike. Only the Nazis and Soviets gained any advantage.

Out of Siberia and the Polish Forces in the West

When Hitler attacked the USSR in 1941, the million-plus Poles who had been deported to Stalin's gulags found themselves in a strange position. The Soviets and the Polish government in exile resumed relations under the pressure of wartime events. Part of the agreement was that Polish captives would be released and there was some discussion of forming a Polish army in the east to fight the Nazis. A quarter of a million Poles in camps all over the USSR were released and began the long trek to transit camps near the Caspian Sea. Starving, sick, beaten and worked nearly to death, many walked or hitched rides on railway trucks. Families were sometimes separated in the chaos, parents never seeing their children again. Tens of thousands died along the way. More died on reaching the transit camps. Although the camps were meant only for potential military recruits, not a single man, woman or child who could make the journey failed to take advantage of the chance to escape Stalin's hell. The initial Polish-Soviet agreement was to cover only ethnic Poles, but many Polish Jews – equally desperate to escape – came as well.

It soon became obvious that the Soviets had no ability to equip a Polish army and Stalin did not want a free Polish force operating in his territory. It was agreed to send the Poles to Persia and then to the British-controlled Middle East. In the spring and summer of 1942, an estimated 115,000 Poles began a second leg of the great exodus, travelling in decrepit steamers across the Caspian Sea. In Persia, more died from disease. From there, the Poles were taken in by British and American authorities. Civilian refugees were sent to British India, others to East Africa, some to Mexico and still others to Palestine. The able-bodied were enlisted in the Polish Army Second Corps under the command of General Władysław Anders. Many had to overcome the effects of starvation before they could endure training. Since whole families had been deported, it was not uncommon for a father and two or three sons to serve in the same unit, while a daughter or mother enlisted in the women's auxiliary, and younger children joined the scouts.

By early 1944, this force, though untested, was considered ready for action. By then, the Allies had driven the Germans out of North Africa and invaded Italy. But the invasion of Italy had bogged down south of Rome along the Germans' fortified Gustav Line. This line of defence was anchored on Monte Cassino, the ancient monastery, which controlled the road north to Rome. Monte Cassino was a mountain redoubt defended by elite Nazi paratroopers. Repeated Allied attacks on the positions had been defeated with bloody casualties. The Americans even bombed the ancient landmark to no effect. Allied landings at Anzio near Rome failed to end the stalemate.

In May 1944, the Allies made one more effort to break the Gustav Line and the untried Polish Second Corps was ordered to storm Cassino. On 12 May the Poles launched their assault. The former concentration camp prisoners fought hand to hand with Nazi 'supermen' in some of the bloodiest close combat of World War II. Positions fell, were retaken, only to fall again. Men fought with knives, shovels, rocks. Finally on 14 May the Polish attack came to a halt short of the monastery. On 17 May, behind a barrage of artillery, the Poles attacked again, gaps in their ranks made up with cooks and drivers. The Poles overran Nazi positions, many of the defenders fighting to the last man, and then repelled fierce counterattacks. By evening, the Poles had broken German defences and the Nazis, facing determined Allied attacks in surrounding sectors, fell back. On the morning of 18 May, Polish forces occupied the ruins of Monte Cassino. At the cost of thousands of dead and wounded, they had broken the Gustav Line and opened the road to Rome. The Polish Second Corps went on to fight the Germans at Ancona in July 1944 and up the Italian peninsula, seizing Bologna in April 1945.

Meanwhile, Polish forces in Britain had been reorganized into two main combat units, the Polish 1st Armoured Division and the Polish Parachute Brigade. The 1st Armoured Division was sent to Normandy in July 1944 to support the Canadian Army Corps. In the two months following the Normandy landings, the Allies had fought bitter battles against the Germans in the Normandy *bocage* or hedgerow country. In late July, American forces under General George Patton broke out from the Normandy beachhead and turned the German flank. With the British and Canadians pushing south and Patton's Americans moving up from the south, the stage was set for a colossal battle of encirclement. Faced with fierce resistance, the British and Canadian advance slowed, but the Polish division broke through German lines on 17 August, its lead elements linking up with Patton's 90th Division. The bulk of the 1st Armoured Division, however, was cut off on a hilltop in the middle of the Germans' line of retreat. The desperate Germans sought to dislodge the Poles from their position. The fanatical SS Adolf Hitler and SS Hitler Youth Divisions launched repeated attacks on the Poles, who directed Canadian heavy artillery and swarms of Allied fighter-bombers down on the Germans' columns on all sides. For four days, the Poles held their ground, as all around Allied fire-power pulverized the Germans. Although some German troops escaped, the Poles had been the cork in the bottleneck that trapped 50,000 Nazi troops.

The 1st Armoured Division went on to fight its way through France and Belgium. In Holland, the division liberated the city of Breda, preventing its destruction by retreating German forces. In April 1945, the division pushed into northern Germany. On 4 May, it broke the German defences around Wilhelmshaven and the following day accepted the surrender of the city and with it a large portion of the German navy.

The incredible courage and sacrifice of the Polish forces on the battlefield against the Nazi foe yielded little political benefit for their country. Although a key ally in 1940 and 1941, following the US and Soviet entries into the war, the Polish position declined. The Polish government in exile was able to hold together but in 1943 things began to fall apart. In April 1943, the Nazis announced to the world that they had found the mass graves of thousands of missing Polish officers. The officers had been in Soviet custody and it was soon apparent to the Poles and even to the Allied governments that the Soviets had committed this atrocity. However, neither the British nor the Americans would acknowledge Soviet complicity. Instead, the crime was laid at the door of the Germans. When the Poles agreed to an investigation by the International Red Cross, sanctioned by the Germans, the Soviets broke off relations with the Polish government and set up a puppet regime made up of Polish communists and Polish-speaking Soviet citizens. The British and American press, which was increasingly pro-Soviet, vilified the Poles as traitors. The Soviets used an extensive network of agents and fellow travellers in the US and Britain to further their propaganda efforts. Within the Polish government, there was serious division over how to handle the Soviets, with commander-in-chief Sikorski taking a fairly moderate approach to appease the Western Allies who were Poland's main hope of resisting post-war Soviet domination.

In July 1943, Sikorski was returning from an inspection tour of Polish forces in the Mediterranean when his aircraft suffered a mysterious crash near Gibraltar. Sikorski and his daughter were killed. Although various theories have been put forward regarding the incident and the possible complicity of Soviet or British agents working for the Soviets, no conclusive evidence of a larger conspiracy has been proven. Regardless of the circumstances, the tragedy ended the life of the one man who had been able to keep the Polish government and armed forces functioning coherently. After his death, the leadership was divided between Prime Minister Stanisław Mikołajczak and the commander of the armed forces, General Kazimierz Sosnkowski (Piłsudski's old associate).

During the Tehran Conference in 1943, the British and Americans largely acquiesced to Stalin's plans for a Soviet sphere of domination in east-central Europe that would include Poland. Although Churchill had a few qualms about betraying his Polish ally, Roosevelt's vision of a post-war world at peace under Soviet and American domination left little room for the self-determination of smaller nations, no matter how loyally they had supported the Allied cause. One of Stalin's key demands was that he be allowed to keep all territory seized under the Nazi-Soviet pact of 1939, to which the Western Allies assented. Churchill would later push Mikołajczak to negotiate with the Soviets in the hope of preserving some semblance of Polish independence, but in the absence of strong Allied backing, the Soviets had no reason to grant the Poles anything and were looking forward to a Poland dominated by or wholly annexed to the USSR.

In Poland, with the tacit approval of the government in exile, the Home Army prepared Operation Burza or Storm. As the Red Army advanced, the underground would rise up, defeat the retreating Germans and greet the Soviets as master of their own country. In Wilno, the AK played a major role in ousting the Germans from the city and helping the Red Army. The Soviet reciprocated by executing the leaders of the Polish resistance and conscripting the rank and file into the Red Army's Polish units. This was an ominous beginning, but the real test would be in Warsaw.

WARSAW FIGHTS

On the evening of 1 August, 1944, shots rang out across the city of Warsaw as some 40,000 poorly armed citizen soldiers, including teenagers, men and women, backed by almost the entire population, attacked the well-equipped, well-fortified German garrison. The first European capital captured by Hitler's armies was fighting back. In the summer of 1944, as the Soviets approached Warsaw, the Poles decided to retake their capital city. Their goal was to drive out the Nazis and welcome the Soviets as masters of their own house, forestalling any effort to impose a Soviet-style puppet regime.

Fierce fighting broke out across the city by the late afternoon. Only one in ten Polish fighters had a weapon, but many went into action hoping to use captured arms from the Germans, or from their own fallen comrades. Units of boy scouts and girl guides, some as young as twelve or thirteen, attacked Nazi panzers armed only with bottles of petrol. The Poles seized large sections of the city, but failed to take many key fortified strong points, including the bridges across the Vistula River. Losses were heavy, but the Polish citizen soldiers quickly learned from their mistakes.

Hitler's reaction was furious. He ordered the completed destruction of the city and the death of all its inhabitants. Heinrich Himmler confidently predicted 'Warsaw will be liquidated; and this city ... that has blocked our path to the east for seven hundred years ... will have ceased to exist.' The Nazi command sent SS police, units of former Soviet soldiers who had deserted to the Nazi cause, and the sweepings of German military prisons – murderers, rapists, child molesters and thieves. Behind them came tanks, aircraft and heavy artillery. Many Nazi units were sent into purely civilian areas where they murdered, raped and pillaged for days on end, killing men, women and children without mercy. German and ex-Soviet troops rampaged through hospitals, even maternity wards, killing every living soul.

Although murdering helpless civilians came easily to the German command, retaking the city did not. Units that were skilled in slaughtering the innocent proved less effective against armed citizenry. Nazi forces seized buildings during the day, only to find that the Poles retook them during the night. Fighting raged from house to house, room to room. Julian Kulski, a teenager fighting in the city's northern suburb, recalled how his unit tricked the Germans into thinking their position was unoccupied:

> The Germans approached our building and, after passing it, started the attack on the barricade.... Then came the long awaited order to fire. We put the muzzles of our rifles, Sten guns, and machine-guns forward through the windows and poured murderous fire down on the Germans who were taken completely by surprise. In addition to this, the detachment at the Health Centre lost no time in firing on the enemy from the other side and launching an attack. One after another, the Germans were struck down by our bullets.

Normally, the Poles spared their ammunition under the slogan, 'one bullet, one German,' but when it came to the SS, a different policy was practised:

> Positioned immediately under the window from which I was firing was an SS police machine gun squad. At the first burst from Cadet-Officer Zawada's Sten gun a machine gunner was shot down. Although he was badly wounded, he tried to retreat, spitting blood and leaving a deadly red trail on the pavement. A rifle shot finished him off.... We did not spare ammunition when shooting at the SS policemen – the men who had been responsible for the slaughter in the Ghetto, for the executions, the street hunts, and the wanton murders.

In the ruins of the Jewish ghetto, a unit of Polish volunteers, using a captured tank, smashed through the walls of the 'Goose Farm' death camp, routing the Nazi guards and freeing about 400 Jewish prisoners. Although small, it was the first Nazi death camp to be liberated by Allied forces. Amid scenes of joy, the Polish officer who led the attack saw a file of men standing at attention. A former prisoner stepped forward, saluted, and announced 'Jewish volunteer company ready for action!' The former prisoners were enlisted in the ranks. As the officer later recalled, the Jewish volunteers were 'exceptionally brave, ingenious, and faithful people.'

As the city fought desperately and the Germans began to bring in reinforcements, the reaction of the Soviets was silence. Soviet forces, which had advanced confidently throughout the summer, stopped within miles of Warsaw. When Allied planes sought to use Soviet airbases to airdrop supplies to the Polish resistance, the Soviets refused. Allied supply planes were forced to make a dangerous return trip and Allied planes that strayed into Soviet-controlled areas were shot at from the ground or even attacked by Red Air Force fighters. Despite the dangers many American, British, Polish and South African aircrews volunteered for this mission.

Denied re-supply from the east, the insurgents were driven back by overwhelming German firepower, and forced to rely on capturing weapons or making their own in secret workshops. To escape German detection, the resistance turned to the city's sewers, using them to move undetected from place to place. This was often highly dangerous, and even skilled guides could become lost or fall into German booby traps.

Although forced onto the defensive, the Poles continued to mount attacks on Nazi positions. On 20 August, the Home Army attacked the State Telephone Exchange, one of Warsaw's few skyscrapers. Special sapper units made up of young women, called *minerki*, led the attack, detonating homemade explosives in the lower part of the building, driving the defenders into the upper floors. Then teams armed with homemade flamethrowers set the building alight. Most of the Nazis inside jumped to their deaths to avoid the flames, shot themselves, or were killed trying to fight their way back down the staircases.

The most savage fighting occurred in the Old Town, Warsaw's historic heart. German heavy weapons smashed building after building, driving the defenders back into an ever smaller area. Civilians were used as human shields for German tanks. The struggle raged around the fifteenth-century cathedral of St John the Baptist. Its medieval walls resisted even point blank fire from tanks. Assault after assault on the church was thrown back with heavy losses. Nazi commanders, certain that the church was garrisoned by some elite commando unit, packed a small remote-control tank full of explosives and rammed it into the building. The explosion collapsed the walls. As the smoke cleared, the bodies of the defenders could be seen lying amidst the rubble, still wearing their Boy Scout uniforms.

As the Germans closed in on the Old Town, the defenders made a daring escape. Thousands of freedom fighters and civilians slipped away single file through miles of sewers beneath the Germans' feet. The wounded were carried through the muck. Some went mad confined in the stinking darkness, others got lost, drowned in sewage, or killed by German booby traps.

As the people of Warsaw fought and died amid the rubble, the Soviets stood by. Stalin was content to let his former ally, Hitler, get rid of the non-communist resistance movement. The Western Allies, who had already secretly agreed to Soviet hegemony over eastern Europe, saw the naked lust for power of their Soviet 'comrades.' Although in public, they maintained a façade of good relations, for many Western leaders Stalin's promises and his goodwill could no longer be trusted. In the eyes of many historians, the struggle for Warsaw was the first battle of the Cold War.

After 63 days of fighting, the defenders of Warsaw, abandoned by their allies and left to face the Nazi army alone, capitulated. The freedom fighters were treated as regular POWs under the Geneva convention – a concession that showed how badly the Germans wanted to end the Uprising. The civilians were to be evacuated without reprisals.

On Hitler's personal orders, Warsaw was systematically levelled, block by block, street by street. By the war's end, one of the great capitals of Europe was a field of rubble, with not a building left standing for miles.

As the Uprising ended, Soviet propagandists and their Western apologists began to sing a different tune: the people of Warsaw were led by 'fascists' who had 'betrayed' them to the Germans. In time, the Soviets would seek to blank the Warsaw Uprising from historical memory, and many Western scholars would go along with this version of events. Many histories of World War II in English lavish fulsome praise on the Soviet leadership but ignore the Warsaw Uprising. Yet, the Uprising destroyed whatever shred of legitimacy the communists might have had over their new eastern European possessions. For all their anti-Nazi rhetoric, they had allied themselves with Hitler at the start of the war, and then stood by while the Nazis killed off the cream of a generation.

Liberation without Freedom

In January 1945, Soviet forces entered what was left of Warsaw. On 17 January, the Soviets struck toward Kraków. Nazi Governor Hans Frank, who had personally supervised the murder and repression of millions, declared that Kraków was German and could never be surrendered and then promptly fled the city. Although Kraków was slated for the same destruction as Warsaw, the speed of the Red Army advance and the actions of local AK prevented the Germans from wrecking the old capital.

On 27 January, Red Army forces reached Auschwitz. The SS had continued killing prisoners until the very end. Other prisoners were sent on death marches toward Germany or packed in railway wagons. The Nazis made a feeble effort to hide their crimes by blowing up part of the camp, but the murder of over one million human beings could not be so easily concealed.

Throughout the winter and spring of 1945, the Red Army overwhelmed one German position after another. Cities such as Gdańsk and Kołobrzeg were turned into fortresses that cost the Red Army dearly in lives, but did not delay the advance. Among the advancing troops were forces of the Polish People's Army, recruited from Poles unlucky enough to not escape to the Middle East, Soviet citizens of Polish extraction and Poles conscripted in regions already conquered by the Soviets. They were often used as shock troops to attack fortified German positions and suffered very heavy losses.

As the Soviets advanced into ethnic German territory, they committed mass atrocities against the civilian population as well as against many of the prisoners they freed from Nazi captivity. Rape was common and of the fifteen million German women living in the eastern half of Germany, the majority between the ages of ten and eighty were raped, often repeatedly. Scenes of madness occurred as terrible crimes were committed against the German civilian population. Mothers with their children in their arms leapt into rivers. Whole families committed suicide. Vast numbers of German civilians simply fled west in terror. Nor were the Germans alone in this suffering. Polish, Jewish and Russian women who had been taken captive by the Nazis were raped on being 'liberated'.

The new Soviet occupation was less horrific than that of the Nazis. However, the living conditions of the population deteriorated. Hunger was rampant and made worse by Soviet food requisitions. Hunger and malnutrition brought on diseases such as typhus that killed and weakened more people. Virtually the entire infrastructure was in ruins and what remained was mostly for the use of Poland's new masters. The Soviets also ended up looting a great deal of Polish property, including artwork that was stolen by the Nazis from Poland and then re-stolen and sent to Russia.

In the face of the Soviet NKVD and its Polish henchmen, the Polish underground quickly abandoned efforts to come out into the open as representatives of Poland's legal government in London. The repression of the Polish underground was severe. For western consumption, the Soviet proclaimed all non-communist members of the resistance to be 'fascists' and 'collaborators'. Many of the most courageous members of the underground were arrested, tortured, imprisoned or killed. For example, Walentyna Stempkowska, a teenage courier for the National Armed Forces, was arrested by the Gestapo in December 1943 and brutally tortured for three weeks. After failing to extract information from her the Gestapo sent her to the infamous women's concentration camp at Ravensbrück. After the defeat of Germany she was re-arrested by the communist secret police and spent six years in prison. Lidia Lwow, a combat nurse with AK's 5th Wilno Brigade, won the Cross of Valour for saving wounded partisans under enemy fire. After the war she was arrested by the secret police and sentenced to life in prison for the 'crime' of belonging to the resistance. August Emil Fieldorf (1895–1953) – known by his code name 'General Zero' – was a highly decorated veteran of the Polish army. He directed the AK's diversion and sabotage operations which wreaked havoc on Nazi military and transport facilities. He, too, was arrested after the war, brutalized, and executed in 1953. Those who had saved the lives of Jews during the Holocaust were especially vulnerable since it was assumed that they were members of the resistance. In some cases, it was necessary for the rescued Jews to come to the aid of their former rescuers who were brought up on false charges in communist courts by providing testimony in their favour. Many rescuers hid their involvement in saving Jews.

The end of Nazi occupation reduced but did not end the arrests, tortures and executions. Nor did it end the fighting and the killing. From late 1944 through 1956, elements of the Polish underground continued to resist the communist regime. Although the AK officially disbanded in 1945, a number of successor organizations continued to function. The best known was Freedom and Independence (known by its Polish initials as WiN), but many others existed. None were able to attain the reach or sophisticated conspiratorial infrastructure of the AK, but they were strong in many areas outside of the major cities. In addition to resistance by Poles, ethnic Ukrainians and Rusyns in Poland continued to field resistance forces, the most notable of which was the UPA. Anti-communist partisans launched raids on communist-controlled facilities and were active in opposing arbitrary acts of power by communist officials. Elements of the secret police and security forces were their major targets.

In response, the Soviet-directed communist regime mounted a major anti-partisan campaign, committing more troops to the struggle than the US committed at the height of the Vietnam War. Communist security forces were especially ruthless, often using summary executions of suspected resistance supporters. In many cases, they simply shot and terrorized people at random. To crush Ukrainian resistance in south-eastern Poland, the government undertook 'Operation Vistula', the forced resettlement of an estimated 140,000 ethnic Ukrainians and Rusyns from their home villages to the new territories in the west. In 1948, the government offered amnesty to resisters and many accepted the offer (although many were later persecuted in contravention of the amnesty agreement). Active resistance, however, continued until 1956 and some individual resisters did not surrender until the late 1960s.

In addition to legitimate resistance there was also a serious crime problem. With the economy in shambles and guns readily available, crime and violence were common. In many areas of the countryside, bandits – sometimes members of the security forces 'moonlighting' from their regular jobs – terrorized the population, stealing and killing almost at will.

Population and Border Changes

At the Yalta Conference in 1944, the US and Great Britain put their official stamp of approval on Stalin's demands in central Europe. The Soviets were granted nearly all the territory they had seized from Poland and its neighbours under the terms of Stalin's agreement with Hitler in 1939 as well as the northern half of East Prussia. Poland was granted pieces of German territory – the southern half of East Prussia, the former Free City of Danzig, and all German land east of the Oder and Neisse Rivers. This left Poland smaller and historic Polish cities such as Lwów (Lviv), Wilno (Vilnius), and Grodno were lost. Silesia and the city of Wrocław, which had not been part of Poland since the late Middle Ages, were again Polish as was Gdańsk.

The fact that Germans had lived in these lands for centuries was of no consequence to the communists. Those who had not fled the Red Army's advance during the war were forcibly expelled afterward. Desperate Poles came to the deserted towns and cities and looted what they could before returning home. In place of the Germans, Poles from the Soviet Union and the annexed territories that formerly made up eastern Poland were forcibly relocated to the so-called Recovered Territories. In all, more than 1.2 million Poles were relocated from Ukraine, along with 274,000 from Belarus and 177,000 from Lithuania. Smaller numbers of Poles were relocated from displaced persons camps in Germany and from the Polish minority in Yugoslavia. Another 3.5 million Poles were relocated from central Poland to the new western lands. At the same time, 483,000 Ukrainians, 30,000 Belarusians, and 17,000 Lithuanians were expelled from Poland to the USSR.

The fate of Poles in the west was especially tragic. Many had fled the USSR and joined the Polish army to fight the Nazis. Others had been taken to Nazi camps as slave labour. Many were fearful of returning to communist-dominated Poland. Despite assurances by the communist authorities and the often hostile attitude taken by Allied governments, many chose to stay in the West. They settled in Britain, France, Canada, Australia, Argentina and most of all in the US. Those who did choose to go back were – as many had feared – persecuted. They were denied housing, jobs, schooling, and in many cases were closely monitored by the secret police. Those who had served as officers in the Polish armed forces in exile were often arrested as 'spies' or on other trumped up charges and sent to prison or labour camps.

Of the approximately 300,000 Jews who survived the Nazi Holocaust, many ultimately found life in Poland unbearable. A significant percentage of Jews supported the new government which promised a Poland free of the scourge of anti-Semitism. Although some attained very high positions in the new regime, for most hopes placed in the communists were misplaced. Poland's new masters accepted Jews not from affection but out of a need for native Polish speakers to fill key positions. Once they were no longer needed in the late 1960s, they would be purged en masse. In the meantime, however, a clear perception arose – building on old stereotypes and the occasional grain of truth – that Jews were a major force behind communism in Poland. The term 'Jew-Communist' became common and sometimes all communists were referred to as Jews regardless of their ethnicity. Although there was great sympathy for Jewish losses on the part of many ethnic Poles, there was also a level of resentment at the prominence of Jews in the new regime.

Most Jews had lost all or the majority of their families and the horror of that fact was often too great to remain in Poland. By 1947, over 200,000 Jews had left Poland for the US, Israel or other countries. Zionism and the desire for a Jewish homeland, which had been only one of many political movements among Jews before the war, now became far more popular. Although many Jews who had lost property were able to regain at least some of it thanks to sympathetic pre-war judges, full-scale restitution was blocked by the Soviet-controlled government which saw this as a perfect opportunity to proceed with nationalizing private business and property. For most Jews, however, the lawlessness, political oppression and economic collapse made rebuilding the lives they had previously known as small businesspeople or craftsmen very difficult. This was exacerbated by instances of anti-Semitic violence. The worst of these occurred in Kielce in 1946 when rioters killed some forty Jews over false allegation of blood libel. The exact course of events is unclear and many historians believe the event was provoked by government security forces (and many documents relating to the event were deliberately destroyed in 1989 prior to the fall of communism); under the desperate conditions in Poland it was nonetheless quite easy to provoke an attack on local Jews.

THE COST OF CATASTROPHE

World War II was a catastrophe for Poland on a scale that few other countries have experienced at any time in human history. A higher percentage of Poles died than in any other country: 21 per cent, more if one counts fatalities caused by war-related diseases. Six million Polish citizens were killed. Of these, three million were Jewish. Poland's ancient Jewish community, with a history stretching back to the early Middle Ages, was virtually wiped out. The Nazis killed two million Polish Christians, the Soviets perhaps between half a million and a million, and over 100,000 by Ukrainian nationalists. The city of Warsaw alone lost more people than Britain and the US put together. Polish military losses were equally appalling: an estimated 360,000 died in battle, of wounds or as prisoners of war, a number greater than any European country save the USSR and Germany.

Cultural and professional elites were the hardest hit: 45 per cent of doctors and dentists were killed by the Nazis; 57 per cent of lawyers; 30 per cent of engineers and technicians; 40 per cent of professors; 15 per cent of teachers; and 20 per cent of clergy. This does not begin to include the number of professionals and community leaders killed or imprisoned by the Soviets and their Polish puppet government.

The country itself was devastated. Warsaw had been the scene of three major battles and what remained after the fighting was systematically levelled on Hitler's personal orders. Other cities, such as Poznań and Gdańsk, were also devastated. Of the main historic centres of Poland only Kraków remained intact. The country's artwork and cultural treasures were stolen or destroyed. Of all the art and cultural artifacts in Poland at the start of the war, 5 per cent remained when it was over. Most major industrial and commercial enterprises were also completely wrecked and what remained was often looted by the Soviets who dismantled whole factories and shipped them to Russia.

The Polish armed forces and the citizen-soldiers of the resistance performed with supreme valour. They fought in every major campaign against Nazism from the first day of the war to the last. Yet, this heroism brought little in way of respect, recognition or consideration for Polish independence. Pro-Soviet feeling and the active work of Soviet sympathizers in the west turned a significant segment of the public and press in the West against the Poles who were routinely described as 'reactionaries' or 'fascists'. In England, the pilots who had defended Britain from the Blitz were sometimes spat on in the streets or beaten up. During the great victory parade in London to celebrate the end of the war, the armies of Turkey and Fiji, who had played no role in the war, were represented. The Poles, however, were not. The British knuckled under to Soviet pressure to keep their old allies out. With large numbers of Poles on British soil, there was a strong desire to deport all of them. Ultimately, about 50,000 would stay in Britain and after an initial period of adjustment were generally accepted by British society. While some of the exiles did well for themselves in the post-war years, others had few resources to fall back on and without any military pension to look forward to, spent the rest of their lives working at menial jobs. General Stanisław Maczek, the brilliant tank commander of the Polish First Armoured Division, hero of Falaise, liberator of Breda, ended up as a waiter in a Scottish pub.

Poland itself effectively ceased to be independent. Although the local communist authorities would gain some measure of autonomy after 1956, virtually all major decisions had to be approved from Moscow. The country's borders were shifted drastically and about a quarter of its population internally displaced.

The war and the Holocaust that had occurred on Polish soil brought forth the best and worst in human nature. There were acts of betrayal and cowardice as well as heroism. People turned in neighbours for money or food. There is no question that Poles could have done more to help Jews facing the final solution, but at the same time Poles did more than any other nation to assist Jews and more Poles died because they aided Jews than any other nation.

The war, then, became a central point of reference for Poland. It would profoundly mark all those who survived and forever alter Poland's historical trajectory.

CHAPTER NINE

'People's Poland,'
1946–78

Poland's new Soviet masters proclaimed the establishment of 'the Polish People's Republic.' The new state retained some of the symbols of the Second Republic, including the flag. The white eagle remained the national symbol but, significantly, without a crown. Yet no effort to cover the new regime with a façade of normality would be enough.

The perfidy and murderousness of the Soviets during the war and the communists' efforts to besmirch and destroy the anti-Nazi resistance movement combined with pre-war memories of the struggle against Soviet invaders in 1920 and the long years of Russian domination during the nineteenth century made winning legitimacy impossible for the new communist regime. No amount of blandishment, propaganda, or coercion would make a regime imposed by force seem acceptable to the majority of Poles. Communism in Poland would always be seen as a foreign imposition. Throughout the subsequent communist period, the regime in Poland would be weaker and more prone to opportunism than to a belief in the ideals of Karl Marx, than any of its counterparts in the so-called Soviet bloc.

Stalinism

The first eleven years of communist rule in Poland is often referred to as the period of 'real socialism.' Stalin's Soviet minions ruled the country with an iron fist. Control was directly in the hands of Soviets, though many of them masqueraded as Poles. Some did not even speak proper Polish. The party that theoretically controlled Poland was the United Polish Workers Party. The original communist party of Poland had opposed Polish independence in 1920 and was banned by interwar Polish governments. Most of its leaders had lived in the Soviet Union until the late 1930s when they were executed on Stalin's orders. In 1942, a small party nucleus emerged in Poland under the leadership of Władysław Gomułka (1905–82). At almost the same time, Soviet authorities created the Union of Polish Patriots which theoretically controlled the Polish Red Army created in the Soviet Union. These two circles would merge by 1945. A rump of the old socialist PPS was also added. After Gomułka showed a flicker of independence, however, he was replaced by Bolesław Bierut (1892–1956) who acted exactly as Stalin wished.

The communists' first task was to defeat the resistance movement and establish a fig leaf of authenticity. This authenticity was designed largely for Western consumption. Although the communists held out the hope that they could win over some sectors of the population, this proved difficult. Moderate policies that might have had a chance were vetoed in Moscow. The Allies had agreed on a government of national unity that would include elements of the London government with Stalin's henchmen. In 1945, Stanisław Mikołajczak (1903–66), the last civilian leader of the legitimate London government and representative of the Peasant Party broke with many of his colleagues in exile and returned to Poland as deputy premier and minister of agriculture. In practical terms, he was simply a figurehead.

In 1946, the communists staged a referendum asking for public support for the elimination of the Senate, nationalising industry and land reform, and the change in Poland's border with Germany. While a majority approved of the third point, the communists falsified the results of the other two questions. In 1947, nationwide elections were held, and the communists falsified the results to show an 80 per cent vote in favour of the party. Mikołajczak, who had become a rallying point for the opposition, fled in fear of his life and lived out the remainder of his days in exile.

Communist rule was reinforced by a wide network of spies and informers. An estimated one in ten Poles informed on their fellow citizens. (This figure, however, was lower than in other communist countries. In East Germany, for example, 30 per cent of the population acted as informers.) Informers came from all walks of life. In the late 1970s secret police even had over 8,000 informers among the Catholic clergy and in Catholic lay organisations. Among other groups, such as journalists, the number of informers was as high as 30 per cent.

With the country in ruins, the party's major task was reconstruction. In this they had the clear co-operation of the population. Thousands of ordinary people attacked piles of rubble in Warsaw, salvaging bricks and anything that could be useful. Bodies were buried and services gradually restored. In one of its most popular moves, the government decided to reconstruct the historic centre of Warsaw. Using old paintings, photos, and architectural drawings that had escaped the destruction, over the course of three decades the Poles would pains-takingly create an exact replica of what the Nazis had destroyed.

In the economic realm the country's new masters had less success. Pent-up demand created by the years of war and its aftermath would help the economy grow for a time, but this would not last long. Polish trade with the West was largely forbidden and trade with the Soviet Union amounted to little more than organised theft. Soviet authorities took Polish commodities, especially coal, at a fraction of their real value. The government also embarked on a crash industrialization programme based on Soviet-style heavy industry. Using Soviet tech-nology from as far back as the 1920s, this new industry proved ineffi-cient and highly polluting. The inefficiencies, however, remained hidden for many decades due to the nature of the command economy and to creative record keeping on the part of the authorities. Never-theless, for the first time in its history, Poland began to develop a sig-nificant industrial base.

Efforts to remake the countryside according to the Soviet model were far less successful. While large estates were confiscated, peasants saw little practical benefit. Attempts to collectivize agriculture failed due to resistance by the peasants and the need to not further antagonise the rural population while the struggle against the anti-communist resistance movement was still in progress. In the so-called Recovered Territories, the communists did set up collective farms, but as usual these resulted in decreasing productivity and low-quality products. The peasant farmers of Poland who kept their own land were denied access to credit and modern equipment and techniques, but still managed to produce more and better produce than their modern, collectivized counterparts. As a result of the government's weakness, Poland remained the only Soviet puppet state to retain a large rural population that controlled its own land.

The regime also attempted social engineering. There was no better example than the town of Nowa Huta outside of Kraków. Designed around a massive new steelworks, Nowa Huta was to be a model communist community where the 'new socialist man' would emerge to lead Poland into the future of Marxism. Workers were to live in soulless concrete apartment blocks and there were to be no churches. It was this latter provision that sparked widespread passive resistance by the new town's residents. Time and again they attempted to build a church, only to be blocked and harassed by the authorities. They held Masses in open fields or journeyed to other towns. This struggle would go on for decades before the authorities were finally forced to give in thanks in part to the archbishop of Kraków, one Karol Wojtyła.

The Church was the only major institution remaining in Poland that was not under government control. The authorities created a host of quasi-Catholic institutions meant to undermine the Church and promoted schismatic movements. An active branch of the secret police worked to undermine the Church and manufactured smear campaigns against popular clergy. All Church property except for church buildings themselves was confiscated and priests and clergy arrested and harassed. During the period, the towering figure of the Primate, Cardinal Stefan Wyszyński, remained defiant. In 1953, he was arrested and imprisoned for over three years. This move only increased his stature.

In the cultural realm, slavish devotion to Stalin was the order of the day. Sycophantic poems extolling Stalin's virtues were composed by the leading writers of the day. For two future Polish Nobel Prize winners, Czesław Miłosz and Wisława Szymborska, as for many, this period would be one of artistic ignominy. In the visual arts, 'socialist realism' was the approved style. Scholarship was systematically given over to Marxism and academics in many fields began their books with quotations from Stalin that could apparently be applied to nearly every field of human endeavour. Poland's history was systematically falsified.

The Polish Primate, Cardinal Stefan Wyszyński

Insignificant communist figures were transformed into national heroes. Poland's non-communist resistance movement and the armed forces that had fought alongside the Allies were vilified as fascists and Nazi collaborators.

COMMUNISM WITH A POLISH FACE

Stalin, one of history's most murderous tyrants, died in 1953. In 1956, following the exposure of a limited number of his crimes at the Twentieth Party Congress in Moscow, Stalin's loyal henchman Bierut died suddenly, possibly by his own hand. The Hungarian Uprising broke out and shortly thereafter workers in Poznań went on strike demanding freedom and bearing banners with slogans like 'Russkies go Home!' The police cracked down hard, killing fifty-three workers, but the writing was on the wall. Those who had served Stalin fell from favour. Władysław Gomułka emerged as the leading figure within the Polish communist party. He managed to gain a slightly longer tether from his Soviet masters. Some of the more overt Russian 'advisors' in the government and army went home and Poland began to get a somewhat more equitable price for the products it shipped to Russia.

Some of the more overt forms of repression were eased in favour of a slightly more subtle form of totalitarianism. Cardinal Wyszyński was released from prison and struck a deal with the authorities. The Church would stay out of politics and the authorities would not interfere with the Church or religious life. In the short run, Gomułka gained a measure of social peace, but in the long run this proved to be communism's undoing. The Church's practical independence created a major loophole in the totalitarian system. While it did not directly challenge the communists, the Church provided an alternative voice and a clear moral beacon in the face of the party's dialectic relativism and corruption.

The economy improved slightly during Gomułka's rule but failed to produce lasting prosperity. The command economy was disastrously inefficient and highly prone to official corruption. Economic imbalances were the order of the day and a black market sprung up to take advantage. Shoes would be plentiful in one city but hats would be impossible to find. In another city, the opposite would be true. A clever or well-connected individual could easily exploit the situation. In all state-run enterprises standards were ignored, corners cut and materials stolen by party officials. If an apartment block was to have twenty floors, a local official might make one floor with a ceiling a few feet shorter and use the extra material to build his summer home in the Mazurian lakes. Apartment buildings for hundreds of families were built without central controls for heating, ensuring that some apartments baked in the winter while others froze. The corruption seeped down from the top. In state-run enterprises workers stole, worked slowly or cut corners. After all, the pay was the same.

Despite these economic disasters, compared to the rest of the Soviet bloc, Poland was a comparative island of prosperity, often referred to as 'the merriest cell in the prison'. Russians and East Germans habitually took their holidays in Poland and shopped for goods that were scarce back home. Poland also benefited from its large diaspora from which, after 1956, people were increasingly encouraged to visit. These visits helped open another small window to freedom.

To escape from the omnipresent state control over the public sphere, Poles retreated into a private world of close groups of family and friends. The exterior of the giant communist apartment blocks were operated by the state and remained gray and forbidding. Inside of the apartments where the people could take care of their own space, there was warmth and laughter. Poles survived by developing a host of jokes that savaged the communist system and made fun of official slogans:

Q. Why do the riot police go around in threes?

A. *One can read, one can write and the third one keeps an eye on the two intellectuals.*

Q. What is a string quartet in Poland?

A. *A symphony orchestra after a concert tour in the West.*

Q. Why are butchers more truthful today than they were in the past?

A. *In the past the sign outside the shop said butcher and the shop contained meat. Now the sign says butcher and the shop contains the butcher.*

Q. Why did the medicine received from an American friend not work in Poland?

A. *The medicine stated: 'Take three times daily after meals.'*

Q. Why would Poland veto a US application to join Comecon [the Soviet economic bloc]?

A. *It could not afford to support the economies of two superpowers.*

Q. What is the difference between capitalism and socialism?

A. *Capitalism is at the brink of the precipice. Socialism is one step further ahead.*

Q. What is the difference between a democracy and a people's democracy?

A. *The same as the difference between a chair and an electric chair.*

1968

The communist system in Poland had few mechanisms for channelling the social and political tensions it created both in society at large and within the party itself. It chose manipulation over daily repression – the iron fist of Soviet power was well gloved in the faux velvet of Polish socialism. After 1956, the party contained fewer and fewer true believers and more and more cynical opportunists. This strange combination of totalitarianism, with corruption, and small windows of freedom would result in periodic and violent upheavals. The two groups who should have been most closely aligned to the regime – the young people who had grown up under communism and the workers whose well-being was supposedly the major concern of the party – were among the first to protest against it.

By 1968, it was clear that Gomułka's economic planning had largely failed. Although the rebuilding of Warsaw was a success, there was little else to which the party could point. Gomułka's prestige within the party began to slip and it took only a few minor incidents to shake the system to it foundations. The first was the reaction of some Polish army officers to the Israeli victory over the Arabs in 1967. Many of the leaders of the Israeli army had received their basic training in the pre-war Polish army while Arab armies had been trained by the Soviets. Some officers gleefully joked about how 'our Jews beat their Arabs.' A group of opportunists within the party led by Mieczysław Moczar seized on such comments as an excuse to purge the country's leadership of 'Zionist' (i.e., Jewish elements). At the same time, a performance of the Mickiewicz play *Dziady* was ordered to close by the Russian ambassador, sparking a wave of student protests in Warsaw and elsewhere. Security forces attacked the students as 'Zionist agitators,' beating and arresting large numbers. Thousands of Jews, most of them party members or relatives of party members, were given one-way passports and left for the United States or Israel. Anti-Semitic rhetoric was once again back in fashion. The majority of Polish society reacted with confusion since the term 'Zionist' had little meaning and most of those being accused were party members themselves. Nevertheless, the campaign did tremendous damage to Poland's international reputation. Those who left were often highly talented individuals who harboured deeply ambivalent feelings due to the experiences of 1968. As they entered western academia and other institutions they brought these attitudes with them and established themselves as experts on all things Polish, often promoting a peculiar view of Poland as a land of inveterate reactionaries and anti-Semites.

In international affairs, the Polish army – though it had occasionally protected students from the security forces – played a shameful role of supporting the Soviet invasion of Czechoslovakia to crush the 'Prague Spring.' This was a test the 'Brezhnev Doctrine' in which the Soviets signalled that any deviation from Moscow's control would result in an invasion.

Despite the upheavals of 1968, Gomułka was able to retain power within the party. Yet, this only staved off the inevitable. In 1970, with the economic situation getting increasingly out of control, the government announced a 20 per cent hike in the price of food a week before Christmas. Workers around the country went on strike and riots ensued. This time, it was the industrial strongholds of the Baltic coast where the worst violence occurred. When the militia ambushed a train full of workers in Gdańsk, shooting scores of unarmed strikers, the workers responded by burning the local party headquarters. Some 300 workers were killed in the riots, but the exact count is unknown since many bodies were buried in secret.

The clashes resulted in Gomułka's fall from power. He was replaced by Edward Gierek (1913–2001), another party functionary who served as regional boss of Silesia. Gierek managed to dampen the flames of revolution and gave a wage increase to placate the workers. The country began to produce more consumer goods to give the appearance of a higher standard of living. Economic growth was funded by borrowing from Western banks who considered coercive regimes a good credit risk because they could always take resources from their own societies by force. The apparent prosperity was brief and illusionary. Exports to the USSR continued to be a losing proposition as in effect Poland was subsidising the Soviet Union's even more serious economic problems. Efforts to create export markets in the West failed as communist managers were rarely able to meet required quality standards. The only advantage of Polish products was their low price, but this was kept down artificially by subsidies. In truth, production was often more expensive due to waste and mismanagement than in the West.

In 1976, Gierek and the party again sought to rectify the situation. They announced a 60 per cent increase in the price of food. Workers across the country walked off the job and riots ensued. A day later, the party repealed the price increases.

By the end of the 1970s, paying the cost of foreign borrowing ate up half of Poland's income. Food and consumer goods were shipped abroad to gain hard currency to pay off the debt. The official rate of unconvertible Polish *złoty* was kept artificially high in an effort to squeeze dollars out of Western visitors, creating a currency black market in which dollars could be sold far above the official rate. The new joke was 'why is the economy of the United States just like the economy of Poland? Answer: In the US you can buy anything with dollars and nothing with *złoty* and in Poland it is the same.' Shortages of basic goods appeared everywhere, fuelling the black market trade. Communist party members were themselves immune from these problems. Despite the party's proclaimed affinity for the working people, only party members and especially high officials had unlimited access to scarce goods, and commodities imported from the west.

MALAISE

As the party's prestige plummeted, the strength of the Church increased. The Catholic Church provided a refuge and a gathering point for new ideas. Intellectuals and workers, people from all walks of life gathered not only to pray and hear the word of God, but also to discuss the problems of society freely. It was the Church's status that allowed it to make a dramatic move: in 1965 Polish bishops reached out to their West German counterparts and called for an end to Polish-German hostility. This stunning move from a society that had suffered so much from German aggression set the stage for opening relations between Poland and West Germany and for Chancellor Willy Brandt's (1913–92) request for forgiveness for the crimes committed by Germans in Poland. This marked the first real Polish-German dialogue in history.

The Polish clergy and laity were the one sector of society bursting with new ideas. In Lublin, the Catholic University was the only independent institution of higher learning in the entire communist world. Church leaders, such as Cardinal Wyszyński, Cardinal Karol Wojtyła of Kraków (1920–2005) and Fr. Józef Tischner, were towering intellectuals who spoke and wrote clearly and forcefully. Their message was first and foremost a moral and ethical one – that good and evil, right and wrong were not relative concepts and that truth would ultimately prevail over lies. Communist party leaders, by contrast, sounded like country bumpkins, babbling a stream of jargon that had no bearing on reality. The contrast could not be clearer. By the

1970s, secular left-leaning intellectuals, including many sons and daughters of party leaders, began to make common cause with the Church and the workers. In 1976, a group of intellectuals formed the Committee to Defend Workers. Illegal publications (which had never really stopped circulating) increased in number, bringing new views and translations of writings from the West.

The Polish diaspora also played an important role. Poles living in Europe and the United States kept the case of Poland's freedom before the attention of western governments. Radio Free Europe proved an important source of information. Journals published abroad, such as the Paris-based *Kultura,* were smuggled into Poland and provided a taste of banned and forbidden writers and ideas. Many Poles read the work of Nobel Prize winner Miłosz in the pages of such publications. Visits from relatives living in the west made clear the material gap that existed between east and west.

Years later the great Polish poet Zbigniew Herbert (1924–98), one

The great poet, Zbigniew Herbert

of the few who refused to compromise with the communists, would diagnose the intellectual malaise:

> A good Marxist, like a good sophist, successfully argued for Helen's virginity, and then equally successfully demonstrated that she was a whore.... The beginning of the present semantic collapse goes back to the 1950s. Those who remained faithful to the principles of dialectic did so after massive training. They do not pronounce intersubjective judgments but instead treat the language as a form of attack or defence: 'Under Bierut I wrote this, under Gomułka something else,' but always following the rhythm of history, or rather, the Politburo guidelines. This amounts to a betrayal of language, a denial of the unequivocal meaning of certain ideas.

Despite such stirrings, however, and despite the periodic protests from Polish society and the incompetence and failure of the communists, nearly everyone agreed that the system backed up by the nuclear armed might of the USSR was in place to stay.

In Kraków, however, there was one man who felt that the situation was not so hopeless or fearful. His name was Karol Wojtyła and all he needed was an opportunity to get his ideas across.

CHAPTER TEN

The Age of John Paul II, 1978–2005

On the evening of 16 October, 1978 communism in Poland died. Although the difference between dead communism and living was not immediately apparent for some time, an autopsy would reveal when and how the fatal wound was incurred. The death of communism in Poland would prove to be the fatal ulcer on the system throughout Europe, a system based on fear, coercion and violence.

From Kraków to Rome and Back

Following the short pontificate of Pope John Paul I, the College of Cardinals of the Roman Catholic Church choose the cardinal-archbishop of Kraków, Karol Wojtyła, to be the first non-Italian pope in 455 years. Although the Polish prelate was well-known in serious Catholic intellectual circles, to most of the world, including in Poland and in Moscow, the choice was a stunning surprise. Cardinal Wojtyła himself at first balked at the thought of the awesome responsibility, but his colleague and mentor Cardinal Wyszyński reminded him of the scene from the Sienkiewicz novel *Quo Vadis?* in which Christ challenges Peter as the first pontiff seeks to save his own life by fleeing Rome. Once again, the power of literature over the Polish heart proved decisive.

Wojtyła had survived the Nazi occupation and had become an increasingly important figure in the Polish church during the 1960s and 1970s. As both an intellectual and a pastor he was able to provide Poles with the moral clarity and the philosophical rigour that had been missing in their lives. Though, like Wyszyński, he never called for direct confrontation with the authorities, he gave back to the people their dignity and the truth of their painful historical experience free of propaganda and government manipulation.

On the evening of 16 October, 1978, the newly elected Pope walked onto the balcony above St Peter's Square in Rome and won over the Roman crowd. As news reached Poland, church bells began to ring out. The ancient Sigismund bell at Wawel Castle, rung only in moments of supreme gravity, tolled out the news. Crowds, cheering and crying, filled the churches. Similar scenes were played out in Polish immigrant communities around the world. In Chicago, at the head-quarters of the oldest Polish organisation in the United States, the Polish Roman Catholic Union, a secretary got a phone call with the news. 'We have Polish Pope. My God. We have a Polish Pope!' she cried. At this the entire staff began to weep.

While ordinary Poles danced in the streets for joy, at party head-quarters in Warsaw and in Moscow there was panic and confusion. The KGB station chief in Warsaw was recalled to Moscow where Yuri Andropov, head of the KGB, demanded to know 'How could you possible allow the citizen of a socialist country to be elected Pope?' State television waited several hours for appropriate high-level clari-fication before broadcasting the news (though by then, everyone knew). In public, official reaction was subdued, but behind the scenes no one was sure what it all meant. Soviet analysis assumed it was a US–German plot to undermine socialist unity. Some felt the new pope would be open to 'dialogue' with the party. Some felt that his election would relieve the communist authorities in Poland of a thorn in their side. Author George Weigel noted that Kremlin anxiety over the election of Pope John Paul II was not confined to the unravelling of the Soviet position in Poland. Poland was the geographic linchpin of the Warsaw Pact. The new Pope's close affinity for the Ukrainian Catholic church and for Catholics in Lithuania was equally alarming to Moscow. In Warsaw, the party sent secret instructions to schools that stated 'The Pope is our enemy. . . . Due to his uncommon skills and great sense of humour he is dangerous. . . .Because of the activation of the Church in Poland our activities designed to atheize the youth must . . . intensively develop.' Years before Stalin had dismissed the Church with the quip

'How many divisions does the Pope have?' His successors were about to find out the answer.

On 2 June, 1979, after protracted negotiations with the authorities, Pope John Paul II returned to Poland. On his first day in Warsaw, a million people packed the streets and squares in the heart of the capital to see the Pope. At that moment, the authorities lost control of the public square, the one asset essential to a totalitarian regime. During his first sermon in Warsaw, John Paul II stressed the theme of his visit: Polish history could not be understood without God, Polish history and culture – given birth at the time of Poland's conversion in 966 – were inseparable from its faith. And only with God could true freedom be attained. The crowds began to chant 'We want God! We want God!' At Mass after Mass as he travelled across Poland, similar scenes were repeated with crowds numbering close to a million at almost every stop. State-run television tried not to show scenes of the massive crowds, but occasionally a cameraman would disobey orders and pan across the sea of humanity. The authorities lost control of their own streets and squares. Workers were denied time off to see the Pope, but simply put down their tools and walked off the job. The crowds remained peaceful and calm, but it was now the turn of the people to feel powerful and the authorities hid in their houses and offices.

John Paul II spoke out forcefully for human rights. At the official reception hosted by the government, he told the authorities that the state was not an end itself but existed only to serve the people. At Auschwitz, he stopped before the inscription in Hebrew and pointedly told Poles that it was impossible to remain indifferent in the face of the great suffering that the Jewish people had endured during the Holocaust. At Nowy Targ, he told young people to commit themselves to a life free of lies and fear.

In nine days, thirteen million Poles had seen John Paul II in person, approximately one in three people. Nearly all of the rest had seen him on television. Thousands of Czech, Slovak, Hungarian, Ukrainian, and Lithuanian Catholics also made it to Poland to see the Pope. As he left, he told Poles never to lose hope or give into despair. From then on, a growing number would act as if the totalitarian regime no longer mattered.

The Shipyard

In 1980 the economy continued to deteriorate and soon the authorities were again attempting to institute sharp price increases on food. Rationing of meat, butter, and cigarettes was ordered in many areas. Food shortages became increasing common, with some stores carrying only pickles and vinegar. Shopping became like a hunting expedition in which shoppers – usually women – tracked down their scarce quarry through a variety of stores and by queuing in line for hours. A cottage industry developed of people who simply joined queues and then sold their place in the line. As more and more people spent more and more time searching for the basics of everyday life, they spent less and less time at work. 'We pretend to work, they pretend to pay us,' was the joke of the day.

The first sparks flew at the Świdnik aircraft factory near Lublin where an 80 per cent increase in meat prices resulted in a work stoppage. In the wake of the Pope's visit, the authorities had become increasingly nervous and realising what the price increases might mean, began to fire or reassign leaders among the workers at key industrial plants. Some were arrested or brought in for interrogation. The workers, too, had become better prepared, creating a host of informal networks, and kept in touch with secretly printed newsletters, flyers, posters. Strikes began to break out across the country, but particularly on the massive shipyards of the Baltic coast.

In late 1979 at the Lenin Shipyards in Gdańsk, the managers let go electrician Lech Wałęsa (1943–), one of the leaders of the workers agitating for the right to form independent unions and receive fair treatment. Then in August 1980 they tried to fire crane operator Anna Walentynowicz (1929–), one of the yard's most popular and respected workers. In addition to being a leader of the workers' resistance, Walentynowicz had been a model worker, receiving awards for her dedication to her craft. Years of the authorities ignoring safety violations and increasingly shoddy work, however, turned Walentynowicz into a dedicated trade unionist.

This was the final straw. The shipyard workers began to stop work spontaneously. Wałęsa climbed over the shipyard wall to rejoin his fellow workers and take charge of the strike. Unlike previous demonstrations, however, this time the workers did not march. They remained calm and peaceful. And they did not accept compromises and half measures from the government officials sent to negotiate the end of the strike. Nor would they accept any agreement that would include only this single shipyard. This time, the spirit of unity found in the streets during the nine days in June of the Pope's visit made itself felt. Students, professors, shop workers, taxi drivers, and workers from all professions began to join the movement in Gdańsk and across the country.

Communist party officials were presented with a list of twenty-one demands that included the right to set up unions independent of the government, the right to strike, the release of political prisoners, the curtailment of censorship, and Sunday Mass for shut-ins on state radio. As the movement expanded peacefully to every corner of Poland, the authorities were increasingly helpless and uncertain. The working class, on whose behalf communism was supposed to be acting, was throwing out communism. On 31 August, the authorities signed an agreement with the strikers that allowed the creation of a free, nationwide free trade union, called Solidarity (*Solidarność*) with Wałęsa as its chairman. Although the party saved face by confirming its 'leading role' in society, its monopoly on power had been challenged and broken.

SOLIDARNOŚĆ

Over the next sixteen months, Poland experienced a heady ferment of freedom. With the effective removal of censorship, Poles were free at last to speak and think for themselves. While access to official media was forbidden, hundreds of new publications appeared, including materials from the west hastily (and often poorly) translated into Polish. New organizations sprung up representing every shade of opinion from cultural and social groups to environmental and political groups.

Solidarity itself struggled to realize the rights it had won in August 1980. A Solidarity organization for farmers, Rural Solidarity, was created and the organization sought to expand into almost every occupation and profession. The party reshuffled its top leadership and replaced Gierek with Stanisław Kania. At every step of the way, the authorities attempted to stall or block implementation of the accords. Official propaganda proclaimed a willingness to work with Solidarity but at the same time blamed the union for the country's economic problems. Few believed the government's explanation. Solidarity increasingly resorted to strikes to force the government to honour its agreements. At the same time, the broad-based decentralised movement suffered dissension within its own ranks due to its diverse make-up as well as to the work of government agents within the movement who acted as agent provocateurs. Solidarity leaders, knowing they were being spied on, continued to work in the open. The most significant split was between relative moderates who feared provoking a Soviet invasion and more radical elements who want to unseat the party.

The Soviet leadership was increasingly alarmed. Poland's neighbours, especially East Germany, urged rapid and violent attacks on Poland to stop the wind of freedom from spreading. Polish authorities tried to reassure their 'fraternal' allies that they had the situation under control, but within the party struggles and divisions over how to handle the situation persisted. Party membership declined and as many as one third of party members actually joined Solidarity. In the West, there was broad-based support for Solidarity, especially in the United States. Parties on the political left and many in the mainstream western media, however, were not enthusiastic about Solidarity's unexpected rise, fearing it would harm détente.

In October 1981, hardliners within the party and government pushed out Kania and replaced him with General Wojciech Jaruzelski (1923–). The general had lost his father to the Soviets during the deportations of World War II and as a youth he had suffered snow-blindness doing forced labour in Siberia, forcing him to wear dark glasses throughout his life. Although he saw himself as a Polish patriot and a soldier he was, nevertheless, supremely loyal to the party and through the party to Moscow.

On 13 December, 1981, Jaruzelski declared martial law. During one television announcement of the state of emergency, a backdrop fell over, revealing a soldier with a gun standing behind the announcer. Army, police and security forces seized control of the country, arresting thousands of Solidarity leaders. The ZOMO, the motorised riot police,

General Wojciech Jaruzelski

beat up and arrested anyone who tried to protest in public. Approximately a hundred people died, including several clergy, some under mysterious circumstances. Some of the worst violence occurred at the Wujek and Manifest Lipcowy mines in southern Poland, where the ZOMO killed nine striking miners. Jaruzelski would later claim that the move had been taken to save Poland from a full-fledged Soviet invasion. Although there is little doubt that the Soviets could have acted, the evidence for an imminent Soviet attack is debatable.

Over the next several months, the government dissolved the union and reversed much of Solidarity's work. In late 1982, Jaruzelski's junta felt sufficiently secure to free Wałęsa, whom it characterized as the 'former leader of a former union.' After gradually easing the most onerous features of the state of emergency, the authorities lifted martial law in July 1983, but Jaruzelski and his generals continued to control the most critical party and government posts. With martial law came economic sanctions imposed by outraged American and Western governments. The government's own efforts did even more damage and the economy began to shut down. Aid in the form of food and clothes sent by the Polish diaspora and Solidarity sympathisers around the world, usually funnelled through the Church, was increasingly necessary for Poles. Horsemeat began to appear in people's diets.

Many Solidarity activists were given one-way passports and faced the choice of a future in which their children might be offered only menial jobs. Others left of their own accord, to escape the intolerable economic situation or in the face of pressure from the secret police who were constantly trying to get people from all walks of life to spy on each other. A new Polish diaspora began, with many Poles going to the United States or Western Europe. Those without good connections often spent time in refugee camps in Europe.

For many Poles, the 1980s were a kind of lost decade. The economy slowly fell apart and government did nothing. People had few options and much time was spent standing in queues or making connections that would allow one to get scarce goods. Faith, family ties, humour and a steady stream of underground publications kept people from losing heart. Within the party, however, things were different. It was clear to most members that aside from the second coming of Karl Marx, communism – whether with a Polish face or a Russian one – was dead. The Polish United Workers Party had always had an unusually high percentage of pure opportunists who had joined merely to advance their careers rather than out of a belief in the historical inevitability of a socialism utopia.

This was illustrated by the historian Norman Davies who took a group of American students from California to Poland for summer study in 1986. Eager to at last be in a socialist country and away from capitalism, one chose to interview communists as her research project. After a week, the student complained that she not yet found a single communist. 'Keep looking,' her professor told her. More weeks passed without a sign of a single communist. Finally, the students attended a talk by a high-ranking member of the Polish politburo. Halfway through his lecture, the student could no longer contain herself. She raised her hand and blurted out, 'Sir, are you a communist or are you not?' 'There was a deathly silence for several instants,' Davies wrote, 'Then he said, "Lady, I'm a pragmatist." '

Throughout the mid-1980s, the 'pragmatists' looked for a way off the sinking ship. Some began to set up private businesses and positioned themselves to buy state-controlled assets. Others took whatever money or property they could get away with.

Periodic strikes and demonstrations added a sense of urgency. Two visits by Pope John Paul II and a steady stream of papal pronouncements kept Poland in the spotlight and steadied the resolve of society. Even the attempted assassination of the Pope in 1981, now known to be staged at the behest of the KGB, did little to dent the spirit of resistance Solidarity had created. Poles looked to John Paul II as their real leader. In 1983, in a televised meeting, the Pope gave General Jaruzelski a dressing down. With the world's press corps watching, TV cameras recorded the general's knees shaking as the Pope spoke, the man of violence quivering before the man of peace. 'There is no freedom without solidarity,' the Pope told his countrymen later, and while he was referring to spiritual solidarity, no one could misunderstand the double entendre. That same year, Wałęsa received the Nobel Peace prize, further embarrassing the government. In 1984, the authorities kidnapped and murdered the popular Warsaw priest Fr. Jerzy Popiełuszko (1947–84), a spiritual advisor to Solidarity. The move only deepened the resolve for non-violent resistance.

In 1988, the authorities reached the end of the line. The rise of Mikhail Gorbachev in the Soviet Union undermined the threat of Soviet military intervention as a justification for the regime's grip on power. The economy had ceased to function. The opposition meanwhile was growing. A new round of strikes in 1988 convinced Jaruzelski that it was time to negotiate with the opposition since the government's position was only going to get weaker.

The Birth of the Third Republic

The communists, however, had one trump card. As they set up the negotiations, they were able to partly split the opposition and negotiated only with the centre and left elements of the opposition, excluding the most anti-communist sectors. The 'Roundtable Talks' dragged on throughout much of 1988. In early 1989, the sides agreed on Poland's first free election since 1938. The communists would have a certain number of seats guaranteed and would retain the presidency. The party and most western media pundits felt that this would likely result in a communist victory, given the party's existing organisational structure versus the ad hoc nature of the opposition.

In June the nation went to the polls. Nearly every single communist candidate was defeated. The 'safe' list of 161 communist candidates which needed only a majority of votes also resulted in defeat with voters preferring no one to a communist. In elections to the new senate, Solidarity won 99 of 100 seats. Because the 161 'safe' communist seats had no one elected to them a second round of elections had to be held. The opposition won all 161 seats. Western journalists who had always assumed that the communists had some support in Poland were stunned. Only the Poles were not surprised. In August 1989, Tadeusz Mazowiecki (1927–), a Catholic intellectual, became the first prime minister of the Third Republic of Poland. The communist party fell apart as the 'comrades' now sought only to feather their own nests and avoid prosecution for their crimes and misdeeds.

That autumn, the communist bloc, once an invulnerable bulwark of Soviet power, fell apart as one country after another followed the Polish example. Poland's old friends, the Hungarians, were the first, dismantling their fortified border with Austria, initiating economic reforms and multi-party elections. East Germany followed and in November tore down the Berlin Wall. Czechs and Slovaks launched the 'Velvet Revolution.' In December 1989, when Romania's communist tyrant refused to hand over power and unleashed his security forces on his own people, a popular uprising ended his bloody rule in a hail of bullets. Within two years, the Soviet Union itself would come apart.

TODAY, TOMORROW

In 1990, the Polish United Workers Party disbanded, with some of its members moving to form the new Social Democratic Party (SLD) that was created with the help of a generous loan from the Soviet Union. Jaruzelski, seeing the writing on the wall, resigned from the presidency, necessitating a new election for president. This move exacerbated splits that had always existed within Solidarity. As elections for president approached, Mazowiecki and Wałęsa squared off and Solidarity began to come apart. Wałęsa was elected president to fill out the rest of Jaruzelski's term.

The new government initiated a programme of rapid market liberalization as a way to rescue the economy. Called 'shock therapy' by some, its immediate effects seemed to exacerbate the situation. However, goods started to appear on shop shelves and a whole new class of small entrepreneurs, many selling products from their cars on street corners, sprang up.

A series of short-lived governments appeared under the aegis of Wałęsa who sought to expand the poorly defined powers of the presidency. As Poland's constitution was an ad hoc mixture of the old communist constitution and new provisions were enacted to ensure the transfer of power, much was up for grabs. In 1992, Hanna Suchocka (1946–) became Poland's first female prime minister at the head of an unstable centre-right coalition.

In 1995, Wałęsa's term ended. The Solidarity leader had become increasingly unpopular with the voters. Although brilliant in creating

Pope John Paul II and Lech Wałęsa

the revolution that ended communism, Wałęsa did not prove to be a good administrator. The new elections brought to power Aleksander Kwaśniewski (1954–) of the SLD, the former communist minister of sports. The youthful, telegenic Kwaśniewski would remain president for two terms, providing a certain measure of stability to the country. After the chaotic early years of democracy, the SLD re-emerged as a significant force in Polish politics. Parties of the right and centre remained divided until after 2000, though they were occasionally able to form electoral coalitions that unseated the SLD.

Economic policies continued the liberalization set forth by economist Leszek Balcerowicz, a socialist convert to Milton Friedman-style market capitalism. Although farmers and pensioners were left out, the Polish economy began to grow in the early 1990s and attract a significant amount of foreign investment. Warsaw became east-central Europe's new centre for business.

In foreign policy, Poland sought to escape any future sphere of Russian domination by re-entering the European scene and building close ties with the United States. In 1999, Poland, along with the Czech Republic and Hungary, joined the NATO alliance, which was a major milestone symbolising the country's acceptance as a democratic, free market country. In June 2003, Poland joined the European Union, completing its 'return to Europe.' There was general agreement across party lines on outlines of foreign policy and after the September 11, 2001 terrorist attacks in New York, Poland emerged as one of the United States' strongest allies and one of the few European countries largely immune to anti-Americanism.

Freedom of movement allowed large numbers of Poles to travel to Western Europe and the US to work or attend college. This had both positive and negative effects. On one hand, it provided a boost to the Polish economy. On the other hand, many of those who stayed abroad were young and well-educated, acting as kind of brain drain on the country.

Education grew dramatically as new private colleges and universities opened up. Many new courses in fields such as business and management appeared and Poles flocked to these in large numbers. While the total number of students grew 3.5 times during the first decade of independence, enrolment in business courses jumped seven fold.

The environment was another area of significant improvement, as old Soviet-style industries were shut down. Air pollution underwent a dramatic reduction, especially in cities such as Katowice and Kraków (though some of these gains were lost to an increase in automobile traffic). As cities implemented modern waste management plans, rivers and streams became dramatically cleaner.

Despite the undoubted successes during the first decade and a half of the Third Republic, significant problems remained. The legacy of communism was not dealt with in a serious way. The former leftist opposition, led by Adam Michnik (who would later become editor of the country's largest circulation daily newspaper, *Gazeta Wyborcza*), had emphasized the 'thick line' in Polish history that was meant to be a symbolic point beyond 1989 when all the crimes and misdeeds of former communists were to be forgotten. Reconciliation, not revenge, was the emphasis. This position was increasingly questioned after the re-emergence of the former communists in Polish politics. Many former communists had enriched themselves at public expense and crimes including murder and torture had gone unpunished. Moreover, some former communists aggressively sought to whitewash the past, portraying themselves as patriots and vilifying their opponents.

The poet Zbigniew Herbert summed up the feelings of many in an interview shortly before his death:

Sometimes I wonder why I feel discomfort when I wake up and remember that I live in a sovereign state. Maybe it has to do with the fact that I did not actively fight for freedom. [This time] we got independence as a gift from history; we did not shed blood for it. It was as if the communists suddenly became smart and said: 'We will not do those nasty things any longer, errr … let's have a drink instead.' Sort of one Pole speaking to another.... Many of us thought that after 1989 we would liberate ourselves from the lie, even if we were not instantly successful in building an ideal society. It did not work out because members of the elite … proved incapable of creating the language of truth. Yet telling the truth is the fundamental obligation of intellectuals, and the only possible justification for society's largesse toward them.... Intellectuals carry the grave responsibility for the use of words [in

society]. Yet today in Poland, they do not wish to shoulder that responsibility.

John Paul II noted a similar tendency. During his 1995 visit to Poland,
he repeatedly admonished Poles not to lose their moral bearings and
exchange the slavery of communism for the slavery of materialism and
consumerism.

The position of the Church in Polish society changed as well. Early
efforts by Church leaders to influence elections failed and the Church
largely withdrew from politics, save for crucial moral issues such as
abortion. One of the few exceptions was the referendum on Polish
entry into the European Union, which Church leaders including the
pope, supported, a fact which provided an important margin of victory.
Although some signs of secularisation began to affect the Church, it
remained stronger than its Western European counterparts.

Freedom also brought an increase in street crime, virtually unknown
for decades, as well as drug abuse, pornography, and human trafficking.
Local gangs and the Russian mafia gained a foothold in the country.

As of 2005, Poland's population stood at 38.6 million. Its average
income stands at about 12,000 USD per capita (PPP). Although the
economy has continued to grow, unemployment and public debt
remain among its most significant problems.

In foreign policy, Poland has achieved good relations with all its
immediate neighbours save for Russia and Belarus. Despite weak
parliamentary governments, its role and importance in world affairs has
increased. In 2004, Poland played an important role in mediating a
peaceful end to the electoral crisis in Ukraine and is among the most
active in protesting human rights abuses in Belarus. Relations with
Russia remain a significant problem, as the Russian leadership has failed
to acknowledge past crimes committed in Poland. Russian energy
conglomerates, working as an arm of the Russian state, have attempted
to control the Polish oil market, often using illegal means. Disputes
over the future of east central Europe and the freedom of Ukraine and
Belarus remain a possibility. Finally, Poland's place within the European Union remains to be seen. Will established Union members treat
Poland as a valued partner and will the Poles see themselves as real

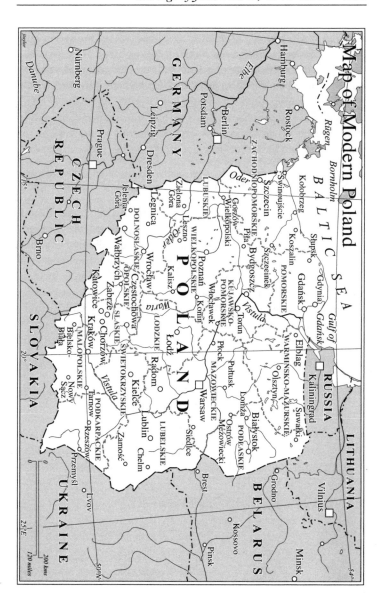

contributors to Europe as opposed to supplicants lacking social, spiritual, cultural or economic resources?

On 2 May, 2005 Pope John Paul II died in Rome amid scenes of global mourning. The man who had fulfilled the prophecy of the nineteenth-century poet Słowacki and led Poland to freedom from the Throne of St Peter was gone. Poles were grief stricken and the country virtually shut down during the days leading up to the funeral. An estimated two million Poles travelled to Rome, the greatest temporary exodus in the country's history, to say goodbye to the man who had shepherded them to freedom and helped them reclaim their dignity. 'What will become us?' many asked. This indeed, remains the question.

Despite all the problems that have arisen since 1989, given Poland's nearly three hundred years of sorrow, the period after 1989 marked a significant improvement in Poland's fortunes. Poland's long road back to freedom was marked with innumerable tragedies, large and small. The Polish people have taken everything fate has to throw at them, including the worst crimes of fascism and communism, and have not succumbed. Though its position in the world is not certain, Poland is no longer a plaything of the great powers. Poles earned the right to govern themselves and make their own mistakes and at last to write their own history.

Notes

Notes

Chronology of Major Events

ca. 5000 BC	Earliest Neolithic farming settlements in what is today Poland.
ca. 4500 BC	Lengyel Culture.
ca. 3900 BC	Funnel Beaker Culture.
ca. 2500 BC	Lusatian and Mierzanowice Cultures.
ca. 1 AD	Arrival of the proto-Slavs in eastern Europe.
ca. 450	Beginning of the Great Slav Migrations.
ca. 800s	Probable origin of the Piast dynasty of the Polanie tribe.
862	Mission of Saints Cyril and Methodius to the Slavic peoples.
922	Birth of Mieszko I.
962	Poland first mentioned in surviving historical chronicles.
966	Poland's conversion to Christianity.
968	Establishment of the first Polish bishropic.
992	Death of Mieszko and accession of Bolesław I.
997	Martyrdom of St Wojciech (Adalbert).
999	Canonization of St Wojciech.
1000	Pope Sylvester II established bishropics in Kraków, Wrocław, and Kołobrzeg. Gniezno raised to an archdiocese. Pilgrimage to Gniezno by German Emperor Otto I.
1002	Bolesław I seized Moravia, Bohemia, and Lusatia.
1005	Emperor Henry I failed in a bid to conquer Poland.
1017	Henry I's second invasion of Poland defeated at Niemcza.
1018	Bolesław I captures Kiev.
1025	Bolesław I crowned first king of Poland. Bolesław I died. Accession of Mieszko II.
1030	Poland invaded. Mieszko II deposed.
1032	Mieszko II restored to power.
1034	Death of Mieszko II. Major pagan revolts.
1038	Czechs sacked Poznań and Gniezno, occupied Silesia, and stole the relics of St Wojciech.
1039	Kazimierz I regained control of Poland and relocated the capital to Kraków.

1050	Poles drive Czechs from Silesia. First monastery established in Poland.
1058	Death of Kazimierz I and accession of Bolesław II.
1076	Bolesław II crowned king of Poland.
1079	Murder of St Stanisław, bishop of Kraków. Bolesław II forced to flee the country due to internal strife and dies in Hungary. Accession of Władysław Herman.
1102	Death of Władysław Herman. Poland divided between his rival sons Zbigniew and Bolesław III.
1107	Bolesław III established as sole ruler of Poland.
1109	Invasion of Poland by Imperial forces. Poles defeat Imperial armies at Glogów and Psie Pole.
1138	Death of Bolesław III; country divided between five of his sons.
1145	Władysław the Exile flees to Germany
1168	Destruction of Arkona, last major pagan Slavic centre.
1170s	Bronze doors of Gniezno Cathedral cast, marking the emergence of Romanesque art in Poland.
1173	Death of Bolesław the Curly. Mieszko the Old became senior prince.
1177	Mieszko deposed. Kazimierz the Just became senior prince.
1194	Death of Kazimierz the Just. Mieszko the Old retakes the post of senior prince.
1202	Death of Mieszko the Old, accession of Leszek the White.
1207	Vincenty Kadłubek elected bishop of Kraków as first independently elected bishop in Poland.
1220s	Large-scale immigration from Germany and Flanders began.
1227	Assassination of Leszek the White, accession of Władysław Spindleshanks.
1228	Teutonic Knights granted land in Mazovia and rapidly expanded their holdings.
1237	Teutonic Order expanded into modern-day Latvia and Estonia.
1241	Mongol invasion of Poland. Battle of Legnica. Death of Henry the Pious. Konrad of Mazovia became senior prince.
1243	Death of Konrad. Bolesław the Chaste became senior prince.
1250s	Arrival of the Cistercian Order in Poland brings Gothic style art and architecture.
1264	Statutes of Kalisz guarantee religious liberty to Jews.
1279	Death of Bolesław the Chaste, accession of Leszek the Black.
1288	Death of Leszek the Black. Accession of Henry the Righteous.
1290	Death of Henry the Righteous. Accession of Przemysł II.

1291	Czech invasion and seizure of southern Poland.
1295	Coronation of Przemysł II as king of Poland in Poznań.
1296	Murder of Przemysł II. Vaclav II, King of Bohemia, occupied all of Poland.
1300	Vaclav II crowned himself king of Poland.
1304	Władysław Elbow-High returned to Poland to oppose Czech rule.
1305	Death of Vaclav II. Accession of Vaclav III.
1306	Assassination of Vaclav III.
1308	Teutonic Knights seized Gdańsk and sacked the city. Pomerania and part of Kujawy lost to the Knights.
1320	Coronation of Władysław Elbow-High.
1333	Death of Władysław Elbow-High. Accession of Kazimierz Wielki.
1340–41	Polish expeditions mounted to control Halicz.
1347	Kazimierz Wielki promulgated new legal code.
1363	Kazimierz Wielki hosted international summit of European leaders.
1364	Poland's first university founded in Kraków.
1370	Death of Kazimierz Wielki. End of the Piast dynasty. Accession of Louis of Hungary.
1377	Jagiełło (Jogaila) became Grand Duke of Lithuania.
1384	Jadwiga of Anjou crowned queen of Poland.
1386	Marriage of Jadwiga and Jagiełło. Jagiełło crowned king of Poland. Lithuania converted to Christianity. Founding of the Jagiellonian dynasty.
1410	Battle of Grunwald ended in defeat of Teutonic Knights.
1413	Union of Horodło.
1434	Death of Władysław Jagiełło. Accession of Władysław III.
1440	Władysław III elected King of Hungary
1444	Władysław III killed in battle with Turkish forces in present-day Bulgaria.
1447	Kazimierz Jagiellonczyk crowned king of Poland.
1454–66	Thirteen Years War with the Teutonic Order. Poland regained Pomerania, Warmia, and Gdańsk.
1473	Birth of Nicholas Copernicus.
1492	Death of Kazimierz Jagiellonczyk, accession of Jan Olbracht.
1497	Royal expedition to Moldova defeated.
1501	Death of Jan Olbracht. Accession of Alexander I.
1505	Parliament of Radom. Statute of *Nihil Novi* enacted.
1506	Defeat of Crimean Tatars at Klecko. Death of Alexander I. Accession of Zygmunt Stary.

1514	Muscovites capture Smolensk but are defeated by the Poles at Orsza. Copernicus published his *Little Commentaries*.
1517	Marriage of Zygmunt Stary and Bona Sforza.
1519	Work began on the Sigismund Chapel in Kraków.
1525	Teutonic state becomes a secularized vassal of Poland.
1530	Birth of Jan Kochanowski.
1543	Copernicus published *De revolutionibus orbium coelestium*.
1548	Death of Zygmunt Stary. Accession of Zygmunt August.
1560s	Poland acquired Livonia.
1569	Union of Lublin.
1572	Death of Zygmunt August. End of the Jagiellonian dynasty.
1573	Election of Henry Valois as king of Poland.
1575	Henry Valois abdicated and fled to France.
1576	Election of Stefan Batory.
1578–82	War with Muscovy.
1579	Kochanowski began work on his *Laments*.
1586	Death of Stefan Batory.
1587	Election of Zygmunt Wasa, beginning of the Wasa dynasty.
1588	Invasion by Habsburg forces defeated.
1589	Founding of Zamość as an ideal Renaissance city.
1594	Zygmunt crowned king of Sweden over the opposition of a majority of Swedes.
1596	Union of Brest. Capital of the Commonwealth transferred to Warsaw.
1598	Zygmunt raised private army to retake Sweden from his uncle Charles IX but failed.
1600	Swedish invasion of Livonia sparked war between Poland and Sweden that would continue on and off until the 1630s.
1605	Polish forces destroy Swedish army at Kircholm. The first False Dmitri, backed by the private efforts of a Polish magnate, was crowned as tsar of Russia after capturing Moscow, reigned briefly and was murdered. Massacre of Poles living in Moscow.
1609	Sweden allied with Muscovy. Zygmunt III declared himself Tsar of Russia.
1610	Second False Dmitri invaded Russia. Polish forces under Stanisław Żółkiewski destroyed Russian army at Kluszyn and captured Moscow.
1611	Uprising against Poles in Moscow. Poles captured Smolensk. Death of the second False Dmitri.
1618–21	Polish Turkish War.
1620	Polish army destroyed by the Turks at Cecora.
1621	Turks stopped at Chocim. Poland and Turkey signed peace treaty.

1632	Death of Zygmunt III. His son Władysław IV elected to the throne.
1648	Beginning of Khmelnicki's Cossack rebellion. Poles defeated at Złote Wody and Korsun. Massacres of Poles and Jews throughout Ukraine. Death of Władysław IV. Election of Jan Kazimierz to the throne.
1649	Cossacks defeated at Zbaraż and Zborów. A truce between the crown and the Cossacks was signed.
1651	Cossacks renew the war against Poland but were defeated at Beresteczko. Khmelnicki put the Cossacks under the authority of Russia.
1655	Russian, Brandenburg, and Swedish armies invaded Poland. The government collapsed and the king fled.
1656	National revolt against the Swedes began. The king returned and royal army harried Swedish invaders. Denmark and Austria joined war against Sweden.
1657	Death of Khmelnicki.
1660	Polish forces scored victories over the Russians and Cossacks.
1667	Treaty of Andrusowo ended war with Russia.
1668	Jan Kazimierz resigned the throne: the end of the Wasa dynasty. Michał Wiśniowiecki elected king.
1672	War with Turkey.
1673	Polish forces under Jan Sobieski destroyed Turkish army at Chocim. Death of Michał Wiśniowiecki.
1674	Jan Sobieski elected king.
1683	Sobieski led allied army to defeat major Turkish invasion of central Europe.
1696	Death of Jan Sobieski. Election of Augustus II the Strong of Saxony.
1700–21	Great Northern War pitted Sweden against Poland, Saxony and Russia.
1702–06	Swedish king Charles XII defeated Polish armies and installed Stanisław Leszczyński as king.
1717	The Silent Sejm established Russian control over Poland.
1733	Death of Augustus II.
1734	Election of Friedrich-Augustus as Augustus III engineered by Russia.
1734–36	War of Polish Succession.
1748	Europe's first public library established in Warsaw.
1763	Death of Augustus III.
1764	Election of Stanisław August Poniatowski as king engineered by Russia.
1772	First partition of Poland.

1773	Europe's first department of education established in Poland.
1788–91	The Four Years' *Sejm*.
1791	Constitution of 3 May promulgated.
1792	Russian and Prussian invasion to overthrow the Constitution. Confederation of Targowica. Second partition of Poland.
1794	Kościuszko led Polish rebellion but was defeated and captured.
1795	Third partition of Poland. End of Polish independence.
1797	First exile Polish Legion formed in Italy.
1807–12	Grand Duchy of Warsaw under French control.
1815	Congress of Vienna.
1822	First textile plant built in Lódz.
1830–31	November Insurrection.
1834	Adam Mickiewicz published *Pan Tadeusz*.
1846	Revolt in Kraków and peasant rebellion in Galicia; Republic of Cracow annexed by Austria.
1848	Poznań revolt; beginning of peasant emancipation in Galicia.
1854	First Polish immigrant community established in the United States at Panna Maria, Texas.
1861	Russian troops massacred demonstrators in Warsaw; Peasant emancipation in Russia.
1863–64	January Uprising.
1893	Polish Socialist Party founded.
1897	National Democratic Party founded.
1905	Henryk Sienkiewicz won Nobel Prize for Literature; 1905 Revolution.
1907	Death of Stanisław Wyspiański.
1914–18	World War I.
1918	Poland declared independence.
1919–20	War with the Soviet Union.
1921	Treaty of Riga set Poland's border with USSR.
1924	Władysław Reymont won Nobel Prize for Literature.
1926	Piłsudski's Coup d'etat; Gdynia founded.
1935	Death of Piłsudski.
1938	Treaty of Munich.
1939	Nazi Germany attacked Poland, starting World War II; Soviet Union attacked Poland; Partition of Poland; Beginning of Nazi and Soviet terror.
1940	Polish troops fought Nazis in Norway and France; Polish pilots defended Britain from Nazi air assault; Nazis created Auschwitz concentration camp; Soviets massacred Polish officers at Katyń and other locations.
1941	Polish troops fought Nazis at Tobruk; Nazi forces attacked USSR; Nazis began mass murder of Jews in eastern Poland.

1942	Poles captive in USSR freed and some escape to Middle East. Beginning of 'Final Solution': German mass murder of the Jews.
1943	Warsaw Ghetto Uprising; Discovery of mass graves at Katyń led to breakdown in Polish-Soviet relations; death of Władysł aw Sikorski; Soviet forces began attempted liquidation of Polish underground; Ukrainian nationalists began massacre of Polish civilians in eastern Poland.
1944	Polish army captured Nazi fortress of Monte Cassino; Polish army defeated Nazis at Falaise in northern France; Warsaw Uprising; Polish paratroopers participate in failed attack on Arnhem, Holland.
1945	Polish army captured bulk of German navy at Wilhelmshaven; Auschwitz camp liberated; beginning of communist terror and armed anti-communist resistance.
1946	Communists falsified results of referendum.
1947	Communists falsified the results of the national election; Amnesty for armed anti-communist resisters declared.
1956	Anti-communist riots in Poznań; Władysław Gomułka became party leader; end of armed anti-communist resistance.
1968	Student demonstrations suppressed by police; anti-Semitic purge campaign within the communist party began.
1978	Election of Karol Wojtyła as Pope John Paul II.
1979	John Paul II made tumultuous visit to Poland.
1980	Solidarity free trade movement staged peaceful nationwide demonstrations and won concessions from the government; Czesław Miłosz won Nobel Prize for Literature.
1981	Attempted assassination of Pope John Paul II, probably carried out by the KGB.
1982	Martial Law declared, government crackdown on Solidarity.
1988	Authorities agree to 'Roundtable Talks' with Solidarity.
1989	Free elections held, communists completely defeated; First non-communist government since World War II formed; Revolutions against communist rule break out across the Soviet bloc.
1990	Lech Wałęsa elected president; process of economic and political reforms began.
1992	Wisława Szymborska won Nobel Prize for Literature. Hanna Suchocka became first female prime minister of Poland.
1999	Poland joined NATO alliance.
2003	Poland joined European Union.
2004	Polish leaders played key role in helping Ukraine regain political freedom.
2005	Death of Pope John Paul II.

Polish Rulers

Władysław II Jagiełło (co-ruler 1386–99, King 1399–1434), King of Poland, Grand Duke of Lithuania
Władysław III, of Varna (1434–44), King of Poland and Hungary
Kazimierz IV, the Jagiellonian (1446–92), King of Poland, Grand Duke of Lithuania
Jan I, Olbracht (1492–1501), King of Poland
Aleksander I (1501–1506), King of Poland, Grand Duke of Lithuania
Zygmunt I, the Old (1506–48), King of Poland, Grand Duke of Lithuania
Zygmunt II, Augustus (1548–72), King of Poland, Grand Duke of Lithuania

Elected Kings of Poland-Lithuania

Henry of Valois (1573–75, abdicated)
Stefan I Batory, 1575–86
Zygmunt III, Wasa (1586–1632; King of Sweden, 1592–1604)
Władysław IV, Wasa (1632–48)
Jan Kazimierz Wasa (1648–68, abdicated)
Michał Wiśniowiecki (1669–73)
Jan III Sobieski (1673–96)
Augustus II, the Strong (1697–1704, 1710–33), Elector of Saxony
Stanisław Leszczyński (1704–10, 1733)
Augustus III, of Wettin (the Fat) (1733–63), Elector of Saxony
Stanisław-August Poniatowski (1763–95)

Following the reign of Stanisław-August Poniatowski, Poland was partitioned and ruled by Austria, Prussia (later Germany) and Russia, with a brief period as a French vassal during the Napoleonic Wars. The Polish monarchy was extinguished. This situation remained until 1918 when an independent Polish republic was re-established.

Second Republic: Presidents and Heads of State

Józef Piłsudski (1918–22, unelected)
Gabriel Narutowicz (1922, assassinated)
Stanisław Wojciechowski (1922–26)
Ignacy Mościcki (1926–39)

Following the 1926 coup, much government power was in the hands of Józef Piłsudski until his death in 1935. After 1935, Poland was ruled by Ignacy Mościcki in combination with General Edward Śmigły-Rydz and other military officers. In 1939, the Polish Second Republic was destroyed by a Nazi-Soviet attack. By the end of the war, there were two separate governments, the legal government in exile in London and the Soviet-controlled government in Poland.

Polish Government in Exile

Władysław Sikorski (1939–43), Prime Minister, Commander-in-Chief
Władysław Raczkiewicz (1939–47), President
August Zaleski (1947–72)
Stanisław Ostrowski (1972–79)
Edward Raczyński (1979–86)
Kazimierz Sabbat (1986–89)
Ryszard Kaczorowski (1989–90)

In 1990, the last president of the Polish government-in-exile, Ryszard Kaczorowski, transferred his insignia of office to President Lech Wałęsa.

Polish People's Republic

Bolesław Bierut (1944–56, President after 1947)
Władysław Gomulka (1956–70, First Secretary of the United Polish Worker's Party)
Edward Gierek (1970–80, First Secretary of the United Polish Worker's Party)
Stanisław Kania (1980–81, First Secretary of the United Polish Worker's Party)
Wojciech Jaruzelski (1981–90, First Secretary of the United Polish Worker's Party, President after 1985)

Third Polish Republic

Wojciech Jaruzelski (1989–90, appointive president)
Lech Wałęsa (1990–95, elected president)
Aleksander Kwaśniewski (1995–2005)
Lech Kaczyński (2005–)

Sources on Polish History in English

1. *General Histories*

Davies, Norman. *God's Playground: A History of Poland*. 2 vols. New York: Columbia University Press, 1984.

————. *Heart of Europe: A Short History of Poland*. Oxford: Oxford University Press, 1984.

Halecki, Oskar. *A History of Poland*. New York: Barnes and Noble, 1993 (reprint of 1942).

Kloczowski, Jerzy. *A History of Polish Christianity*. Cambridge: Cambridge University Press, 2000.

Lukowski, Jerzy, and Hubert Zawadzki. *A Concise History of Poland*. Cambridge: Cambridge University Press, 2001.

Milosz, Czeslaw. *The History of Polish Literature*. Berkeley: University of California Press, 1983.

Wandycz, Piotr. *The Price of Freedom: A History of East Central Europe from the Middle Ages to the Present*. London: Routledge, 1992.

Zamoyski, Adam. *The Polish Way: A Thousand-Year History of the Poles and Their Culture*. New York: Hippocrene, 1993.

2. *Medieval and Early Modern Poland*

Carpenter, Bogdana. *Monumenta Polonica: The First Four Centuries of Polish Poetry, a Bilingual Anthology*. Ann Arbor: Michigan Slavic Publication, 1989.

Fiszman, Samuel. *The Polish Renaissance in its European Context*. Bloomington: Indiana University Press, 1988.

Górecki, Piotr. *Economy, Society, and Lordship in Medieval Poland, 1100–1250*. New York: Holmes and Meier, 1992.

Halecki, Oskar. *Jadwiga of Anjou and the Rise of East Central Europe*. Boulder, Colo.: Social Science Monographs, 1991.

Hundert, David Gershon. *Jews in Poland-Lithuania in the Eighteenth Century: A Genealogy of Modernity*. Berkeley: University of California Press, 2004.

Jasienica, Pawel. *A Commonwealth of Both Nations.* Miami: American Institute of Polish Culture, 1987.

———. *Jagiellonian Poland.* Miami: American Institute of Polish Culture, 1978.

———. *Piast Poland.* Miami: American Institute of Polish Culture, 1985.

Knoll, Paul. *The Rise of the Polish Monarchy: Piast Poland in East Central Europe, 1320–1370.* Chicago: University of Chicago Press, 1972.

Maniura, Robert. *Pilgrimage to Images in the Fifteenth Century: The Origins of the Cult of Our Lady of Częstochowa.* Woodbridge, UK: Boydell, 2004.

Ostrowski, Jan, et al. *Art in Poland, 1572–1764: Land of the Winged Horsemen.* Alexandria, Va.: Art Services International, 1999.

Reddaway, W. F., O. Halecki et al., eds. *Cambridge History of Poland.* Cambridge: Cambridge University Press, 1950.

Turnbull, Stephen. *Tanneberg: Disaster for the Teutonic Knights.* London: Osprey, 2003.

3. *Partitions and Diaspora*

Cavanaugh, Jan. *Out Looking In: Early Modern Polish Art, 1890–1918.* Berkeley: University of California Press, 2000.

Kieniewicz, Stefan. *The Emancipation of the Polish Peasantry.* Chicago: University of Chicago Press, 1969.

Morawska, Ewa. *For Bread with Butter: The Life-worlds of East Central Europeans in Johnstown, Pennsylvania, 1880–1940.* Cambridge: Cambridge University Press, 1985.

Opalski, Magdalena, and Israel Bartal. *Poles and Jews: A Failed Brotherhood.* Hanover, N.H.: Brandeis University Press, 1992.

Pula, James S. *The Polish Americans: An Ethnic Community.* New York: Twayne, 1995.

Radzilowski, John. *The Eagle and the Cross: A History of the Polish Roman Catholic Union of America, 1873–2000.* New York: Columbia University Press, 2003.

Wandycz, Piotr. *The Lands of Partitioned Poland, 1795–1918.* Seattle: University of Washington Press, 1974.

4. *The Second Republic*

Abramowicz, Hirsz. *Profiles of a Lost World: Memoirs of East European Jewish Life before World War II.* Detroit: Wayne State University Press, 1999.

Buell, Raymond L. *Poland: Key to Europe.* New York: Knopf, 1939.

Carpenter, Bogdana. *The Poetic Avant-Garde in Poland, 1918–1939.* Seattle: University of Washington Press, 1983.

Concise Statistical Year-Book of Poland. Warsaw: GUS, 1938.

Davies, Norman. *White Eagle, Red Star: The Polish-Soviet War of 1919–20.* London: Random House, 2003.

Karolewitz, Robert F. and Ross S. Fenn. *Flight of Eagles: The Story of the American Kosciuszko Squadron in the Polish-Russian War, 1919–1920.* Sioux Falls, S.D.: Brevet Press, 1974.

Karski, Jan. *The Great Powers and Poland, 1919–1945: From Versailles to Yalta.* Lanham, Md.: University Press of America, 1985.

Modras, Ronald. *The Catholic Church and Antisemitism: Poland, 1933–1939.* Amsterdam: Harwood, 2004.

Polonsky, Antony. *Politics in Independent Poland, 1921–1939: The Crisis of Constitutional Government.* Oxford: Clarendon Press, 1972.

Watt, Richard M. *Bitter Glory: Poland and Its Fate, 1918–1939.* New York: Barnes and Noble, 1998 (reprint of 1979).

Wynot, Edward D. *Warsaw between the World Wars: Profile of the Capital City in a Developing Land, 1918–1939.* Boulder: East European Monographs, 1983.

5. *World War II and the Holocaust*

Baluk, Stefan Starba. *Poles on the Fronts of World War II, 1939–1945.* Warsaw: Ars, 1995.

Chodakiewicz, Marek Jan. *After the Holocaust: Polish-Jewish Conflict in the Wake of World War II.* New York: Columbia University Press, 2003.

———. *The Massacre in Jedwabne, July 10, 1941: Before, During, After.* New York: Columbia University Press, 2005.

Courtois, Stephane, et al. *The Black Book of Communism: Crimes, Terror, Repression.* Cambridge, Mass.: Harvard University Press, 1999.

Cynk, Jerzy. *The Polish Air Force at War: the Official History, 1939–1945,* 2 vols. Atlgen, Pa.: Schiffer Military History, 1998.

Czech, Danuta. *Auschwitz Chronicle, 1939–1945.* New York: Henry Holt, 1989.

Davies, Norman. *Rising '44: The Battle for Warsaw.* New York: Viking, 2003.

Garlinski, Jozef. *Fighting Auschwitz.* Greenwich, Ct.: Fawcett, 1975.

Gross, Jan T. *Revolution from Abroad: The Soviet Conquest of Poland's Western Ukraine and Western Belorussia.* Princeton, N.J.: Princeton University Press, 1988.

Hilberg, Raul. *The Destruction of the European Jews.* New York: Harper, 1961.

Jolluck, Katherine. *Exile and Identity: Polish Women in the Soviet Union during World War II.* Pittsburgh: University of Pittsburgh Press, 2002.

Korbonski, Stefan. *Fighting Warsaw.* London: Allen & Unwin, 1956.

———. *The Polish Underground State: A Guide to the Underground, 1939–1945.* New York: Hippocrene, 1981.

Kurek, Ewa. *Your Life is Worth Mine.* New York: Hippocrene, 1997.

Lukas, Richard. *Forgotten Holocaust: The Poles under German Occupation, 1939–1944.* Lexington: University Press of Kentucky, 1986.

Paul, Allen. *Katyn: The Untold Story of Stalin's Polish Massacre.* New York: Scribners. 1991.

Paulsson, Gunnar S. *Secret City: The Hidden Jews of Warsaw, 1940–1945.* New Haven: Yale University Press, 2002.

Piotrowski, Tadeusz. *Poland's Holocaust: Ethnic Strife, Collaboration with Occupying Forces and Genocide in the Second Republic, 1918–1947.* Jefferson, N.C.: McFarland, 1998.

Rossino, Alexander B. *Hitler Strikes Poland: Blitzkrieg, Ideology, and Atrocity.* Lawrence: University Press of Kansas, 2003.

Stirling, Tessa et al., eds. *Intelligence Co-operation between Poland and Great Britain during World War II.* London: Vallentine Mitchell, 2005.

Zaloga, Steven and Victor Madej. *The Polish Campaign of 1939.* New York: Hippocrene, 1985.

Zamoyski, Adam. *The Forgotten Few: The Polish Air Force in the Second World War.* New York: Hippocrene, 1995.

6. *Memoirs, Biographies, Autobiographies*

Adamczyk, Wesley. *When God Looked the Other Way.* Chicago: University of Chicago Press, 2004.

Frister, Roman. *The Cap: The Price of a Life.* New York: Grove Press, 1999.

Grabowski, Stanislaw. *Follow Me: The Memoirs of a Polish Priest,* J. Radzilowski, ed. Roseville, MN: White Rose, 1997.

Klukowski, Zygmunt. *Diary from the Years of Occupation, 1939–44.* Chicago: Illinois University Press, 1993.

Kulski, Julian E. *Dying We Live.* New York: Holt, Rinehardt, Winston, 1979.

Nowak, Jan. *Courier from Warsaw.* Detroit: Wayne State University Press, 1982.

Perechodnik, Calel. *Am I A Murderer?* Boulder, Colo.: Westview Press, 1996.

Piotrowski, Tadeusz. *Vengeance of the Swallows.* Jefferson, N.C.: McFarland, 1995.

Pope John Paul II. *Memory and Identity: Conversations at the Dawn of a Millennium.* New York: Rizzoli, 2005.

Szpilman, Wladyslaw. *The Pianist.* New York: Picador, 1999.

Walesa, Lech. *A Way of Hope: An Autobiography.* New York: Henry Holt, 1987.

Weigel, George. *Witness to Hope: The Biography of Pope John Paul II.* New York: Cliff Street Books, 1999.

Wood, E. Thomas and Stanislaw Jankowski. *Karski: How One Man Tried to Stop the Holocaust.* New York: John Wiley and Sons, 1994.

7. *Communist and Post-Communist Poland*

Barnett, Clifford. *Poland: Its People, Its Society, Its Culture.* New York: Grove, 1958.

Chodakiewicz, Marek Jan, John Radzilowski, and Dariusz Tolczyk, eds. *Poland's Transformation: A Work in Progress.* Charlottesville, Va.: Leopolis, 2003.

Kaufman, Michael T. *Mad Dreams, Saving Graces: Poland, a Nation in Conspiracy.* New York: Random House, 1989.

Kostrzewa, Robert, ed. *Between East and West: Writings from Kultura.* New York: Hill and Wang, 1990.

Michnik, Adam. *The Church and the Left.* Chicago: University of Chicago Press, 1993.

Milosz, Czeslaw. *Nobel Lecture.* New York; Farrar, Straus, and Giroux, 1980.

Penn, Shana. *Solidarity's Secret: The Women Who Defeated Communism in Poland.* Ann Arbor: University of Michigan Press, 1995.

Steinlauf, Michael C. *Bondage to the Dead: Poland the Memory of the Holocaust.* Syracuse: Syracuse University Press, 1997.

Weiser, Benjamin. *A Secret Life: The Polish Officer, His Covert Mission, and the Price He Paid to Save His Country.* New York: Public Affairs, 2003.

Historical Gazetteer

Numbers in bold refer to main text

Auschwitz (Oświęcim). A small community west of Kraków that during World War II was chosen by Nazi officials as a site for a concentration camp for Polish prisoners. During the course of war, it developed into one of the largest killing centres for mass murder of European Jewry. With scores of subcamps located throughout the surrounding region, it was also one of the largest concentration camp complexes in Nazi-occupied Europe. Over one million people were murdered in Auschwitz, Jews being the largest group. **194–96, 206, 207, 221–22, 243**

Białowieża Forest. Located on the present-day border between Poland and Belarus, this area is the last remaining stand of primeval forest in all of Europe. Used as a hunting preserve for royalty, it is one of Europe's most important natural preserves and is the home to the only wild herd of European bison. **4**

Białystok. An important economic and political city in eastern Mazovia founded in the fifteenth century. This city had an ethnically mixed population with Poles and Jews pre-dominating but also containing Lithuanians, Germans, and Belarusins. During the partitions of Poland, Białystok was located outside the Congress Kingdom of Poland and incorporated directly into the Russian empire. Due to tariffs placed on goods from the Congress Kingdom, the city developed a significant textile industry serving the Russian market. Today, it is an industrial and regional centre and the largest city in north-eastern Poland. **152, 174, 211**

Biskupin. Located on a lake near Żnin in west-central Poland, Biskupin is one of the best preserved examples of an early Iron Age settlement in Poland. The site was first settled sometime in the 700s BC and was occupied for centuries. The site was rediscovered in 1933 and has since become one of the best-known archeological and museum sites in Poland illustrating the region's pre-historic cultures.

Brześć (Brest-Litovsk). Located on a bend in the Bug River and today part of Belarus, Brześć was founded in 1019 as a minor princely city. Alternately under Polish and Lithuanian rule, in the late 1500s it hosted one of the major synods that resulted in a partial reunion of part of the Orthodox church with the Catholic Church. During the Russian empire, it was a major fortress town. In 1918, it was the site of a peace treaty between Germany and the new Soviet Union that ended the First World War on the eastern front.

Bug River. One of the major tributaries of the Vistula River, the river's name derives from the ancient Slavonic word for 'god.'

Bydgoszcz. Endowed by Casimir the Great in 1346, Bydgoszcz was a major trading post on the Vistula River between Gdańsk and central Poland. It was incorporated into the Prussian empire during the Partitions. During the Second Republic, it had a very large ethnic German minority. This minority staged an unsuccessful revolt against Polish authorities during the first days of World War II.

Carpathian Mountains. Forming Poland's southern boundary with the Czech Republic and Slovakia, the Carpathian Mountains are home to the unique culture of the Polish highlanders or *górale*. Though not as high as the Alps, the Carpathian mountains are rugged and craggy and many areas remain wild. Others are suitable for winter and mountain sports. The Polish Carpathian range has two main parts: Sudety in the west and the Beskids in the centre and east. **2, 4, 7, 14, 15**

Chicago (Czykago). The Windy City is home to more people with Polish surnames than any city outside of Warsaw. Almost one million Poles and people of Polish ancestry live in Chicago and its environs. As it has for more than 130 years, the city continues to attract Polish immigrants and visitors who support a large infrastructure of shops, media, and cultural activities in both Polish and English.

Częstochowa. A city in south central Poland, it is home to the famous Jasna Góra (Bright Mountain) monastery of the Pauline Fathers. Founded in 1364, the site houses the famous icon of the Virgin Mary known as the Black Madonna. It is the most significant and visited religious pilgrimage site in Poland. **72, 119, 120**

Elbląg (Elbling). A trading centre for the ancient Balts by the ninth century, the present city was founded by German colonists in 1237. Located near the mouth of the Vistula, the city was an important commercial point for the Teutonic Knights. Absorbed by Poland after the Thirteen Years' War, it was second only to Gdańsk as a Polish maritime port. Elbląg and its environs developed a significant German and Dutch influence due to immigration and trading ties. After the partitions, it remained part of East Prussia until 1945 when it was transferred to Poland.

Galicia. A name applied to southern Poland, especially Małopolska, the term derives from ancient Celtic inhabitants. This archaic term was given new life in the nineteenth century when it became the designation for the Austrian partition region of Poland. **8, 14, 19, 34, 148, 149, 154, 161, 174**

Gdańsk (Danzig). Founded in 998 at the mouth of Vistula, the city of

Gdańsk developed into Poland's major maritime commercial port. A melting pot of Slavs, Balts, and Germans, Gdańsk was a powerful member of the Hanseatic League and had close trade ties to Holland, Scandinavia, and England. During the era of the Polish Commonwealth, the city enjoyed unique political and economic rights. After the destruction of independent Poland, the city declined in importance. Following the Treaty of Versailles, it was designated the Free City of Danzig under the League of Nations, while Poland was granted some commercial and customs privileges. During the 1930s, the city's German community was a hotbed of pro-Nazi sympathy and the city became a flashpoint for German-Polish tensions. On 1 September, 1939, German and Danzig forces fired the opening shot of World War II by attacking a small Polish garrison on the Westerplatte peninsula. The majority of the German population fled or was expelled at the end of World War II and the city returned to Polish rule. In the 1970s, the city's shipyards became the site of a significant anti-communist workers' movement. In that year, communist security forces massacred unarmed workers demonstrating against government price hikes. In 1980, Gdańsk became known around the world as the birthplace of the Solidarity Free Trade Movement which played an important role in overthrowing communist rule in Poland. **18, 31, 38, 43, 69, 74, 90, 91, 127, 131, 166, 188, 190, 224**

Gdynia. This humble fishing village north of Gdańsk was transformed into a major modern port by the Polish Second Republic in the late 1920s. By the 1930s it was the busiest port on the Baltic Sea. Like neighbouring Gdańsk it was a hotbed of Solidarity activity in the 1980s. **183, 192**

Gniezno. This town in west-central Poland east of Poznań was the first capital of Poland. From the 800s AD, it was the seat of the Piast princes whose rule gradually extended over most of present-day Poland. Gniezno was also the site of Poland's first bishropic and cathedral. In 1000 it became the seat of the primate of Poland. **11, 14, 20, 24, 35, 36**

Grunwald. This picturesque area near Olszytn was scene of the largest battle of the European Middle Ages. On 15 July, 1410 the armies of Poland and Lithuania won a crushing victory over the forces of the Teutonic Order, breaking the might of the most formidable military state of its day and setting the stage for Poland's rise to the ranks of Europe's foremost powers. **64–7, 70, 161**

Holy Cross Mountains (Góry Świętokrzyskie). An old, small mountain range in central Poland, its main peak Lysa Góra (Bald Mountain) was an ancient pre-Christian cult site. The mountain's reputation as a place of witchcraft and legend endures to the present. During World War II, it was the site of significant partisan activity against the Nazis and later the Soviets. **7, 11**

Kalisz. One of the oldest-known cities in Poland, Kalisz was mentioned in Claudius Ptolomeus' geography from the second century BC. It was located on the amber trade routes running south from the Baltic. The present city received its charter in 1237. In 1264, Prince Bolesław of Sandomierz issued the Statutes of Kalisz, guaranteeing Jewish freedom of worship, movement, and trade. The city became a minor industrial and agricultural centre. **8**

Kaminets Podolsk (Kamieniec Podolski). Located in Ukraine near the Moldovan border, the city's name translates literally as the 'Rock of Podolia.' Long a seat of local Ruthenian princes, during Poland's Golden Age it became one of the Commonwealth's greatest fortresses, protecting south-eastern Poland and Ukraine and guarding routes into the volatile regions of Moldavia and Transylvania.

Katowice. The capital of Poland's coal mining region of Upper Silesia, Katowice was founded in the mid-nineteenth century as the region's coal production expanded dramatically. Although the mines and factories were developed by German entrepreneurs, the workforce was largely Polish. Following World War I, three Polish uprisings resulted in Katowice's inclusion within the borders of independent Poland where it became one of the country's most important industrial towns.

Katyń. Located in Belarus, outside of Minsk, this isolated site was a killing ground for the Soviet authorities who murdered and buried their internal and external opponents there. In 1940, it became indelibly linked with Polish history when thousands of Polish reservists were murdered there by the Soviets. **199, 213**

Kazimierz Dolny. Named after King Casimir the Just in 1170, this town on the Vistula south of Warsaw is one of the best preserved and most charming medieval-Renaissance towns in east-central Europe.

Kielce. This city in south-central Poland is located near the Holy Cross Mountains and was an ancient centre for iron smelting. Early Celtic inhabitants may be the origin of its name. The present town was founded by the bishops of Kraków in the twelfth century and it became known for metallurgy and glass making. **226**

Kiev (Kyiv). The ancient capital of modern-day Ukraine was the heart of Orthodox Kievan Rus culture from the tenth century until its destruction by the Mongols in 1240. It was liberated by Lithuanian forces in the fourteenth century and later became part of the Polish-Lithuanian Commonwealth. Kiev developed a significant Polish presence and was a meeting place of eastern and western ideas. It was a major Polish outpost until the Deluge when it gradually fell into Russia's sphere of influence. During the nineteenth century its population was one fifth Polish and it retains a Polish minority to this day. **21–3, 29, 41, 42, 43**

Kraków (Cracow). The old capital of Poland from 1038 to 1596. Kraków was originally the seat of the Wislanian people and its original settlement stretches far back into prehistory. It had historically close ties to Bohemia and was the first major city north of the Carpathian Mountains to have a significant Christian presence. It gained a bishopric in 1000. In 1241 it was sacked by the Mongols, but recovered to become an important commercial and political centre. In the sixteenth century, it was a major location for the Polish Renaissance. Following World War II, the city was designated as one of the first UNESCO World Heritage Sites. **14, 15, 19, 20, 25, 36, 42, 44, 48, 57, 64, 68, 69–70, 118, 135, 139, 148, 192**

Kresy. The Kresy (or 'borderland') refers to the vast region of present day Lithuania, Belarus, and Ukraine once ruled by Poland but lost due to the partitions and subsequent border and ethnic changes. **4, 112, 113, 117**

Kujawy. Located along the middle Vistula between Toruń, Gniezno, and Bydgoszcz, the rich farming region of Kujawy is one of the original provinces of the first Polish state. Under German rule during the partitions, it returned to Poland in 1918. **49**

Lithuania (Litwa). This ancient princedom was the last pagan state in Europe until its merger with Poland which began in the late fourteenth century when it converted to Christianity thanks in part to Polish missionaries. Polish language and culture have had a significant impact on Lithuania and most of the elite were Polonized. It was an integral part of the old Polish Commonwealth that ruled over east-central Europe from the fifteenth to the seventeenth century. Modern Lithuania retains a significant Polish ethnic minority. **2, 41,**

43, 45, 53, 59, 60–6, 70–3, 80–1, 94, 125, 142, 144, 172

Livonia. The archaic name for modern Latvia, this land came under Polish rule as a separate royal province in the sixteenth century and remained in the Polish kingdom until the end of the eighteenth century. A small Polish minority has survived the intervening centuries of war and political upheaval to help build an independent Latvia. **94–6, 99, 104, 106**

Łódź. Once a small village whose name means 'boat,' it was probably a spot where a ferry helped travellers across a local river. Beginning in the 1820s, Polish, Jewish, and German businessmen set up textile mills to weave cloth for the Russian market. Known as the 'Polish Manchester,' the city grew dramatically in size, becoming one of Poland's largest cities by the early twentieth century with a mixed Jewish, Polish, and German population. **152, 161, 174, 191**

Lublin. Settled as early as the sixth century, Lublin emerged as an important Polish town in the twelfth century. Its easterly location made it a regular target for attacks by the Lithuanians and the Tartar horde. During the fourteenth and fifteenth centuries, Lublin became a major trading post between Poland and Lithuania and developed one of the Commonwealth's largest commercial fairs. Many parliaments were held in Lublin and the final union of Poland and Lithuania was concluded there in 1569. The city was also home to a major Jewish community that was distinguished by its tradition of learning and as the seat of the self-governing body for Jews throughout Poland and Lithuania, the Council of the Four Lands. During the communist period, Lublin was home to the Catholic University of Lublin, the only independent university in the communist bloc. **3, 7, 70, 238**

Lwów (Lviv). An ancient Ruthenian city, capital of the land of Halicz (Galicia), Lwów came under Polish rule during the reign of Casimir the Great. Located on the trade routes between Central Asia and Europe, it became one of the leading cities of Poland with diverse population of Poles, Jews, Armenians, Germans, and Ukrainians. During the partitions it came under Austrian rule as Lemberg. After World War I, it was fought over by Polish, Ukrainian, and Soviet forces, but remained in Poland hands. As a result of the Nazi-Soviet alliance, it was lost to Poland and today is part of independent Ukraine, though it retains a large Polish community. **123, 165, 167, 171**

Majdanek. Located virtually within the city of Lublin, Majdanek was one of the largest Nazi death camps of World War II. At least 78,000 people were murdered there, Jews and Poles constituting the largest and second largest groups respectively. **207**

Malbork (Marienburg). Located on the River Nogat south of Elbląg, Malbork was once the capital of the Teutonic Order whose powerful and rapacious armies menaced Poland and Lithuania for centuries. The fortress of Malbork is one of the most powerful and impressive castles built in

Europe. It fell to Polish forces during the mid fifteenth century and remained in Polish hands until 1772. It returned to Polish control after World War II. **74**

Małopolska (Little Poland). The region of Małopolska stretches from Kraków in the west to Lwów in the east. This hilly land of small farms and towns is one of the historic provinces of Poland. **19, 24, 42, 44, 47, 126, 148**

Mazovia. Once a semi-independent border province, Mazovia is today in the centre of Poland, around the capital city of Warsaw. **25, 43, 54, 57, 60, 92, 135, 139**

Mazurian Lakes. Long a part of Prussia, the Mazurian Lakes region became part of Poland in 1945. The area's water, woods, and wildlife make it a favourite holiday destination for Poles and foreign tourists. **4**

Modlin. Located north of Warsaw at the confluence of Narew and Vistula Rivers, Modlin was developed as fortress by the Imperial Russian army during the nineteenth century and passed to Polish hands in 1918. In September 1939, it was a major Polish strongpoint that held off repeated Nazi attacks before surrendering at the end of the campaign.

Mokra. This small village near Częstochowa became the scene of legendary resistance during the German invasion of Poland in 1939 when two regiments of the Wolyńska Cavalry Brigade defeated the Nazi 4th Panzer Division in one of the opening battles of World War II.

Narew. A tributary of the Vistula, the Narew is the major river of north-east

Poland. The north parts of its course contain important wildlife habitats.

Odra (Oder). One of the major rivers of Poland and central Europe, the Odra runs from the Carpathian Mountains in the south, through Silesia, emptying into the Baltic Sea at Szczecin.

Ojców National Park. Located in south central Poland, Ojców's major feature is the craggy limestone valley of the Jura Krakowska, which is a unique natural reserve. The park also contains numerous historic and cultural sites.

Palmiry. This thick forest north-west of Warsaw has long been a nature preserve, but during World War II, it was the site of mass killings by the Germans. Tens of thousands of Poland's political, cultural, and professional elite were murdered there.

Panna Maria. This humble community on the Texas Gulf Coast of the United States was the first complete overseas Polish community created by mass emigration from Poland. In 1854, a shipload of Silesian immigrants, led by a Franciscan priest, Fr. Leopold Moczygemba, founded what would become the mother community of the vast Polish diaspora in the Western Hemisphere.

Pińsk. This city was the capital of the Polesie region and is today in Belarus. A part of the Polish-Lithuanian Commonwealth and the Second Republic (1918–39), it had a majority Jewish population that was destroyed during the Holocaust.

Podolia. Now part of western Ukraine, Podolia was one of the historic regions of old Poland. This flat, fertile land had a significant Polish population until the population transfers following World War II.

Polesie. This region, now part of Belarus and Ukraine, was once home to Europe's largest marshland, the Pripet Marshes. Part of Poland for centuries, it remained very isolated until quite recently.

Pomorska (Pomerania). Bordering the Baltic Sea and stretching from the Odra River in the west to the Vistula in the east, this region was originally inhabited by a series of west Slavic tribes whose sole remnants are the Kashubian people west of Gdańsk. Alternately independent under native princes or under direct Polish rule, the west part of this province was gradually lost to Poland during the late Middle Ages under the pressure of Germanic expansion. The eastern part (also called West Prussia) was part of the Commonwealth and later the Second Republic. The entire region again became part of Poland again after World War II. **18, 19, 25, 29, 30-1, 43, 48, 52, 53, 74, 166**

Poznań. The capital of Wielkopolska, Poznań was founded on an island in the Warta in the eighth century. It remained an integral part of Poland until the second partition in 1793 when it was taken by Prussia. It returned to Poland in 1918 and is today the country's fifth largest city. **17, 25, 37, 46, 49, 69–70**

Psie Pole. Located near the Odra River in central Silesia, Psie Pole or 'field of the dogs' was the site of King Bolesław II, the Wrymouth's victory over the army of the Holy Roman Empire in 1109 which effectively ended the imperial effort to subdue Poland.

Radom. An ancient tribal centre south of Warsaw that developed into a medieval market town, Radom's recorded history dates back to the 1150s. Under Russian rule during the partitions, in modern times Radom developed into an industrial town specialising in metallurgy, food processing, and leather working.

Riga. Now the capital of independent Latvia, Riga came under Polish rule in the sixteenth and seventeenth centuries. Until it was lost to the conquering armies of Gustavus Adolphus, it was an important Polish port city. **94, 104, 106, 171**

Rzeszów. Endowed by Casimir the Great, Rzeszów is located in southeastern Poland in the foothills of the Carpathian Mountains. It developed as an important trading town between Lwów and Kraków as well as with Hungary to the south. During the partitions it fell under Austrian rule but return to Polish control in 1918.

Sandomierz. First settled in Neolithic times, Sandomierz is one of the oldest cities of Poland. Sacked by the Mongols and later the Lithuanians, the city was rebuilt by Casimir the Great. Because it was never a major industrial centre, it has retained much of its late medieval and Renaissance architecture. **34, 42, 44, 48**

Silesia (Śląsk). One of the original provinces of Poland, Silesia was lost to Poland in the late Middle Ages, though a large part of its population remained culturally Polish. Part of Silesia was granted to Poland in 1922

and the rest of the province after World War II. **4, 18, 19, 24, 25, 34, 37, 43–4, 48, 52, 53, 72, 151, 166, 172**

Sopot. A popular resort town located on the Baltic coast north of Gdańsk, after World War II Sopot became the site of a major summer music festival.

Szczecin. Originally founded in the eighth century by a local Slavic tribe at the mouth of the Odra River, Szczecin came under German influence early in its history. It was refounded as a German law town in 1243. As Stettin, it was a member of the Hanseatic League and later fell under Brandenburg, Swedish, and Prussian rule. In 1945 it became part of Poland and under the communist authorities was developed as a major shipbuilding location. During the early 1980s it was a stronghold of Solidarity. **18, 31**

Tatra Range. The highest and most picturesque mountains in the Polish section of the Carpathian Mountains. Located south of Zakopane along the Polish-Slovak border.

Toruń. Founded in 1233 by the Teutonic Knights, Toruń's early history was heavily influenced by its German community. It became an important trans-shipment point in the Vistula grain trade after it became part of Poland in the 1450s. Its ties to Germany made it one of the first cities in Poland to be significantly affected by the Reformation. It was also the birthplace of the famous astronomer Nicholas Copernicus. In 1997, the old city was designated a UNESCO World Heritage Site. **7, 8, 28, 35, 79, 85, 99, 122**

Treblinka. Located east of Warsaw, Treblinka was turned into a killing centre by the Germans. During the Holocaust, it became one of the worst Nazi death camps. Between 700,000 and 900,000 Jews, most of them from Poland, were murdered at Treblinka. **207**

Upper Silesia. The south-east part of Silesia, called Upper Silesia, contains one of the largest concentrations of hard coal in Europe. In 1922, this area officially rejoined Poland and has since been one of the country's leading industrial regions.

Warmia. A province of Poland, located west of the Mazurian Lakes and east of the Vistula, it became part of Poland following the Thirteen Years War in 1466 and remained so until the partition of 1772. In 1945, it again became part of Poland. **74**

Warszawa (Warsaw). A provincial town and main city of Mazovia until the 1590s, when its geographic location made it the ideal place for the new capital of the Polish-Lithuanian Commonwealth. It quickly grew into an important city and the heart of Polish national life. Repeatedly attacked, fought over, destroyed, and resurrected, its history reflects modern Poland in microcosm. During World War II, its Jewish population – the largest and most significant in Europe – was virtually wiped out by the Germans. In 1944 the city's inhabitants rose up to overthrow the Nazi occupation, the largest urban uprising in history. Following the uprising's defeat, the city was systematically levelled on Hitler's personal orders. During the war, Warsaw suffered heavier casualties than the United States and Britain put together. After the war the city was rebuilt and today it is one of the most significant business centres of central Europe. **91–2, 103, 118–19, 128, 134, 135, 161–2, 169–72, 191–2, 207–10, 217–21, 227, 231, 236**

Warta. A tributary of the Odra, the Warta flows through the heart of the original Piast patrimony in central Poland.

Wielkopolska (Greater Poland). One of the historical provinces of Poland and the cradle of the first Polish kingdom, Wielkopolska is located between Silesia, Pomerania, and Mazovia along the present-day German-Polish border. **43, 48, 49, 174**

Wilno (Vilnius). The ancient capital of Lithuania, Wilno became an important city in the Commonwealth as the capital of the Grand Duchy of Lithuania. It also became an important focus of Jewish life in Europe, known as the 'Jerusalem of the North' for its famous Talmudic scholars. Under Russian rule during the partitions, it was disputed by newly-independent Poland and Lithuania, but the fortunes of war placed it in Poland. After World War II and the destruction of its Jewish community by the Germans, it became the capital of the Lithuanian SSR of the Soviet Union. In 1991, it became the capital of independent Lithuania. It retains one of the largest Polish minority populations in the former Kresy region. **60, 118, 144, 161, 167, 217**

Wisła (Vistula). The largest and most

historically significant river in Poland. From its origins in the Carpathian Mountains, the Vistula runs through Kraków, Warsaw, and reaches the Baltic Sea near Gdańsk. **2–4, 15, 74, 99**

Wołyn (Volhynia). Located today on the Ukrainian side of the Polish-Ukrainian border, Wołyn became part of Poland as early as the fourteenth century, although its population was largely Orthodox. Poland ruled Wołyn until the partitions. It was part of the Second Republic after 1918. Its population was mixed with a Ukrainian majority and large Polish and Jewish communities. During World War II, the Nazis exterminated most of the Jewish population while Ukrainian nationalists massacred tens of thousands of Poles. Most of the remaining Polish population fled or were later forcibly relocated by the Soviets. **10, 31**

Wrocław. Founded in the ninth century on an island in the Odra River, Wrocław emerged as the most significant city of Silesia. It came under Polish rule by 990 and was made a bishropic in 1000. Alternately under Polish, German, and Czech rule, its original Polish population was augmented with a significant influx of German immigrants in the thirteenth century. During the fourteenth and fifteenth centuries it fell under Bohemian and Habsburg control and was largely Germanized by the nineteenth century. In 1945, after its German population fled or was expelled, the city was given to Poland by the Allies. **18, 20, 31, 37, 38, 42, 43–4, 225**

Zakopane. A regional town in the Tatra Mountains of southern Poland, in the late nineteenth and early twentieth centuries Zakopane became an important resort and famous as a centre for the unique folk art of the Polish highlanders. Today, it is one of Poland's best known skiing and vacation spots. **157, 185**

Zamość. Founded by the Zamoyski family in the late sixteenth century, Zamość, in south-east Poland, was designed as an ideal Renaissance city and retains its original character and mix of central European and Italian influences. The old town was designated a UNESCO World Heritage site in 1992. **85, 211**

Index